WITHDRAWN
HARVARD LIBRARY
WITHDRAWN

The Sacred in the City

Also available from Continuum

Postsecular Cities Edited by Christopher Baker and Justin Beaumont
Religion in a Secular City Edited by Arvind Sharma
Sacred Space Edited by John North and Philip North

The Sacred in the City

Edited by
Liliana Gómez and Walter Van Herck

Continuum International Publishing Group
The Tower Building   80 Maiden Lane
11 York Road   Suite 704
London SE1 7NX   New York NY 10038

www.continuumbooks.com

© Liliana Gómez, Walter Van Herck and Contributors, 2012

All rights reserved. No part of this publication may be reproduced or transmitted in any form or by any means, electronic or mechanical, including photocopying, recording, or any information storage or retrieval system, without prior permission in writing from the publishers.

Liliana Gómez, Walter Van Herck and Contributors have asserted their right under the Copyright, Designs and Patents Act, 1988, to be identified as Authors of this work.

British Library Cataloguing-in-Publication Data
A catalogue record for this book is available from the British Library.

ISBN: HB: 978-1-4411-7295-2

Library of Congress Cataloging-in-Publication Data
The sacred in the city/edited by Liliana Gómez and Walter Van Herck.
  p. cm.
 Includes bibliographical references and index.
 ISBN 978-1-4411-7295-2 (hardcover)
 1. Cities and towns–Religious aspects. I. Gómez, Liliana. II. Herck, Walter Van, 1962-
 BR65.C57S23 2011
 201'.7–dc23   2011035788

Typeset by Deanta Global Publishing Services, Chennai, India
Printed and bound in Great Britain

Contents

Notes on Contributors   vii

Framing the Sacred in the City: An Introduction
Liliana Gómez & Walter Van Herck   1

Part One: The Sacred and the City: Theoretical Approaches

Chapter 1: Sacred *Horror Vacui*: A Philosophical Reflection   15
Walter Van Herck

Chapter 2: The Urbanization of Society: Towards a Cultural Analysis of the Sacred in the Modern Metropolis   31
Liliana Gómez

Chapter 3: The Lingering Smell of Incense: Exploring Post-secular Public Space   52
Pieter Dronkers

Part Two: Religion, Built Environments and Urban Societies

Chapter 4: Religion in the Built Environment: Aesth/Ethics, Ritual and Memory in Lived Urban Space   73
Sigurd Bergmann

Chapter 5: *Kinhin* in a Megacity – Implicit Meanings of the 'Walking-in-the-Park'-Movement in São Paulo   96
Frank Usarski

Chapter 6: Life Stance and Religious Identity in an Urbanized World: The Meaning of Life as Modern Predicament   108
Rik Pinxten & Lisa Dikomitis

Part Three: Sacred Symbols, Sacred Spaces

Chapter 7: Sacred Symbols of the City: Babel, Barbara and their Towers   127
Anne-Marie Korte

Chapter 8: Communicating the Elemental Cosmos: The Hereford *Mappa Mundi*, Sacred Space and the City   141
Renée Köhler-Ryan

Chapter 9: Relocating and Negotiating the Sacred: The Reception of a Chapel in a Shopping Mall   161
Peter Nynäs & Anne Birgitta Pessi

Part Four: Politics of the Sacred in Contemporary Urban Spaces

Chapter 10: Kinshasa and its (Un)Certainties: The Polis and the Sacred   191
Filip De Boeck

Chapter 11: The Politics of a Sacred Place: Revisiting an Israeli Development Town   208
Haim Yacobi

Chapter 12: The Sacred in the City: Havana. Alejo Carpentier or 'Fieldwork' in the Urban   227
Liliana Gómez

Chapter 13: Remaking Sacred Spaces after Socialism in Ukraine   244
Catherine Wanner

Index   263

Notes on Contributors

Sigurd Bergmann holds a doctorate in systematic theology from Lund University and works as Professor in Religious Studies at the Department of Archaeology and Religious Studies at the Norwegian University of Science and Technology in Trondheim. His previous studies have investigated the relationship between the image of God and the view of nature in late antiquity, the methodology of contextual theology, visual arts in the indigenous Arctic and Australia, as well as visual arts, architecture and religion. He is chair of the "European Forum on the Study of Religion and Environment" and ongoing projects investigate the relation of space/place and religion and "religion in dangerous environmental/climatic change". His main publications are *Geist, der Natur befreit* (Mainz 1995, Russian ed. Arkhangelsk 1999, rev. ed. *Creation Set Free*, Grand Rapids 2005), *Geist, der lebendig macht* (Frankfurt/M. 1997), *God in Context* (Aldershot 2003), *Architecture, Aesth/Ethics and Religion* (ed.) (Frankfurt/M, London 2005), *Theology in Built Environments* (ed.) (New Brunswick/London 2009), *In the Beginning is the Icon* (London 2009), *Så främmande det lika* ("So Strange, so Similar", on Sámi visual arts, globalization and religion, Trondheim 2009) and *Raum und Geist: Zur Erdung und Beheimatung der Religion* (Göttingen 2010). Bergmann was a co-project leader of the interdisciplinary programme "Technical Spaces of Mobility" (2003–7) and co-edited recently *The Ethics of Mobilities* (Aldershot 2008), *Spaces of Mobility* (London 2008), *Nature, Space & the Sacred* (Farnham 2009), *Religion Ecology & Gender* (Berlin 2009), *Religion and Dangerous Environmental Change* (Berlin 2010), *Religion som rörelse* ("Religion as movement", Trondheim 2010), and *Ecological Awareness* (Berlin 2011).

Filip De Boeck is a professor of anthropology and the coordinator of the Institute for Anthropological Research in Africa (IARA), a research unit of the University of Leuven, Belgium. He has carried out long-term field research in both rural and urban communities in the Democratic Republic of Congo. Recent publications focus on the role of youth in Central Africa (see for example Honwana and De Boeck (eds.), 2004, *Makers and Breakers. Children and Youth in Postcolonial Africa*) and on the conditions of urban living in the Central-African context (see De Boeck and Plissart, 2004, *Kinshasa. Tales of the Invisible City*). Together with architect and critic Koen Van Syngyhel, De Boeck also curated several exhibitions about Congo's capital, and in 2010 he directed 'Cemetery State', a documentary film on life in and around a Kinshasa graveyard.

Lisa Dikomitis works as a postdoctoral researcher at the Department of Comparative Sciences of Cultures (Ghent University, Belgium). Her monograph, *Cyprus and Its Places of Desire. Cultures of Displacement among Greek and Turkish Cypriot Refugees* (IB Tauris, forthcoming) is based on long-term fieldwork on both sides of the border on Cyprus. The book explores questions of justice, suffering, ethnic conflict and notions of place and home. She has also published several book chapters and journal articles and edited (with Rik Pinxten) *When God Comes to Town* (2009, Berghahn Books, Oxford). Lisa is currently working on a new comparative project on Cyprus and Belgium.

Pieter Dronkers is a PhD student in Ethics at the Protestant Theological University, Utrecht, the Netherlands. In his research, he investigates how religious freedom is affected by the contemporary political and social pressure on citizens to demonstrate and prove their allegiance to the civic community and the nation-state. The Dutch debate on religious expressions in the public domain serves as a case study. In 2008, he published a non-specialist book in Dutch on the controversies in Turkey, France and the Netherlands about the visibility of Islam in public life.

Liliana Gómez is an assistant professor of Latin American literary and cultural studies at Martin-Luther-University Halle-Wittenberg. Trained as philosopher and architect, she received her doctorate in Latin American studies from Freie Universität Berlin. Her main research fields are cultural and spatial histories and theories, urban studies, Latin American epistemologies, and transatlantic knowledge circulations. Selected publications: 'El discurso colonial en la iconografía cubana: Paisaje, urbanización y narrativas de lo rural del siglo XIX', in: O. Ette & G. Müller (ed.), *Caleidosocopios coloniales. Transferencias culturales en el Caribe del siglo XIX* (2010, Iberoamericana, Madrid). She is editor with C. Rincón & S. de Mojica of *Entre el olvido y el recuerdo. Iconos, lugares de memoria y cánones de la historia y la literatura en Colombia* (2010, Universidad Javeriana CEJA, Bogotá), and with

G. Müller of *Relaciones caribeñas. Entrecruzamientos de dos siglos/Relations caribéennes. Entrecroisements de deux siècles* (2010, Peter Lang, Frankfurt). Her book on urban epistemologies, the cultural and political theory on the Latin American city is forthcoming.

Renée Köhler Ryan is a senior lecturer in philosophy on the Sydney campus of the University of Notre Dame in Australia. Before this, she was an academic assistant and researcher at the Katholieke Universiteit Leuven, where she defended her doctoral dissertation, entitled *From Head to Foot Set in our Place: Sacred Space as the Expression of Religious Experience and Imagination*. She has also worked as an adjunct instructor in Philosophy for the Rome programmes of the Erasmus Institute of Liberal Arts, and for the Thomas More College of Liberal Arts. Her publications reflect her main research areas of philosophy of religion and philosophy of culture and range from reviews of current writings about christian architecture and applied ethics to articles concerning the continuing influence of Augustine and the work of contemporary philosopher William Desmond.

Anne-Marie Korte is professor of religion, gender, and modernity at the Faculty of Humanities of Utrecht University, the Netherlands, and scientific director of the Netherlands School for Advanced Studies in Theology and Religion. She is a member of the steering committee of the National Research Programme 'The Future of the Religious Past' of the Netherlands Organisation for Scientific Research (2002–11) and she initiated the international research cooperation 'Interdisciplinary Innovations in the Study of Religion and Gender: Postcolonial, Post-secular and Queer Perspectives' (2011–14). She is Editor in Chief of *Religion and Gender* (religionandgender.org). She (co-)edited *Wholly Woman, Holy Blood: A Feminist Critique of Purity and Impurity* (Harrisburg: Trinity Press International, 2003); *Women & Miracle Stories: A Multidisciplinary Exploration* (Leiden: Brill, 2004); *The Boundaries of Monotheism: Interdisciplinary Explorations into the Foundations of Western Monotheism* (Leiden: Brill, 2009). She currently studies the role of gender, sexuality and human materiality in contemporary images and performances that are accused of blasphemy and sacrilege. See a.o. Anne-Marie Korte 'Madonna's Crucifixion and the Female Body in Feminist Theology,' in: Rosemarie Buikema & Iris van der Tuin (eds.), *Doing Gender in Media, Art and Culture* (New York: Routledge, 2009), pp. 117–33.

Peter Nynäs is professor of comparative religion at Åbo Akademi University. His main research areas are psychology of religion, intercultural encounters and place and religion. Important publications in English: A hermeneutic perspective on intercultural communication: interpretative models of estrangement and identification, in: *Bridges of Understanding. Perspectives on Intercultural Communication*, (ed. Øivind Dahl, Iben Jensen & Peter Nynäs, Oslo: Oslo Academic Press, 2006); Spatiality, practice and meaning: the existential ambiguity of urban chapels, in: *Theology in Built Environments: Religion, Architecture & Design*, (ed. Sigurd Bergmann, New Jersey: Transaction 2009); From sacred place to an existential dimension of mobility, in: *The Ethics of Mobilities. Rethinking Place, Exclusion, Freedom and Environment*, (ed. Sigurd Bergmann & Tore Sager, Aldershot: Ashgate 2008).

Anne Birgitta Pessi is a docent (adjunct professor) in theology/church and social studies (University of Helsinki) and in sociology (University of Kuopio). She works as an academy research fellow and a deputy director at the University of Helsinki, Collegium for Advanced Study. Pessi's research interests cover particularly altruism, communality, church social work, volunteerism, and urban religion as well as individualized religiosity. Pessi is extensively involved in various international research projects and directs a Finland´s Academy funded research project RiTS (Religion in Transforming Solidarity for 2008–11) that involves seven researchers, both doctoral and post-doctoral fellows. Pessi has been awarded several academic prizes, such as the Nils Klim prize. Selected publications: Pessi, A.B. (2010). "Privatized Religiosity Revisited: Building an authenticity theory of the individual-church relations." Social Compass. [forthcoming in 2012.]; Pessi, A.B. (2011). "Religiosity and Altruism: Exploring the link and its relation to happiness." *Journal of Contemporary Religion* 26(1), 1–18; Pessi, A.B. & Nicolaysen, B. (2010). "Towards Good Life by Volunteering? Bringing the Work of Charles Taylor into Dialogue with Sociological Research on Volunteering." *Diaconia: Journal for the Study of Christian Social Practice*, Vol. 2, 128–55; Jeppsson Grassman, E. & Pessi, A.B. & Whitaker, A. & Juntunen, E. (2010). "Spiritual Care in the Last Phase of Life: A Comparison between the Church of Sweden and the Church of Finland." *The Journal of Pastoral Care and Counseling*, 1–10; Pessi, A.B. (2008). "Religion and Social Problems: Individual and Institutional Responses." *The Oxford Handbook of the Sociology of Religion*. Ed. P. Clark. Oxford University Press, 941–61.

Rik Pinxten is senior professor in anthropology and the comparative study of religion at Ghent University. He has published widely on the anthropology of knowledge (e.g. *Anthropology of Space*. U Penn Press, 1983), on epistemology and anthropology (e.g. *When the Day Breaks*, P. Lang Verlag, Frankfurt,

1997) and on the comparative study of religion and of knowledge (e.g. *De Strepen van de Zebra*, Houtekiet 2007). Recently, he published a book on comparative study of religion: *The creation of god*. Frankfurt: P. Lang Verlag (2010). He is editing a series on anthropology and politics with Berghahn Publishers, Oxford. Current research focuses on formal thinking and culture (in line with the 1983 book), to yield a book on the scope and limits of ethnomathematics.

Frank Usarski, PhD, lectured on the Science of Religion at the universities of Hannover, Oldenburg, Bremen, Erfurt, Chemnitz and Leipzig, all in Germany, between 1988 and 1997. Since 1998, he is professor at the Pontifical Catholic University (PUC) of São Paulo, in Brazil. Among the projects he has undertaken at the PUC was to found "REVER – Revista de Estudos da Religião", the first fulltext online-journal on Religious Studies in Latin America and the research group CERAL (Centro de Estudos de Religiões Orientais no Brasil) that is investigating the history and contemporary situation of traditional and "new" oriental religions in Brazil. His publications include: *O Budismo e as outras – Ewncontros e desencontros entre as grandes religiões mundiais*. Aparecida: idéias & letras 2009; "Merkmale der frühen deutsche Buddhismusrezeption. Ein revidierter systematischer Aufriss", in: Thomas Hase et. alii (eds): *Mauss, Buddhismus, Devianz - Festshrift für Heinz Mürmnel zum 65.Geburtstag*, Marburg: Diagonal 2009, pp. 233–52; "The Last Missionary to Leave the Temple Should Turn Off the Light" – Sociological Remarks on the Decline of Japanese "Immigrant" Buddhism in Brazil, in: *Japanese Journal of Religious Studies*. 2008, v.35, pp. 39–59.

Walter Van Herck obtained his PhD in Philosophy in 1996 at the Institute of Philosophy of the Catholic University of Leuven with a dissertation on *Metaphors, relativism and religious belief*. He is an associate professor of philosophy of religion at the University of Antwerp and member of the Centre Pieter Gillis at the same university. His research interests concern mainly religious epistemology, religious language, and the interaction between culture and religion. He recently edited together with Hans Geybels a volume on *Humour and Religion* (Continuum, 2011). Together with colleagues he translated work of Hume and Kant into Dutch. He is editor-in-chief of *Bijdragen. International Journal in Philosophy and Theology*.

Catherine Wanner is a professor in the departments of history and anthropology at the Pennsylvania State University. She received her doctorate in cultural anthropology from Columbia University. She is the author of *Burden* *of Dreams: History and Identity in Post-Soviet Ukraine* (1998), *Communities of the Converted: Ukrainians and Global Evangelism* (2007), which won four prizes and was named Choice Outstanding Academic Title, and co-editor of *Religion, Morality and Community in Post-Soviet Societies* (2008). She is currently writing a book on religion and secularization in the Soviet Union, *The Sacred and the Secular in Soviet Borderlands: Commemorating the Living and the Dead*, and editing another, *New Religious Histories: Rethinking Religion and Secularization in Russia and Ukraine*. Her research has been supported by awards from the National Endowment for the Humanities, the National Science Foundation, and the Social Science Research Council among others.

Haim Yacobi is a senior lecturer at the department of politics and government at Ben Gurion University and a Marie Curie fellow at Cambridge University. As an architect and planner who specialized in politics, his academic work focuses on the urban as a political, social and cultural entity. The main issues that stand at the center of his research interest in relation to the urban space are social justice, the politics of identity, migration, globalization and planning. His latest books *The Jewish-Arab City: Spatio-Politics in a Mixed Community was published recently* (2009 Routledge, London) and *Rethinking Israeli Space* (co-authored with Erez Tzfadia, 2011 Routledge, London). In 1999, he formulated the idea of establishing "Bimkom – Planners for Planning Rights" (NGO) and was its co-founder.

Framing the Sacred in the City: An Introduction

Liliana Gómez & Walter Van Herck

The City

Costa's naturalization of the origins of the plan stresses the symbolic significance of the figure of the cross. As a sign, the cross functions in the plan as both an index and an icon . . . . It points to a spatially defined place (but in this case, any place), indicating the presence of human beings and their attributes of property, settlement, and civilization. It is an indexical sign because it indicates the presence of a city and civilization as the source of the crossing axes in the same way that smoke indicates fire as its source. The cross of the plan is also an iconic sign in that it geometrically resembles several other well-known symbols, and this resemblance of form calls their meaning to mind. In a graphic medium, the cross of the plan resembles the cross of Christianity. The formal, iconic association evokes the idea of a sacred site for the city of Brasília and a divine benediction for the founding of the capital, an evocation based on the conventional association in the Christian world of crosses and things sacred. (Holston, 1989, p. 70).

With the foundation of the city of Brasília, in 1957, realized in a design competition for the new capital of Brazil, a novel Master Plan was projected in a most ambitious and ambivalent way: the modernist city. The new city, both utopian and foundational, became a paradigmatic model of a modern city for the new (Brazilian) society. Looking at the 'plan's hidden agenda', Brasília signifies as icon and index the realization of the modernist credo of a social change, of the modernization of society through urban design and architecture, that is, through the urbanization of society. What Brasília certainly makes clear is an overlapping or superposition of ancient traditional 'sacred' planning devices, in the way it represents symbolically in its Master Plan and urban structure the cross as an ordering principle and a modernist 'hidden agenda' of the 'city's design as a means to radical social transformation' (Holston, 1989, p. 59). It has been widely recognized that Lúcio Costa, Brasília's urban planner and architect, seems to have intended something analogous to the foundation of a city through the power of sacred symbols. But the realization of Brasília profoundly questions the rupture or ideological opposition. An opposition that has been articulated between, on the one hand, what has been conceived, in the realm of the cities, as a rational modern discourse, corresponding to the process of secularization of society and the idea of modernity and modern thinking following the Enlightenment. On the other hand, the irrational non-modern inherent in those religious phenomena have been opposed to this type of modernity to which the 'sacred' has always signified the counterpart. In his anthropological critique of the modernist city Brasília, James Holston observes that ' . . . if we are to believe Costa's myth of legitimation, the plan contains all the world's architecture, past, present, and future. The ecumenical scope of this legitimation is indeed extraordinary'. (Holston, 1989, pp. 73–4). So it seems that Costa gives the plan of the new city Brasília 'the suggestion of a legendary foundation, to give technical planning devices the aura of sacred symbols, and to invest Brasília with a world mythology of cities and civilizations' while concealing the city's origin as a modernist city (Holston, 1989, pp. 74).

Taking this rupture and ideological opposition as a starting point, we question today the relationship between the sacred and the city which we propose to (re)frame, looking at both historical and contemporary cultural and religious phenomena and the different theoretical approaches that configure this question. The urbanization of the world and the secularization of society not only provoke new cultural phenomena and a radical social transformation, which have shaped the idea of the modern, but also repositions the question of understanding these transformation processes at the foreground of our times. In these dynamics the relationship between the sacred and the city seems far more relevant to the understanding of modernization and modernity than might be thought on first reflection. The sacred in the city is (re)articulated as an emerging and meaningful relationship, politics of the sacred and cultural reinvention. We want to bring this re-articulation to the forefront by mapping its negotiations and making this relationship visible in a manifold and critical way. What has been increasingly made important by the so-called spatial turn has been to comprehend and discuss differently (social, cultural, political and economic) phenomena through their constitutive relationship to (urban) space, so the sacred and its different transformations constitute a challenge that only can be discussed within its epistemic entanglement. We will therefore focus on the relationship between the city and the sacred from a broader perspective. Only a multidisciplinary approach of philosophers and historians, architects and social geographers, sociologists and anthropologists and others, dealing with this question, offers the possibility of drawing a nuanced picture of the different layers of the sacred and its diverse manifestations in the city.

The Sacred

According to the historical encyclopaedia of philosophy, *Heilig/Heiligkeit* (sacred) refers in Greek to αγιος and in Latin to ‹sanctus›, originating from *sancire* which means to enclose, to encircle, that is, to delimit an area or district, while what is outside of the district (fanum) is referred to as pro-fanum. This origin is also present in Hebrew taking it from ‹qadôš›, referring to 'to separate' (Ritter, 1974, p. 1034). The city originally a delimited area, both physically and symbolically and by city-rights, always opposed to the non-city (country). Today, in times of dissolution of the opposition city-country (or urban-rural), it does certainly not represent such a clearly defined area against something else comprehended as the pro-fanum. Still, we consider it valid to keep this trace of 'encircling' and 'delimiting', a 'demarcation', which signifies a process or phenomenon, as a moment to define the 'sacred' today. Politics of meaning, of limits/borders, of inclusion and exclusion, certainly mark and unmark, in this sense, the 'sacred'. Roger Caillois has observed, in a more systematic study of the sacred and the man (Caillois, 1939), an intrinsic 'ambiguity of the sacred' in (modern) society that, we suggest, may be taken as a starting point to the study of the city.

It is central to the approach of this book that the notion of 'religion' is not given preference. 'Religion' has too many connotations with belief structures, institutions, hierarchies, while the 'sacred' as a category is more connected to an embodied attachment to symbols, buildings, monuments and other cultural manifestations. Emphasizing the experience of material religion, world religions are treated on an equal footing with all other expressions of spiritual allegiance. The city has a constitutive effect on our relation with the sacred and interacts with the human search for meaning in life and with the sacred in all its many guises. This constitutive dimension has hitherto not received much scholarly attention. Given the fact that the process of the urbanization of society is accelerating – thus giving an increasing importance to cities and the metropolis – it will become relevant to investigate the social or cultural cohesion that these urban agglomerations (still) manifest. New symbols of sacred ties to religious, political and ideological ideals emerge and are inscribed in urban spaces worldwide, thus changing the outlook of the processes of the urbanization and secularization of society. The sacred has become an important category of a new interpretation of social and cultural transformation processes, for example, taking into account how nature has always been understood in religious terms 'even where nature is apparently secularized through technology' (Szerszynski, 2005, p. xi). The city, both as *polis* and as a built environment, certainly reclaims a sort of 'second nature'. Following this observation, the city as *the* cultural, technological, political realization and horizon of meaning becomes the primary object of understanding the sacred in a broader sense. Bronislaw Szerszynski observes:

> With the *modern* sacred, the transcend axis is pulled into the very empirical world that was constituted by its ejection . . . . in the late twentieth century we start to see the emergence of a *postmodern* sacred, where multiple orderings of the sacred are grounded in the very individual subjectivities that had been made possible by the transcendent axis. (Szerszynski, 2005, p. xiii).

While rural community life – as more likely mono-cultural and mono-religious – is considered more propitious to a virtuous lifestyle, the city, as the habitat of the liberal individual, usually invokes associations with a secularized and hedonistic lifestyle. Given, however, the diversity of contemporary cultural contexts, it is in the city that different religions and quests for meaning confront one another, ignore one another, communicate with each other and compete with each other. The relics of the sacred might provide unity and union, but they also bring conflict and division. The impact of religions and their functional substitutions on the private and public life of individuals is undeniable. Understanding contemporary societies and their challenges requires attention to the way in which spiritual meaning, religion and world views are shaped within urban space. The sacred relates to the hidden forces of social and cultural cohesion, related to the meaning of life, which is not necessarily embedded in a particular religious system or practice. The focus on the sacred makes clear that within the cultural transformations due to modernity, particularly characteristic of the rise of the metropolis, the sacred did not disappear but emerged in a more complex way in new and different forms that are negotiated in urban settings. In this sense, the sacred in its manifold and ambivalent forms helps us to develop a better understanding of the processes of secularization that are characteristic of (post)modern cultures, of power structures in democracies and nations, of decolonization, as well as of other forms of the social imaginary of the city.

Our book aims to look at the relationship between the sacred and the city. So, we decided to describe the phenomena related to the sacred in its divergent forms and along the processes of its manifestations and negotiations in urban spaces. That the sacred is an important analytical and descriptive tool to understand social, cultural and political processes is an underlying assumption in most chapters. There is another assumption active here that we would like to make explicit – and which is shared again by most contributors – that is that the sacred did not disappear with the modernization of society, but instead has always existed and has (re)emerged as inherent to modernity. As has been observed, (modern) cultural and social phenomena today could not definitively confirm that religious belief would be 'superfluous' to the progress of Enlightenment reason (Zingerle and Mongardini, 1987, p. 99). But instead, as the example of the modernist city of Brasilía claims, the inscription of the sacred in the city must be looked at carefully.

The potential to comprehend the sacred as a category lies in its analytical quality to decipher both modernity and modernization. Birgit Meyer and Peter Pels focused on magic and modernity as a dynamic of revelation and concealment. They suggest here that 'one needs to ask what are the specific forms of the magic of modernity itself – those enchantments that are produced by practices culturally specific to modern states, economies, and societies – practices labelled as representation, commodification, and discipline' (Meyer and Pels, 2003, p. 5). In particular they argue that magic should be 'theorized as being explicitly of modernity' taking into account that the magic itself is 'culturally at home in the institutions and practices' of the Western world (Meyer and Pels, 2003, p. 4). In relation to this, it becomes important to unfold the concept of the sacred from within its two constitutive dimensions: first, that the modernization of Europe and its modern social and cultural constitution have to be read in the context of the world colonial experience and, today, from within the complex decolonization processes. The second has to do with the configuration of what has been started to be perceived and conceptualized as the 'modern metropolis', that is, the urbanization as an experience of the modern and the complete urbanization of society worldwide (Lefèbvre, 1970). Both dimensions unmask the ideological stance of the 'disenchantment of the world' through which Max Weber once determined the rationalization of society and in which the split between modernity and the sacred has been grounded. While the relationship between magic and modernity has been brought to our attention, the focus on the sacred in the city seems to offer a particularly important relationship through which the comprehension of emergent contemporary cultural and political phenomena may be possible. Examples include the emergence of new powerful religions, like Neo-Pentecostalism in postcolonial societies, or sacred forms in secular dynamics, such as the post-socialist movement of new urban meaning and the negation of the past in the present. The city in its complex forms represents here a necessary conceptual frame to discuss these cultural, religious and social phenomena, and allows us to (re)conceptualize the sacred as a category for understanding modernity and modernization and its processes beyond.

Mapping the Sacred in the City: An Overview

The book has four parts which approach the sacred in the city from four different angles. Part One 'The Sacred and the City: Theoretical Approaches' proposes some theoretical approaches. The three chapters in this first part can be seen as extensions of the introduction as they discuss the central notions of this book from philosophical and historical perspectives. The second part 'Religion, Built Environments and Urban Societies' offers an overview of current contexts of the debate and orients itself towards the discussion of religion in an urbanizing world, and of the built environment in a broader sense. Part Three, 'Sacred Symbols, Sacred Spaces', presents a more historical-conceptual analysis discussing the relation of Christian iconography, visual and spatial culture and the sacred in regard to the (medieval) order of knowledge. And the last part, 'Politics of the Sacred in Contemporary Urban Spaces', addresses the question of the sacred in contemporary urban spaces, such as Israel, the Congo, Cuba, and post-soviet Ukraine, to focus on the negotiation of the sacred today.

In his chapter Walter Van Herck starts from Marc Augé's analysis of non-places which expel any reference to the sacred. In an attempt to answer what we lost in losing the sacred old style, he looks at the procession of the Holy Blood in Bruges. One way in which the sacred returns is in the museum as a modern and postmodern temple of values. His itinerary in the end reveals how the sacred in the city is connected to issues of recognition and pluralism. Liliana Gómez offers in her chapter a path to draw a cultural analysis of the sacred in urban space. She argues that with the emergence of the modern metropolis the relationship between the sacred, the profane and everyday life has been radically changed. To understand the constitutive character of the sacred within modernity, she suggests (re)conceptualization of the sacred from within the perspective of the College of Sociology's sacred sociology: the sacred as an aesthetic experience helps us to understand non-rational and non-intentional social binding forces as forms of primary sociality. The recognition of the constitutive role of symbolic structures in social life implies that we understand the perception of society as a type of imagination, based on the actualization and transformation of individual and collective traditions. Approaching this relation differently, Pieter Dronkers observes, that long ago the sacred constituted a source of public order and social cohesion. But in the post-secular city religious, he argues, diversity is increasingly perceived as threatening the survival of the public domain. He proposes to look at the public role of religion that has provoked a lot of discussion among political philosophers, referring to Habermas or Frase. In accordance with them, this space should function as the integrating force of the political community. But Republican scholars phrase the importance of the public sphere in more radical terms, a position the author will look at, questioning the public domain as a platform that unites people and liberates them from archaic group identities, while other thinkers, such as Marcel Gauchet, define the public as sacred space. So the author examines the different theoretical reflections to these specific circumstances and the spatial impact of different political theories on the place of the sacred in the metropolis: how is the public reconstructed in different political theories? It is especially in the crowded, multicultural and post-secular cities that this interplay between public domain and the sacred becomes apparent. Since the metropolis functions as the site of this identity construction, it is important to assess, he argues, how religion finds its place in the city and can become material for identity construction. Finally, his argument builds on the work of critical philosophers who understand the city itself as a philosophical model. The metropolis here is the expression of difference and the site for inspiring discoveries, but at the same time appeals to a shared responsibility for the public accessibility of the city of the post-secular society.

In the second part, 'Religion, Built Environments and Urban Societies', Sigurd Bergmann's chapter proposes to think of religion in (cor)relation to the built environment by focusing on the 'aesth/ethics', ritual and memory in lived urban space. Specifically he asks: how does 'postmetropolis' interact with religion? How is 'lived religion' affected by 'lived (urban) space'? Should one interpret religion itself as a spatial phenomenon? Drawing on concepts from ecological phenomenology, anthropology, critical urban studies, theology and ritual theory, he explores how to catalyse the spatial turn of religion in built environments with regard to 'aesth/ethics', ritual and remembrance in particular. In Frank Usarski's contribution '*Kinhin* in a Megacity – Implicit meanings of the 'Walking-in-the-Park'-Movement in São Paulo' the label 'Caminhada no parque' ('walking in the park') refers to sessions of walking meditations (*kinhin*) undertaken periodically since April 2001 in the few green areas of the city of São Paulo. Behind these activities is Claúdia Souza de Murayama, alias 'Monja Coen', one of the central figures of Zen-Buddhism in Brazil. This chapter elaborates the hypothesis that the phenomenon in question is representative, not only of Brazilian Buddhism in general, but also of other segments of the highly diverse religious life for which Brazil is known. In their chapter on 'Life Stance and Religious Identity in an Urbanized World: The Meaning of Life as a Modern Predicament', Rik Pinxten and Lisa Dikomitis claim that the urban condition of mankind, basically living in vast metropolitan concentrations around the world, is at the very least a parameter to be reckoned with. The question they address is: what can be understood through the impact of this altered way of living on the growing majority of humanity with respect to the meaning of life and on the way life stances and religions are transplanted? More poignantly, they pose the question of whether the loosening grip and the decrease of control by kin and/or small communities in the urban context produce freedom, anxiety, creative potential or other reactions in the new generations growing up in larger urban areas. It may not be a moral or existential loss, but it certainly makes for new forms to deal with the meaning of life. From the perspective of the model of identity dynamics the learning processes in religions can be characterized as identity-forming paths, where religion is a vehicle for the construction of identity. It states that it gives an insight (which has comparative potential) of how religious traditional practices and/or beliefs work in the process of socialization. Safeguarding a local identity may safely be regarded as one role of religion: the small group (village, lineage group, clan, age groups, etc.) or genealogy. The claim that urbanization is impacting on religion as a vehicle for identity formation is theorized.

In the third part 'Sacred Symbols, Sacred Spaces', Anne-Marie Korte looks at the image of the Tower of Babel, which has an extraordinary history and meaning in Western religious culture, both literary and visual. She suggests that the Tower of Babel concerns a religious symbol that addresses the highest ambitions as well as the greatest failures of the metropolitan way of life. She focuses on this two-sided impact of the story of the Tower of

Babel, taking the tension between both sides as a productive means to explore the imaginative power of the Tower of Babel as a sacred symbol of the metropolis. By doing so, she elucidates 'gendered aspects' of the visual and textual interpretations of the story of the Tower of Babel and deciphers those aspects the Christian legends and depictions of Saint Barbara offer as an alternative interpretation, that is of the fundamental ambivalence towards the reality of ethnic and cultural diversity of the great cities the biblical story of the Tower of Babel represents. From the perspective of a more intrinsic relation of sacred symbols and sacred spaces, Renée Köhler-Ryan deciphers the nature and importance of sacred space considered as an 'elemental microcosm' which is taken here to mean a three-dimensional representation of the world that is composed of the elements so as to form a valuable, coherent and communicable whole that mirrors those same qualities of the cosmos. When a sacred space is considered as an elemental microcosm, she argues, it can intensify and mediate significant sacred aspects inherent to the city. She suggests that in this way, the false antithesis between the city and what is sacred comes to light. Taking a hint from modern space theory, she discusses the imagination of the (abstract) space or the space of rationality (for example, Descartes) that tends to separate us from imaginative ways of understanding our place in the cosmos. So she brings together the most important aspects of rational thought and lived bodily experience (place theory) for a kind of median way between these two positions to offer an understanding of the (modern) city. Anne Birgitta Pessi and Peter Nynäs in 'Relocating and Negotiating the Sacred: The Reception of a Chapel in a Shopping Mall' indicate how the intertwined processes of secularization and re-sacralization point to a shift away from religion in its traditional form. Instead, both tend to foster a spirituality that corresponds to personal needs fulfilled through consumption. This can be observed in the way religious architecture has been marginalized and made more invisible in society. Thus a relocation of facilities for worship, prayer and contemplation can be witnessed. They are, for instance, found in airports and shopping malls. Moreover, it is not only the location but also the character of these new prayer rooms that is changing. They are often intended to be used by people of all faiths, or by people of no faith at all, i.e., they are designed to be inclusive. Given the blurred boundaries between sacred and profane the authors examine the role of relocated facilities for worship among people. Pessi and Nynäs make a case study of a particular chapel, the Chapel of Silence, which is situated in a shopping mall in the fastest growing area of Finland, a suburb around Helsinki. The focus is placed on the reception of this chapel. How is the chapel within the specific context of a shopping mall appreciated and experienced by the presumed users? From this perspective they shed light on how the sacred dimension is negotiated in post-secular urban settings.

The last part, 'Politics of the Sacred in Contemporary Urban Spaces', focuses on the politics of the sacred in contemporary urban spaces, by looking at four cities as examples: Kinshasa, capital of the Democratic Republic of Congo, Netivot, an Isreali development town, Havana in Cuba, and the post-socialist cities in the Ukraine. Filip De Boeck observes in his contribution 'Kinshasa and its (Un)Certainties: The Polis and the Sacred', in Kinshasa, one of Africa's most vibrant urban environments, the notions of the polis and of the sacred do not offer steady ground. First of all, in the Congolese context, it is not clear what the notion of the polis, in its double meaning of urban community and of political community, might mean. Kinshasa as polis, in the double meaning of the word, has never belonged to its inhabitants: In terms of the polis most Kinois have never had a real right to the city. During the colonial period Kinshasa, then still Léopoldville, developed along strictly defined racial and gender lines, turning into a model of urban segregation. Today, Kinshasa has long outgrown the contours of La Ville, the former colonial city, and lacks the most basic urban infrastructure. Kinshasa and the country at large were thereby condemned to a perpetual state of exception, in which the Congolese citizens became homines sacri, to adopt Agamben's notion, people caught in a politicized form of natural life, whose lives are desacralized, constantly exposed and subjugated to death, and who are placed outside both the divine and profane law. This brings the author to the second term, that of the sacred. By discussing the specific ways in which the polis and the sacred have become intertwined in Kinshasa, as well as the contradictions, paradoxes and uncertainties, the author looks at how, unlike the government, the churches, such as those of the Neo-Pentecostalism, seem to have a clear urban project: to turn Kinshasa into a New Jerusalem, and to reconfigure the city and its public sphere through the sheer power of prayer. The negotiation and the politics of the sacred are especially focused by Haim Yacobi by looking at Netivot, an Israeli development town located in the peripheral Negev region. From the perspectives of both political theory and architecture and planning history, he deciphers some principles of development towns in Israel to comfort a modernist layout of space. He observes that a modernist schematic urban morphology is visually and spatially disrupted by indications of a different layer of urban life, memory and sacred experience that reflects diverse perceptions of what constitutes a city. By focusing specifically on the case of Netivot, Yacobi argues that how an alternative sense of sacred place is linked to a diasporic memory and Mizrahi identity functions to undermine the Israeli production of sovereign space. More specifically, he discusses the role of the built environment in the production of Jewish places in the 'old-new space', in which top-down power creates counter-reactions that do not adhere to the desire to modernize/Westernize space. In this part, Liliana Gómez looks at how the city of Havana (Cuba) has been incorporating the modern project and how the city has perpetuated cultural practices of syncretism and of the sacred that are rooted in a culture of resistance. Through the lenses of the Cuban writer Alejo Carpentier she offers a decipherment of these hybrid phenomena of an urban popular culture. The sacred is here no less than the experience of the heterogeneous, the incongruent and the hybrid. This approach to decipher the city is supported by a series of both theoretical and methodological questions that help to relocate the sacred as a main source of social cohesion, both as a hidden force and as a counter-discourse of resistance. Her contribution focuses on the interweaving between the sacred and everyday life that is the key to understanding Havana's modern urban spaces. Finally, Catherine Wanner observes the practices of remaking sacred spaces after socialism in Ukraine by contrasting the construction of urban sacred space in the former Soviet Ukraine with how these sacred spaces have been remade in the post-Soviet period to promote a new nationalized Self. She argues that as conflated as Soviet ideology was with a sacred vision of worldly salvation, urban life revealed an ongoing presence of the sacred in public space as well as lived domestic space. By contrasting the divergent aesthetics, sites and meanings of monumental representations of history from the Soviet to the post-Soviet periods, she suggests that we see how sacred visions have been articulated in the urban landscape over the course of the twentieth century. Since 1991 it has become incumbent on the new Ukrainian state to articulate a new sense of individual and collective identity. She suggests that these new monuments, depicting pivotal events in Ukrainian history, are forging a new aesthetic and creating new forms of experience that tap into religious sensibilities by appealing to the sacred to cultivate a sense of allegiance to a newly redefined national community.

This book is partly the outcome of an international workshop 'The Sacred in the Metropolis' held on March 24, 2009 at the University of Antwerp. A short lecture series 'From Kinshasa to Havana' was part of that event. The workshop and lecture series were organized by the University Centre Saint Ignatius Antwerp (UCSIA). UCSIA also granted a scholarship to Liliana Gómez for a research stay at the University of Antwerp. Our thanks go to the director and staff of UCSIA for their generous support: Prof Christiane

Timmerman, Prof Luc Braeckmans, Geert Vanhaverbeke and Barbara Segaert. We would also like to thank Nathan Van Herck for helping us with the preparation of the index. Last, but not least, we thank the contributing authors for the fruitful and most enjoyable collaboration.

Bibliography

Bergmann, S., Scott, P., Jansdotter S., M. and Bedford-Strohm, H. (eds) (2009), *Nature, Space and the Sacred.* London: Ashgate.
Caillois, R. (1939), *L'homme et le sacré.* Paris: Leroux.
—. (1995), 'L'ambigüité du sacré', in Hollier, D. (ed.), *Le Collège de Sociologie 1937–1939.* Paris: Gallimard, pp. 364–402.
Durkheim, E. (1912), *Les formes élémentaires de la vie religieuse.* Paris: Alcan.
Eliade, M. (1959), *The Sacred and the Profane. The Nature of Religion.* New York: Harcourt Brace.
Holston, J. (1989), *The Modernist City: An Anthropological Critique of Brasilia.* Chicago: University of Chicago Press.
Kamper, D. and Wulf, C. (eds) (1987), *Das Heilige. Seine Spur in der Moderne.* Frankfurt am Main: Athenäum.
Lefèbvre, H. (1970), *La révolution urbaine.* Paris: Gallimard.
Mauss, M. (1968), *Les fonctions sociales du sacré.* Paris: Édition de Minuit.
Meyer, B. and Pels, P. (eds) (2003), *Magic and Modernity. Interfaces of Revelation and Concealment.* Stanford: Stanford University Press.
Rincón, C. (2001), 'Magisch/Magie', in Barck, K. et al. (eds), *Ästhetische Grundbegriffe. Historisches Wörterbuch in sieben Bänden.* Stuttgart: Metzler, pp. 724–60.
Ritter, J. (ed.) (1974), 'Heilig, Heiligkeit', in: *Historisches Wörterbuch der Philosophie*, Vol. 3. Darmstadt: Wissenschaftliche Buchgesellschaft.
Szerszynski, B. (2005), *Nature, Technology and the Sacred.* Malden: Blackwell.
Zingerle, A. and Mongardini, C. (eds) (1987), *Magie und Moderne.* Berlin: Guttandin & Hoppe.

Part One

The Sacred and the City: Theoretical Approaches

Chapter 1

Sacred *Horror Vacui*.
A Philosophical Reflection

Walter Van Herck

By 'sacred *horror vacui*' I mean the impossibility of complete profanation or perfect secularity. However much public space is rendered devoid of symbols, ritual and the sacred, there is an ineradicable dynamics to fill the vacuum. I explore these dynamics by reflecting first on the category of 'non-place'. Second, I take a closer look at medieval processions in order to see what we have lost in dealing with the sacred in the public domain. Third, the suggestion that our contemporary museums are ritual sites is investigated. Could this be a genuine retrieval of the sacred? And last: the sacred underwent many transformations in our time, but the urge to externalize our highest values and seek recognition for these symbols of what we deem holy, remains unchanged.

Two Exemplary Places

A city is a locus of transformation. People, businesses, professions change in the city. But the city itself changes too. In comparing two paradigmatic places the ways in which the urban public space has changed and changes, becomes clear. James Frazer's portrayal of the city of Rome of his day is juxtaposed with a clip from *2001: A Space Odyssey* (Stanley Kubrick, 1968).

James Frazer, the famous armchair anthropologist, is the writer of the magisterial study *The Golden Bough*. As is well known, the book starts with a sketch of the priesthood of Nemi. Near the lake of Nemi – south of Rome – there was in ancient days a temple for the Goddess Diana. The priest taking care of the sanctuary would, as a rule, be replaced by his murderer, thus leading a stressful, vigilant and short life. Frazer is baffled by this phenomenon and dedicates the rest of his extensive work to resolving the riddle of the priesthood of Nemi by tracing comparable customs in other cultures and in history.[1] After all his reflections on heathen forms of religion, Frazer ends his book on a more Christian note. So, I'm here not interested in pagan notions of the holy, but in what Frazer – a bit off guard – says about Rome in the last sentences of his book:

> Once more we take the road to Nemi. It is evening, and as we climb the long slope of the Appian Way up to the Alban Hills, we look back and see the sky aflame with sunset, its golden glory resting like the aureole of a dying saint over Rome and touching with a crest of fire the dome of St. Peter's. The sight once seen can never be forgotten [. . .] But Nemi's woods are still green, and as the sunset fades above them in the west, there comes to us, borne on the swell of the wind, the sound of the church bells of Rome ringing the Angelus. *Ave Maria!* Sweet and solemn they chime out from the distant city and die lingeringly away across the wide Campagnan marshes. "*Le roi est mort, vive le roi!*" (Frazer, 1976, p. 934).

Frazer must have seen in Christianity part of the solution to the mystery he is trying to solve. Christ is a king who dies and saves the world. Frazer's walk to the Alban Hills stays within hearing distance of the church bells of Rome. Rome is for Frazer a landmark of Christian meaning and as such it overarches his inquisitive searches in antiquity. The place where he stands on the Via Appia, looking back at Rome, is a space interwoven with meaning. Sacred reference points like Saint Peter's seat give orientation. The sound of the bells[2] tolling penetrates every space within its vibrant circle.

The movie *2001: A Space Odyssey* offers us an entirely different experience of 'space'. In one scene, just after the opening scene in which primates discover the use of utensils, a scientist Dr Heywood Floyd (William Sylvester) is on his way to the moon. A shuttle brings him to a space station to the tunes of a Straussian waltz. In the space shuttle almost complete silence reigns. Once he arrives in the space station Floyd traverses different waiting rooms and is attended by charming, but impersonal hosts. He follows computer instructions for identification and uses a phone booth to speak to his little daughter. After being brought from the space station to the moon base, Dr Floyd steps into a conference room where a company of officials awaits him. When first describing this scene the word 'impersonal' comes to mind, given the uniform type dresses of all characters and the quasi-clinical environment. No signs of collective values or symbols are present. The only meaning here is functional.

Place and Non-place in Supermodernity

In *Non-places: An introduction to supermodernity* the ethnologist Marc Augé (Augé, 2008) undertakes to study the city in its most recent appearances. In order to do this he distinguishes between place and non-place. His thesis is that the last category is starting to dominate urban life.

Place can also be described with the more accurate term 'anthropological place'. It is defined in several ways. Among these definitions is the characterization that it is a space in which inscriptions can be found of social bonds and collective history (Augé, 2008, p. viii). A place is therefore a symbolic universe where everything is a sign or part of a code:

> . . . universes of meaning, of which the individuals and groups inside them are just an expression, defining themselves in terms of the same criteria, the same values and the same interpretation procedures. (Augé, 2008, p. 25)

The identity of place is a crucial factor in the establishment and unity of a group. Of course, this cultural community localized in time and space is partly the product of an illusion. Cultures create myths concerning their origin, sometimes blind to the diversity and relativity of their history. This indigenous fantasy often corresponds to the illusions of the ethnologist concerning the autarkic character of culture, but, however much an illusion, the experience of the identity of place is a reality. Through the organization of space and the founding of places identity is built (Augé, 2008, pp. 37–41).

'Anthropological places' are places of identity, of relations and of history. The place of birth for example is often mentioned as a constitutive element of one's identity. 'I'm originally from X (specifying a city, region, state, country)' or 'I was born in X' are standard ways of giving autobiographical information that is seen as throwing light on who one is. The spatial position one is given, situates one in a configuration of relations and loyalties. To live in an anthropological place means to live in a place which was built by one's ancestors.

The simplest example that can be given of an 'anthropological place' is perhaps a village or town. Its roads and paths come together at intersections where marketplaces and crossroads receive people for commercial, political and religious interactions. Inhabitants of these town centres erect monumental buildings like churches and town halls. With these monuments they try to give permanence to their culture and conceive themselves as part of something bigger: '. . . monuments . . . give every individual the justified feeling that for the most part, they pre-existed him and will survive him' (Augé, 2008, p. 49). In such a context people are proud of their citizenship of a particular town. In some countries, people use joke names to indicate citizens of specific cities. Due to the Spanish rule of Antwerp, residents of that town are called 'sinjoren' (derived from 'señor') and other city dwellers in Belgium have received names like 'chicken eaters' (Brussels), 'moon extinguishers' (Malines), 'onion eaters' (Aalst). These names also testify to reciprocal prejudices. But due to an increase in mobility and migration, less and less people identify with their residential city, forsaking to call it 'my town'.

Augé's notion of non-place (*non-lieu*) refers to the postmodern space which stops radiating identity, thus being the exact opposite of anthropological places. Examples of such non-places are: hospitals, holiday clubs, trains and train stations, subways, airports, waiting rooms (Sayeau, 2010), shopping malls, supermarkets, educational institutions, office buildings, conference rooms, highways and their rest stops, transit areas, etc. Of course, Augé is conscious of the fact that neither place nor non-place exist in pure form. But still he has reasons to conclude: 'non-places are the real measure of our time; . . .' (Augé, 2008, p. 64).[3]

Non-places are typically instrumental spaces. One enters them in order to attain certain ends like transport, transit, commerce or leisure. While anthropological places are organically social, non-places create solitary contractuality.[4] Passport, credit card, boarding pass, driver's license and the like open the gates of the non-place. Word and text accompany one's passage in the form of instructions for use: prescriptive signs ('stand on the right, walk on the left'), prohibitive boards ('no smoking') and informative panels. Once inside one is one of many; a passenger, a customer, a driver, a visitor, a tourist. Unlike anthropological places where people are present in their full individual identity (being greeted in the street; craftsmen in their workshops; recognizable uniforms, toga's, soutane's) one is here freed from one's defining qualities and can enjoy 'the passive joys of identity loss' (Augé, 2008, p. 83). Even a traveller feeling homesick in a strange country can experience relief upon entering non-places like gas stations or airports.

In opposition to modernity that integrates old and new, pre-modern and modern, 'the chimneys and the spires', postmodernity fails to do this. The churches and monuments are classified to the status of 'places of memory and assigned to a circumscribed and specific position' (Augé, 2008, p. 63). These monuments are approached with a specific attitude of people in search of a past and an identity. This is what we once were. Buildings and monuments have become nothing more than 'heritage' – sites of symbolic interest that lack vital involvement. 'City marketing' is the commercial exploitation of urban historic sites.

It seems clear that if Augé is right in thinking that the postmodern cityscape is dominated by non-places, two conclusions can be drawn. The first is that the predominance of non-places is the material correlate of a certain type of liberalism that highly values the neutrality of the state. The state should not force any conception of the good on its members. Non-place is above all a neutral space: no symbolizations, no local references, no community (that always excludes some people). The second conclusion is only the next step: the sacred is absent from non-places. This absence is an essential absence. When anything sacred would enter a non-place, it would immediately stop being a non-place.

Losing the Sacred

What exactly did we lose in losing 'anthropological place'? Lilley (2004) offers an interesting perspective on the ways in which religious identity is present in medieval towns. What is original about his iconographic and morphological approach is that he wants 'to look at medieval urban landscapes more from the point of view of those who were there at the time, to see them through medieval Christian eyes' (Lilley, 2004, p. 308).

Many towns in the Christian world have legendary descriptions of their origins that connect them with the realm of the sacred. Textual sources often have references to intervening angels and saints. Descriptions of the position of walls, streets, churches and gates also mirror descriptions of Holy Jerusalem and incorporate symbols like the cross or the number of evangelists and apostles. The city-cosmos thus becomes a representation of the wider cosmos, thereby connecting heaven and earth.

This urban Christian symbolism enters the lives of the populace through the 'participation in processions that punctuate the Christian calendar in honour of Christ and his saints' (Lilley, 2004, p. 304). These processions are in many cases imitations of the liturgies of Jerusalem where Christians follow the (literal) path of Jesus. Jesus' birth is celebrated in Bethlehem, the resurrection of Lazarus in Bethany, the suffering on Golgotha, the ascension on the Mount of Olives. Next to the carrying around of relics in honour of saints on their feasts, there are Eucharistic processions in which the Body of Christ (*Corpus Christi*) is carried through towns. The routes of these processions commonly connect the periphery to the centre where a cathedral (or something akin) functions as an *axis mundi*. The mystery plays or *tableaux vivants* which are performed on these occasions enact the whole of history from creation to judgement day. In the Body of Christ this history is condensed: creation, fall, salvation.[5]

A fine example of the way in which the sacred physically engages people is the procession of the Holy Blood in Bruges, Belgium. By 1256, a relic of the Holy Blood, which originated from Constantinople, had fallen into the hands of Bruges' magistrates (Boogaart, 2001, p. 74). The relic was incorporated into an already existing festival of the Holy Cross and eventually supplanted it. After a vigil in the chapel of St. Basil the evening before, the procession started at 4 a.m. when the relic was taken from its tabernacle and put on display. In the same way as the sound of a bell marks the transubstantiation in the Eucharist, the city bells of Bruges signalled the liquefaction of Christ's Blood (Boogaart, 2001, p. 87). At about 10 a.m. the Holy Blood was placed in its carriage and taken out under a canopy. A circumambulatory procession started that went from the city centre to its southern gate and then followed the walls of the city alternating between the outside and the inside. Boogaart analyses the dynamics of the procession using Arnold van Gennep's threefold phases of rites of passage: detachment, liminality and reincorporation. The procession cuts the residents off from their profane occupations. All the while the city bells kept resounding, 'infusing the urban landscape with a pulsating rhythm, punctuated only occasionally by the horns and trumpets of city minstrels and guild musicians as well as psalms sung by celebrants' (Boogaart, 2001, p. 89). Once outside the city gates with rural plains before them they looked upon their habitat from an external point of view. As such the procession induced the reflective experience that underneath their differences a more fundamental social bond existed between them. After reentering the city and returning the relic to the chapel the procession dissolved as all the artisans went to their guild halls for a festive meal.

Consensual Unity versus Ritual Unity

Historians do not seem to agree on the question of whether these processions promoted cohesion and relieved social tension or whether, on the contrary, these processions were only a superficial varnish which hid unresolved conflicts and tensions in medieval society (Boogaart, 2001, p. 92). Much depends here on how one would want to understand the notions of 'cohesion' and 'unity'. The most obvious and modern way of conceiving this unity is to equate it to 'consensus'. People are unified, or form a community when they think largely the same or have identical opinions on a number of issues. In order to achieve unity dialogue is needed and democratic discussion. This type of unity is partial in at least two senses. First, it is partial because people will keep on disagreeing on some issues. Second, it is partial because a consensus between a majority is sufficient to proceed. The consequence of this is that some people still feel left out.

Next to this consensual type of unity, there is 'ritual unity'. For some anthropologists there is little difference between consensual and ritual unity, because they conceive of ritual as essentially communicative and expressive of ideas. I follow, however, a theory of ritual which is less intellectualist (Humphrey and Laidlaw, 1994, p.73; Moyaert, 2001, 2003). Any action can form part of a ritual, so what is characteristic of ritual must not be sought in *what* one does, but rather in *how* one does it. This modification (or ritualization) concerns the intentionality of action. In normal action, intentionality determines the identity of an action. What did I do, when raising my hand? Depending on my intentions it was an act of calling someone, of stretching a muscle, of feeling whether there is a draft in the room. In ritual, however, the actions are prescribed in a kind of scenario and the identity of the actions is fixed independently of the celebrant's intentions (wishes, emotions, accompanying thoughts). The validity of a wedding is not dependent on the vicar's intentions and thoughts (*ex opera operato*). These words and actions in this sequence entail marriage. This is not to say of course that intentions are absent or not valued, but only that they do not determine the identity of the actions in question. Acting out a ritual means to step into something that is larger than (my) life. In most religions the origins of ritual are situated in a mythic past as a gift from God or the gods. For this reason they count as irreplaceable and are never seen as man-made. 'Celebrants' acts appear, even to themselves, as "external", as not of their own making' (Humphrey and Laidlaw, 1994, p. 89). They must be performed with precision and scrupulousness. Rituals can be enormously impressive, because they take away the weight of intentions and desires that rests upon our everyday actions. Rituals free us of ourselves. In this sense, rituals must be opposed to ceremonies or parties (like celebrations, valedictory ceremonies, etc.) that are designed and made by people. Such ceremonies have impact because they express and evoke emotions with the intention of getting a message across. Essentially substitutable, these ceremonies revel in emotions, while ritual frees us from them.

All this has consequences. The point of ritual is not to get a message across. This means that different people attribute different meanings to rituals. Standing at the exit door of a church or temple and asking celebrants what the meaning of their ritual actions was, one receives myriad interpretations: liturgical, theological, metaphysical, realist, idealist, materialist, ethical... all smart, wise or simplistic. Ritual is, therefore, essentially poly-interpretable. It 'tends towards a dispersal of meaning' (Humphrey and Laidlaw, 1994, p. 265) and '(...) a custom does not become "a ritual" until people can disagree about its meaning' (Humphrey and Laidlaw, 1994, p. 12). It brings together people notwithstanding their very different views and interpretations. It allays diversity, tensions and differences in common adherence to sacred symbols. Although some rituals (or fragments of rituals) nowadays survive, no single ritual seems to be able to mobilize a complete city as was the case in Bruges in the late thirteenth century. Are we left with an endless search for consensus?

Retrieving the Sacred

Collective rituals, unifying symbols and a shared sense of the sacred have disappeared, but there are instead functional alternatives for religion and its social role. These alternatives are sometimes called 'invisible religions'. An example of such a functional alternative is the museum (Duncan, 1995). Museums in the contemporary cityscape remind us of the significance which temples, churches and cathedrals once had.[6] Museums have become sanctuaries of contemplation, filled with treasures, through which one strides with a feeling of awe and deep respect. In a sacrosanct silence (using a loud voice in a museum feels like a desecration) one contemplates from low seating the painting or work of art that makes such an impression as if it were the shrine of a favourite saint. The architecture of contemporary museums is often spectacular (see Kiasma in Helsinki, the Metropolitan and Guggenheim in New York, museums in Linz, Toledo, Boston, San Francisco, etc.) and defines the cityscape in the same penetrating way as cathedrals once formed the landmarks of European cities. One could extend the comparison up to the opening hours on Sundays, the presence of ushers or attendants and the 'devotion cards' sold in the museum shop.

As is pointed out in an insightful essay by Sharon Macdonald (2006) the established nineteenth century public museum can be contrasted to a museum of a newer type. The established museum was an expression of the identity of the nation state, of progress and the achievements of the arts and sciences and of the ambitions of civil society. Egyptian collections in Western museums, for example, traced a cultural genetic line in which the ancient Egyptians, as testators to the Greeks, are part of the European civilization – an approach that remains blind to the African roots of Egyptian culture (Bouquet and Porto, 2006, pp. 8–9). Under pressure of increasing criticism and dropping visitor numbers, this type of museum gave way to a newer type that has redefined its role in public culture. Since there is no canon anymore and no unifying ideal, this newer type focuses on the individual (rather than on the community) and it's craving for experiences. Museums aid in the search for the deeper, truer self. Hence, changed display forms comprise 'total environments', 'interactive exhibits', drama and visual effects. The visitor walks inside a computer or inside the human body and is taken by the hand through fascinating and passionate science adventures. The disenchanted individuals can feel re-enchanted in the magical museum.

Macdonald notes the similarity between, on the one hand new religious movements with their attempt to arouse deep individual spiritual experiences *à la carte*, and on the other hand the new museum type. 'The demise of a canon and the attempt to provide variety and novelty also have implications for the role of the museum priesthood' (Macdonald, 2006, p. 215). The role of the curator is evidently redefined as subject expertise and scholarship have only a partial say in the new museum. Although the individual visitor and his search for unmediated experiences is the prime focus of the museum, the fact that 'museums have been one of the key institutions through which collective identities have been imagined' (Macdonald, 2006, p. 217) cannot be dismissed. So, museums want to reach out to the community or bring the community to the museum.

The established museum had such a community, but in the case of the newer type of museum the target group has diversified to such a degree that lots of examples can be given of museums that get entangled in ambiguities and sensitivities. The museum is given a political vocation as an instrument of civil society, but at the same time the museum can no longer be a museum for all. Creationists of Christian and Muslim lineage refuse to enter a natural history museum; a holocaust documentation centre must be careful not to venerate what it remembers; ethnological museums can raise controversy concerning the representation of colonialism; museums of contemporary art get questions about whether this 'art' is worth the taxpayers money; and so on.

The conclusion must be that only certain layers of the population visit museums and that within this category many eclectically choose the museum of their liking. The retrieval of the sacred through, for example, the museum as a ritual site is therefore limited. The sense of being part of something bigger, of being freed from the trivialities of one's own individuality in the light of something infinitely more important is undoubtedly rare in the modern museum. One finds what one was looking for. Rather than calling the museum a ritual site, it is perhaps more appropriate to emphasize the ideological role of museums which started out in the nineteenth century with a nationalist vocation and is now adapted to the context of pluralism and ecological problems that characterizes contemporary society. The new museum provides experiences as a mediator of messages with a political, cultural or 'scientific' content. As such the museum in its present form promotes dialogue and understanding. It is directed at consensual unity.

Non-place and the Urban Jungle

The Latin word for city, *civitas*, has a double sense. It can refer to a political community of people living together and it can refer to the material city. Insofar as Augé's analysis suggests that part of our public urban spaces have developed into non-places, this reveals the partial destruction of the city-community. The rise and frequent use of the metaphor of an 'urban jungle' signals this comparable change. Non-place demands an inconspicuous ethos. Inferring the wealth, standing and profession of someone by his way of dressing and moving has become increasingly difficult. The contemporary city dweller seems to choose a kind of camouflage which makes him blend in with the masses in the street. A more common, more anonymous and egalitarian way of dressing masks economic and social differences. It also matches the neutrality of non-place. Characteristic is the use of small backpacks to carry computers, books, documents, lunch boxes, etc. One takes the subway and crosses streets in anoraks which are said to be appropriate to traverse dark forests and to climb mountains – even on the north face. Less anonymous, but emanating the same message of being in a hostile environment is the use of SUVs.

From whence this desire to camouflage, to blend in, to leave home only well-equipped? The image of an 'urban jungle' presents itself at first sight as a *contradictio in terminis*. Jungle and urbanity are opposites, but 'urban jungle' points to the resemblances these original opposites have started to develop. Instead of an exemplification of the civilized world, the city has been overgrown by uncontrollable nature. The law of the jungle reigns in the city, the law of survival of the fittest, of unlimited egoism. The jungle starts where the human community ends. An 'urban jungle' testifies to an experience in which the city threatens to lose its humanity.

Far too little do we realize that our humanity, our freedom, our properties are only possible within a community. Having a car, for example (and the freedom it still represents for some), would be utterly useless without the roads, the laws and traffic rules, the petrol supplies, and other things that the community provides. What's more: driving a car is only possible in a community where people *respect* property laws and traffic rules. Free riders – as they are called – make use of the community provisions and facilities in order to break its rules. They depend on the obedience and docility of all the others to have their selfish interests served. As such any free rider behaviour (like not paying fares on public transport, leaving litter in the street, not paying due taxes, etc.) undermines the community. The offender wants the pleasures and benefits of the social contract, but not its problems and expenses. His lack of respect for the law equals his lack of respect for the community which carries and supports him in innumerable ways. This explains the enormous sensitivity people have concerning vandalism and hooliganism. However insignificant the material damage may be, acts of this kind signal a breach of the social contract placing the self above the community. On a very local scale these acts signify a relapse into a state of nature or a condition of war. Having to live with the constant possibility of such a relapse turns the city into an urban jungle.

Perhaps the instrumental nature of non-place, the fact that it is there and I am in it to serve my private goals, induces this egotistical, pragmatic use of public space. 'Private vices, public benefits' may be a principle that works within the confined space of capitalist markets, it cannot be the motto of civil society. Some have sought the solution for the lack of communality in a restoration of politeness, decency, manners, etiquette and courtesy (Sennett, 1977). As such, this was the sociological recognition of the importance of ritual. Thanks to manners and courtesy we do not need to be or think the same, but can still live together in the city. Manners used to characterize urban culture. The peasant lacks dignified behaviour. Doing away with politeness was a mistake of the sixties committed in the name of authenticity and truthfulness.[7] Indeed, politeness is more than formality or masquerade. Decency makes social interaction possible where there are considerable differences on the level of politics, religion or even personality. The manners of a 'civil' lifestyle are not redundant at all. Although it is difficult, even impossible, to force people by law to be polite and decent, it is clear that life would be utterly unliveable without. This rehabilitation of manners view neglects, however, the fact that manners and 'good breeding' still emanate from a shared culture or set of values. When this common ground fails, city life disintegrates and turns for some into an 'urban jungle'.

Craving for Recognition in the City. Towards a Deepened Understanding of the Complexities of Pluralism

Scholarly literature on contemporary pilgrimage points out that the powers of sacred contiguity remain strong. People want to be there, at the exact spot and in close physical contact, where great events have taken place and where their heroes and saints once were. A special issue of the journal *Crosscurrents*[8] devoted to 'The Varieties of Contemporary Pilgrimage' gives an exemplary overview: the gravesite of Elvis in Memphis, Tennessee; the settings of the film 'The Lord of the Rings' in New Zealand; the Atomic Test Site in New Mexico; ground zero in New York City. A sense for the sacred was never lost, but we do not seem to share the same sense for the sacred. This reveals the intricacy of postmodern pluralism.

Understanding what is at stake in the pluralist setting of Western society, implies attention for this specificity of the human experience of what is valuable beyond measure, i.e., of what is sacred. Values could be defined as that which people deem more important than themselves. When a person is willing to make sacrifices for something or someone, it is correct to conclude that this something or someone embodies a value for the person in question. Many examples of this can be given: family, friends, native country, money, success, etc. The highest values of people are associated with their religion (or more broadly, their worldview). Two characteristics of human values are important here: first, the highest values are represented in a material, symbolic form (statues of leaders and artists; religious buildings; flags; symbols like crosses; relics; specific clothing) and, secondly, values tend to be shared on a social level, partly in the public domain.

An intellectualist view of pluralism believes that the best strategy to cope with diversity is openness and dialogue. It treats religions and worldviews as a kind of hypotheses that can be discussed, entertained, adapted or abandoned and on which a consensus can be reached. It doesn't take account of the fact that man is a symbolic animal who is deeply attached to the symbols that embody his values (De Dijn, 1999). The pluralist setting clearly involves more than individual people having divergent opinions. Coping strategies for pluralist settings therefore necessarily must go beyond the level of public debates where diverging opinions are expressed and given argumentation.

Understanding public space has often been limited to understanding the logic that rules public debate, understood as the intellectual exchange as it is conducted in democratic societies in parliament, in courts, in newspapers and other media. But when focusing on the way people negotiate their values and what is sacred to them, a broader, more material, notion of public space comes into play. Public space in this sense comprises the streets and squares, the building and parks, the statues and monuments, the behaviour and clothing of the people moving about these places and, of course, the demonstrations, the organic structuring of the urban (in ghetto's, quarters etc.).

In societies where the presence of traditional religious communities is most influential, this symbolic determinedness of the public space is evident. In Jerusalem, the 'sacred city' *par excellence*, symbolic spatiality shows its conflicting and multilayered nature. Similarly, in Indian society forms of conflict and peaceful coexistence are often attached to factors related to symbolic spatiality (e.g., the Aydohya dispute). Western multicultural societies also experience such conflicts and need to come to terms with fundamental dilemmas related to issues concerning symbolic spatiality. One can think of referendums concerning building mosques and minarets; the general controversies over the appearance of religious symbols in public spaces (sculptures, crucifixes, Christmas trees etc.).

The emptiness of the non-places of supermodernity as described by Augé sets a sacred *horror vacui* in motion. The neutral void is instantly filled with symbols and specific clothing, with billboards and texts on t-shirts, with flyers and announcements. Places without symbolic traces of what is deemed sacred are inhumane. We only survive non-places because we also live in anthropological places.

This *horror vacui* reveals a desire for recognition. Beyond the formal ways of recognizing people (Honneth, 1996; Taylor, 2005), like giving minority groups equal rights, a craving for a certain type of recognition still remains. People don't want to be just tolerated, they want to be respected for who they are, as they live out their identities. They obey ambiguous impulses in doing this. By seeking identity and uniqueness people desire to be set apart (*liberté*), but by seeking recognition they testify of the desire to be included in a larger community (*fraternité*). Typically, they seek this recognition not merely in the form of disputes over rights but also in a symbolic way (Van Herck, 2011).

In our postmodern urban environments different groups play a delicate game of symbolically displaying their values in a quest for recognition. Not one procession of the Holy Blood, but several, very divergent processions and parades are going on continuously in our cities. Now, recognition has a triadic structure: I feel recognized whenever someone appreciates what I appreciate.

Precious Public Space

Perhaps it is worthwhile to think about a kind of ecology of our urban public spaces. How can it be kept, on the one hand, from being divided up by different groups which each retreat to their symbolically conquered areas and quarters, and on the other hand, from sterile neutrality?

Man as a rule-follower is not just an information processor, but a being that strives to meet certain norms and standards; that makes the distinction between what he does and what he ought to do. Only public standards of correctness can give sense to a distinction between what is right and what seems to be right (O'Hear, 1991, p. 51). Public space is exactly the place where these public standards are formed and used in processes of evaluation. Wittgenstein tells us that language – and by way of extension any rule guided activity – can't do without a public space. This public space is constitutive of our speaking, moral acting, religious feelings, and so on, even when these activities, this speaking and acting concerns the most intimate and the most personal.

> What this distinction [between deviant and non-deviant applications of a rule] requires, . . ., is the existence of a community, united in education, training and judgment and at one in the application of rules and the use of concepts. (O'Hear, 1991, p. 51)

From this it follows, that public space must be seen as the oxygen room that makes private and individual life possible. It is not the other way round: as if individuals would make communal, public life possible. An empty or neutral public space is nothing to be wished for. Without a community of scientists, there is no individual scientific thinking; without a community of citizens, there is no individual citizenship; and so on. In this light, the sacred 'in' urban public space can only survive when a certain sacredness 'of' public space has meaning for us.

Notes

[1] 'The object of this book is, by meeting these conditions, to offer a fairly probable explanation of the priesthood of Nemi' (Frazer, 1976, p. 3).

[2] Compare also Chateaubriand, *Génie du christianisme ou beautés de la religion chrétienne*, Quatrième Partie Culte, Livre Premier, Chapitre I. Des cloches (Chateaubriand, 1978, p. 893). Its quality consists mainly in 'par un seul coup de marteau, de faire naître, à la même minute, un même sentiment dans mille cœurs divers,

et d'avoir forcé les vents et les nuages à se charger des pensées des hommes' (with one stroke of the hammer it gives birth in the same moment to the same feeling in a thousand different hearts and it forces the winds and the clouds to charge themselves with the thoughts of men; my translation).

³ Compare (Augé, 2008, p. 86): 'places and non-places intertwine and tangle together'. Also: 'But the fashionable words – those that did not exist thirty years ago – are associated with non-places.'

⁴ 'Alone, but one of many, the user of the non-place is in contractual relations with it (or with the powers that govern it)' (Augé, 2008, p. 82).

⁵ '... the town as a social body performed His Body as the embodiment of the whole World, tracing through the town's centre an axis symbolizing the course of the world's linear history, as foretold by Holy Scripture' (Lilley, 2004, p. 306).

⁶ 'Museums and religious sites may also share an aesthetic: hushed tones, dimmed light, a sense of reverence – of being in communion with the sacred; they emanate an aura of age, the past, anachronism. There are also similarities in contemporary debates about them: in particular, a prevalent concern with demise – the anxiety that they are institutions of yesterday which are unlikely to have much place in the world of tomorrow' (Macdonald, 2006, p. 209).

⁷ See in this context the chapter on politeness (Comte-Sponville, 1995, ch. 2).

⁸ See *Crosscurrents*, Vol. 59 (2009), Issue 3 (September).

Bibliography

Augé, M. (2008), *Non-places. An Introduction to Supermodernity*. London: Verso.

Boogaart, T. A. (2001), 'Our Saviour's Blood: Procession and Community in Late Medieval Bruges', in Ashley, K. and Hüsken, W. (eds), *Moving Subjects. Processional Performance in the Middle Ages and the Renaissance*. Amsterdam: Rodopi, pp. 69–116.

Bouquet, M. and Porto, N. (eds) (2006), *Science, Magic and Religion. The Ritual Processes of Museum Magic*. New York: Berghahn.

Chateaubriand, F.-R. (1978), *Essai sur les révolutions – Génie du christianisme* (ed. Maurice Regard). Paris: Gallimard.

Comte-Sponville, A. (1995), *Petit traité des grandes vertus*. Paris: Presses Universitaires de France.

De Dijn, H. (1999), 'Values and Incarnation', in Olivetti, M. (ed.), *Incarnation*. Padova: Cedam, pp. 371–9.

Duncan, C. (1995), *Civilizing Rituals: Inside Public Art Museums*. London: Routledge.

Frazer, J. G. (1976), *The Golden Bough. A Study in Magic and Religion*. London: Macmillan.

Graham, G. (2007), *Re-enchantment of the World: Art Versus Religion*. Oxford: Oxford University Press.

Guelf, F. M. (2009), *Stadtluft macht frei. Von der Polis zur Cyberstadt. Philosophische Auseinandersetzungen*. Frankfurt am Main: Peter Lang.

Honneth, A. (1996), *The Struggle for Recognition: The Moral Grammar of Social Conflicts*. Cambridge: Polity Press.

Hubbard, K., Kitchin, R. and Valentine, G. (eds) (2005), *Key Thinkers on Space and Place*. London: Sage.

Humphrey, C. and Laidlaw, J. (1994), *The Archetypal Actions of Ritual*, Oxford: Clarendon.

Lilley, K. D. (2004), 'Cities of God? Medieval urban forms and their Christian symbolism'. *Transactions of the Institute of British Geographers, New Series*, 29(3): 296–313.

Macdonald, S. (2006), 'Enchantment and Its Dilemmas: The Museum as a Ritual Site', in Bouquet, M. and Porto, N. (eds), *Science, Magic and Religion. The Ritual Processes of Museum Magic*. New York: Berghahn, pp. 209–27.

Meagher, S. M. (2008), *Philosophy and the City. Classic to Contemporary Writings*. Albany: SUNY Press.

Molendijk, A., Beaumont, J. and Jedan, C. (eds) (2010), *Exploring the Postsecular. The Religious, the Political and the Urban*. Leiden: Brill.

Moyaert, P. (2001), 'Incarnation of Meaning and the Sense for Symbols', in Boeve, L. and Leijssen, L. (eds), *Sacramental Presence in a postmodern context*. Leuven: Peeters, pp. 112–29.

—. (2003), 'The Sense of Symbols as the Core of Religion', in Faulconer, J. (ed.), *Transcendence in Philosophy and Theology*. Bloomington: Indiana University Press, pp. 53–69.

O'Hear, A. (1991), 'Wittgenstein and the Transmission of Traditions', in Phillips Griffiths, A. (ed.), *Wittgenstein Centenary Essays*. Cambridge: Cambridge University Press, pp. 41–60.

Sayeau, M. (2010), 'Waiting', in Beaumont, M. and Dart, G. (eds), *Restless Cities*. London: Verso, pp. 279–99.

Sennett, R. (1977), *The Fall of Public Man*. New York: Knopf.

Taylor, C. (2005), 'The Politics of Recognition', in Taylor, C. (ed.), *Philosophical Arguments*. Cambridge, MA: Harvard University Press.

Van Herck, W. (2007), 'A Friend of Demea? The Meaning and Importance of Piety', in A. F. Sanders (ed.), *D.Z. Phillips' Contemplative Philosophy of Religion*. Aldershot: Ashgate Publishing, pp. 125–38.

—. (2008), 'Lift up Your Hearts. On Emotionalism in Religious Experience', in W. Lemmens and W. Van Herck (eds), *Religious Emotions. Some Philosophical Explorations*. Newcastle: Cambridge Scholars Publishing, pp. 75–86.

—. (2010), 'Religion, Democracy and the Empty Shrine of Pluralism. Some Reminders', in P. Losonczi and A. Singh (eds), *From Political Theory to Political Theology*. London: Continuum, pp. 101–10.

—. (2011), 'Humour, Religion and Vulnerability', in Geybels, H. and Van Herck, W. (eds), *Humour and Religion: Challenges and Ambiguities*. London: Continuum, pp. 191–203.

Ward, G. (2000), *Cities of God*. London: Routledge.

Chapter 2

The Urbanization of Society: Towards a Cultural Analysis of the Sacred in the Modern Metropolis

Liliana Gómez

On the Conceptual History of the Sacred

In his history of knowledge, Michel Foucault pointed out that initially magic and erudition belonged together and complemented each other until the modern rationalization of the world removed the sacred and magic as valid aspects of knowledge, since which time they seem to have been dissolved by the modern sciences and have disappeared forever.[1] Before exploring the sacred in the modern city and following the hypothesis of the urbanization of society, I would like to briefly outline aspects of the conceptual history of the sacred and to describe the sacred as magic, wonder, or enchantment, which re-emerges in different forms in modern life as an aesthetic experience. As the urbanization of society belongs to the process of cultural modernization, which has been accelerating since the end of the nineteenth century and was particularly intense at the beginning of the twentieth century, I would like to pay attention, in the first instance, to the colonial expansion of Europe which redefined the relationship between periphery and metropolis and made it necessary to elaborate new concepts that would describe this and its implications for new formations of knowledge. It was this colonial experience that was to lead to the emergence of two important modern disciplines, namely ethnology and sociology, in particular with respect to French expansionism. The necessity to introduce new analytical and descriptive categories which aimed at describing the many new social phenomena in Europe and the outer-European world made clear that nothing less than European identity itself was negotiated and reformulated. One of these concepts is the 'sacred', which is part of a range of (sub-)concepts such as animism, fetishism, totem, *mana* and shamanism, all of which describe the transcultural history of magic as an aesthetic concept (Rincón, 2001, p. 724). It is necessary to recall here that at the beginning of the twentieth century, after the apotheosis of the colonial expansion of European empires and the transference of the anthropological fiction of 'primitive society' onto tribal societies, in particular by the French and the English, a new general classification needed to be invented due to the diverse 'artefacts brought to Europe through conquest, pillage, and collection zeal' (Rincón, 2001, p. 724, my transl.). As has been discussed, in the course of the twentieth century 'magic' became part of a popular cultural delimitation in aesthetics. In relation to the concept of fetish, the concept of magic became central to aesthetic theories, economics and politics in societies of mass consumerism (Rincón, 2001, p. 724). From within this perspective, it is important to understand that the concept 'sacred' is ascribed to two movements which characterize the beginning of the twentieth century: first, the modernization of Europe and its modern social and cultural formations, in which the European colonial and imperial experience played a constitutive role through the manifold processes of exchange and circulation of culture and knowledge, secondly, the configuration of what started to be perceived and conceptualized as the modern metropolis. It is a context that particularly seems to characterize the emergence and institutionalization of French sociology. I would like to specify here that I understand *metropolis* in a twofold way. On the one hand, as the modern city which is an effect of the modernization process and the urbanization of society and, following Henri Lefèbvre, as the emergence of the 'phénomène urbain'. On the other hand, I understand it as 'metropolis' in respect to the outer-European world formed by European colonies. It seems important to take this double discursive context into account when trying to understand the key concepts 'sacred', 'magic' and 'fetish' as they determined the struggle of disciplinary debates. in particular in France. These concepts dealt with an epistemological necessity to focus on the analysis, both of the cultural modernization of European societies and urbanization, against the background of what Max Weber once called the 'disenchantment of the world', a formulation that for a long time shaped the imagination or dogma of the split between 'modernity' and 'magic'. It has been acknowledged following Max Weber that the disavowal of magic, which is rooted in Judeo-Christian religion, is one of the principles of the articulation of Western civilization. In the same way, rationalization is characterized by a cognitive control of reality by means of the natural sciences, which displaced magic and myth from life and forms of knowledge. This formulation by Weber was taken up later by Max Horkheimer and Theodor W. Adorno to define one of their basic theses in the 'Dialectic of Enlightenment': '"The disenchantment of the world is the eradication of animism"' (Rincón, 2001, p. 727, my transl.).

Regarding the conceptual history of magic, it has been acknowledged that a definition of the concept represents manifold problems, and due to the constitutive heterogeneity of magic no semantic invariance exists. Instead there are different discursive orders and constellations of problems in accordance with whether 'magic or enchantment, wonder, the fantastic or automatism is in correlation'. It has been observed further that 'at the level of the object, this correlates with a diversity which constitutes the meaning of the practices of magic' (Rincón, 2001, p. 727, my transl.). In a similar way, the concept of the sacred cannot be described easily by any conceptual history, as it is constituted by a heterogeneity that is negotiated at the different levels of its practices and uses. But what we can say here is that 'sacred' represents an important concept that was introduced in the context of the formation and constitution of modern sciences, in particular sociology and ethnology, and which I try to reclaim as a key concept for a cultural analysis of the modern metropolis – as a form of knowledge of modern society – relating back to 'the magical form' as inherent in knowledge (Foucault, 1966, p.48).[2] Once divination and knowledge were not in a competitive relationship, but instead constituted a unity (Foucault, 1966, p.47). Both 'sacred' and 'magic' are heterogeneous categories 'embracing diverse practices whose only common characteristic is that they rest on interpretive premises contrary to our own, [so] it is unreasonable to expect that a single theory will fit all cases' (Lewis, 1994, p. 580).

Without doubt two 'realities' embedded these theories of modernization and rationalization of society in the context of sociology and ethnology: one is the city, the urban metropolis, which is an effect of the processes of rationalization and accelerated industrialization in the second half of the nineteenth century, and the other is the complex relationship 'metropolis-periphery', that is, the expansion of the modern space that constitutes itself as 'modern' because of the specific processes of colonial expansion and Western epistemologies. We can certainly observe that 'magic' and its (sub) concepts, in particular the fetish, which directly refers to a socio-cultural dimension of the sacred, describes an irrational materialization opposed to enlightened Reason. As has been observed, the sacred and the fetish thus became, due to a reversal of the projection, the interior of modernity (Kamper and Wulf, 1987). It is not surprising that in the different cultural theories of anthropology, sociology, political economy, psychoanalysis and, to a lesser extent, philosophy, in the course of the nineteenth century, fetishism represented a religious as well as an economic, sexual and aesthetic value

(Rincón, 2001, p. 735). While 'fetish' seems to be a key concept in several cultural theories of modernity, it becomes clear that the sacred as opposed to modernity certainly did not vanish completely, but re-emerges in specific and transformed ways in modern societies and characterizes the modernization and urbanization of European society. This re-emergence, particularly with respect to the reciprocal but asymmetrical relationship between metropolis and periphery, has not yet been fully discussed. One of my objectives is, thus, to determine some elements of the sacred in order to forge a key concept for a cultural analysis of the modern metropolis with which I will look at the urbanization of society.

The 'sacred', in the context of the French and German debates on ethnology, sociology and philosophy, in the traditions of Émile Durkheim and Georg Simmel in the first decades of the twentieth century, and later of their disciples Marcel Mauss and Ernst Cassirer, is ascribed to the research fields and (sub)concepts of magic, *mana*, myth and symbol which all refer to processes of exchange, circulation and relation. To outline the importance of the 'sacred' as a concept for a cultural analysis of the modern metropolis and, hence, modern society, it is worth recalling what Marcel Mauss once observed on the concept of *mana* – one that later oriented the operationalization of the 'sacred' in the work of the College of Sociology and its programme of sacred sociology which I will discuss in a moment:

> . . . the magician is a functionary of society, often instituted by it, and he never finds the source of his own power in himself.. . . Finally, these powers, these qualities all have a similar character and proceed from the same general idea. In the Malayo-Polynesian languages, this notion is given the name *mana*. . . . It is at the same time that of power, of cause, of force, of a quality, and of a substance, of a milieu. The word mana is at the same time noun, adjective, verb, designates attributes, actions, natures, things. It is applied to rites, to actors, to matters, to spirits of magic, as well as to those of religion. It so happens that the rites and the magical representations have the same social character as the sacrifice and that they depend on an identical notion or an analogous one, to the notion of the sacred. (Mauss and Hubert, 1929, pp. XVIII–XIX)[3].

Mana, magic, and sacred seemed to form a nucleus of interest in this context, not only to describe so-called 'primitive society' or 'sociétés inférieures', but serving in fact to distinguish certain phenomena of the modern European metropolitan and urban societies. In the course of the late twentieth century debate 'magic' and its sub-concepts were erased altogether from the ethnographical and sociological vocabulary and no longer served to describe rational or modern social behaviour.[4] In the 1980s, due to the impact of postcolonialism and its revisions, magic and modernity were thought together again. In particular, two attempts – apart from the postcolonial literary and cultural theory debates that determine 'magic' as part of a history of identity and mimicry (Rincón, 2001, p. 730) – focused on the sacred and magic in their intrinsic relationship to modernity and modernization. Today this relationship has been receiving scholarly attention only very tentatively, while the sacred in the modernization and urbanization of society, that is, the city, has almost not been discussed at all.[5]

The Sacred and the Modern Metropolis

What made the ethnographic interest in the 'sacred' strangely pertinent at this time was that Leiris and his friends wondered aloud whether that ethnographic sacred to which Durkheim had introduced them might not be hard at work as a living force in the modern world about them. This was the basis of their College of Sociology, dedicated as it was to sacred sociology. But this had little to do with religion as a church. Instead 'the sacred' pointed to a replay of a spirit world thought to be long since obliterated by what had come to be called the 'disenchantment of the world.' The spirit-force sacred is what I wish to reclaim, too, what Burroughs called the 'magical universe,' as opposed to the OGU or One God Universe. (Taussig, 2009, 33).

The sacred, in accordance with Marcel Mauss and Henri Hubert, is essentially a social concept or a product of collective action (Moebius, 2006, p. 66). As a concept it serves to identify social aspects, which are also relevant in looking at the modern metropolis and the cultural modernization processes we identify as urbanization of society, such as the emergence of the modern city. From this perspective, it is particularly relevant as Georges Bataille, a member of the College of Sociology, suggests to focus on the relationship of the gift, which is part of an economy and of the sacred; a relationship that also determines our modern processes of exchange and circulation. Bataille pointed out, by referring explicitly to Mauss's essay on the gift, that the gift is of broad significance for the general understanding of an economy, that is, for understanding how forms of destruction, of excess and productive production are bound together. The modern city, as a complex phenomenon of processes of excess, circulation, exchange and manifold relations could be a preferred object of analysis, one for which the concept of sacred, as a social one, could be reintroduced.

With the urbanization of society as an experience of the modern, we can also observe how relations between space and knowledge have been changed. In this respect, the sacred is no longer related to 'religion as church', but becomes interesting and pertinent, as Michael Taussig outlined it, as 'spirit-force sacred' and 'magical universe' (Taussig, 2009, p. 33). This observation makes the work of the College of Sociology particular interesting because it emphasizes the different and diverse experiences of the sacred. To rediscover the sacred as a concept for a cultural analysis of the modern city means to look at the relations between the sacred in its various transformed manifestations in urban spaces which was experienced as 'modern'. What is the sacred? How is it manifested and experienced in the spaces of the modern metropolis? And what do we (re)discover when looking at the sacred in its displaced modern forms? Certainly the sacred has been either analyzed, mostly by ethnographers who looked at so-called 'primitive societies', or it has been part of the sciences of religion, which comprehend its function as part of a religious system. It has been said that 'every (archaic) society is based on violence and crime'. Modernity has always been opposed to this relation. Modernity was/is the attempt to be founded on an unequivocal reality and to construct the world following some comprehensive categories: economy versus sacrifice, sense versus madness, etc. (Kamper and Wulf, 1987, p. 3). Labour, rationality and the public speech are all strategies of disenchantment that aim at constructing a continuous space and time in order to avoid paradox, antinomy and the *fascinans-tremendum* of a given reality and at substituting for it (Kamper and Wulf, 1987, p. 3). The modern metropolis and the modernization of urban spaces, explicitly through a modern urbanism, make those attempts very clear, while they are simultaneously based on irrational eruptions of modernity by showing different forms of the sacred inherent in modernity itself, such as luxury or war. The modern metropolis can be characterized, on the one hand, by the individualization of its subjects, that is, the birth of the so-called modern subject, and on the other, by the emergence of new collective forms and energies. In these forms, in this 'spirit-force sacred' and 'magical universe' the College of Sociology aimed at constituting itself. The sacred, indeed, may be a key concept in understanding those modern cultural and social transformations experienced through the city.

I want to reclaim, therefore, this heterogeneous concept of the sacred in order to better comprehend both the urbanization of society and the modern metropolis. My point of departure is the project of the College of Sociology (1937–9) and its theoretical programme called 'sacred sociology'. I will focus, on its main protagonists, such as Georges Bataille, Roger Callois, Michel Leiris and their 'conceptual encounters' later, with the French sociologist Henri Lefèbvre who retrieved the decipherment of the urbanization of society and of everyday life which the members of the College of Sociology comprehended as an experience for the understanding of the sacred, the 'magical universe'. The College's sacred sociology is of particular interest as it proposes the sacred as a conceptual entity with which to understand these cultural transformations, and hence, to comprehend it from within the perspective of a cultural anthropology of modernity (Baxmann, 1995).

Regarding the sacred and its transformed manifestations in modern life, and in particular in urban spaces, it may be fruitful to focus on the sacred in its intrinsic relations to general economics. Following Bataille, it means to comprehend the sacred as a function of social cohesion and sociality and as part of the 'accursed share', which is an integral part of an economy of expenditure. Bataille observes here that the sacred emerges out of economy as an unproductive expenditure that is constitutive of the modern metropolis, and reappears as luxury, war, urban cults, magnificent buildings, theatres, or sexual practices of desire which all have their objective in themselves. The modern metropolis as a *fait urbain* certainly makes this unproductive expenditure clear and makes manifest that the urban is the modern space where multiple exchange processes are realized, determining its irrational dimensions and its qualities of the heterogeneous and heterological. If we ask what it is that binds together urban societies or communities we are questioning social or cultural cohesion. Then we should possibly acknowledge the sacred and its different forms, which re-emerge with modernity. The sacred in its manifold modern forms is part of those urban cultures which have been characterized by a performative element, such as celebrations or festivities, or other (para)religious ceremonies and which are relics of the sacred. I would like to identify here the city as a complex cultural and social phenomenon, which is part of an economy of expenditure. For that reason, I would like to explore the sacred as a key concept to describe the city's cultural transformations, or the urbanization of society.

The metropolis can certainly be understood as a laboratory where it is possible to observe processes of social constitution whose heterogeneous elements produce certain new social configurations which we identify as 'modern'. In this sense, we can observe that the perception or the experience of the modern metropolis not only exercises its effects on the level of the characteristics of a sociological view, but also that the construction of sociological concepts themselves refers to the perception of the modern city. The sacred and its spaces used to be understood as counterparts to the everyday life and as closely linked to 'religion as church'. The College of Sociology, instead, rediscovered the sacred as related to the 'magical universe', as an experience of the everyday life and conceived of the sacred in its ambivalent relationships. For a perspective of the conceptual history of the sacred, I would like to recall here Henri Lefèbvre's lucid hypothesis of the complete urbanization of society in order to approach modern urban relations with the sacred and their cultural transformations. Following this path, some questions come up: why does the everyday life play a key role in the College's sacred sociology? How can we rely on it for a cultural analysis of the sacred in the modern city? How is the sacred manifested in the modern metropolis and its urban spaces?

Sacred Sociology as a Cultural Analysis of Modern Society

> Sacred sociology can be considered as the study not only of religious institutions but of the whole of the *mouvement communiel* of a society: this is why it includes, among other objects, as its proper object instances of power and the army, and takes account of all human activities – sciences, arts, and technology – in their capacity of having a *valeur communiel*, in the active sense of the word, that is in their capacity of *creating* unity. (Bataille and Caillois 1995a, p. 36)[6].

The College's theoretical programme, or sacred sociology, points out two important aspects worth taking into account for a cultural analysis of the modern metropolis. First, this has to do with the sacred and its intrinsic relations to an economy, that is, its nature as a culture of exchange which has been observed primarily in the so-called 'primitive societies', and was studied and interpreted by ethnologists and sociologists such as Marcel Mauss and Émile Durkheim. Durkheim recognized, for example, the sacred as a system through which men imagined their society and their relationship within society. He understood society as a 'collective conscience'. In this sense, the 'collective conscience' could describe the sacred as a *communiel* dimension in modernity, manifested in particular in collective ideals such as the nation or the city, both objects of religious adscription. It is Mauss's and Durkheim's great merit in particular to understand the sacred in its function of social cohesion which the College later emphasized. The College understood the sacred principally as an experience which still remains in modernity so that the sacred is not necessarily linked to religious communities or religion at all. In this sense, sacred sociology is not the sociology of religion but rather sociology of the *mouvements communiels* and their specific forms of social imaginaries which may produce 'modern' social cohesion and manifest themselves in collective myths, representations and other social and symbolic practices. The modern city seems to be, par excellence, the space for such modern collective representations and social practices.

Secondly, Mauss's cultural analysis of the gift leads to another aspect that George Bataille took up explicitly. He lucidly observed that the sacred is part of an exchange system, that it is its cultural dimension which allows it to function as an exchange economy. These two aspects of the proper objects of sacred sociology determine the sacred as a key concept, which seems to be useful in understanding the modern metropolis's cultural transformations and with it society's process of secularization, which is also its urbanization. Within this perspective, it becomes clear that the sacred reclaims the irrational dimension of modernity, which has been thought of predominantly as rationality and Reason. In this sense, the sacred as an experience includes both sides of what has been called *mysterium tremendum* and *mysterium fascinans* (Otto, 1947; Eliade, 1959), or what the Latin word *sacer* wants to say, referring both to the sacred and the accursed or taboo. The 'left' and 'right' sides of the sacred, once distinguished by Robert Hertz (Hertz, 1928), are part of the College's conception of the sacred and in particular of Caillois's and Bataille's work, without ever becoming polarized, but instead manifesting a creative ambivalence:

> I admit that it was a vague anti-Marxian undertaking. But I clarify that this anti-Marxism did not imply any political engagement, let us say to the right. Only that we did not support the systematic reduction of history to an economic determinism, that is, the fight for life from strictly utilitarian motivations. For us, it was not about contesting the legitimacy of these motivations, but they seemed to us too limited in comparison with the instincts of luxuriousness, delirium, prestige, which have an enormous importance even at the collective level. The College of Sociology studied these instincts and passions, and it tried to explain how they are composed as social forces. (Caillois in Baxmann, 1995, pp. 281–2)[7]

Let me go back therefore to Bataille's work on the sacred, which I would like to read in relation to the modern metropolis, against the background of his interventions in the journal *Documents* between 1929 and 1930. I will also take into account Bataille's reflections on general economics which are unfolded explicitly in 'La part maudite' and in 'La notion de la dépense'. Bataille had a particular interest in an economic analysis of the irreducible surplus value, which he translated into the notion of expenditure. This conceptualization of economics has also been discussed in another context as phantasmagoria which radically changes the system of equivalence and identity. At one point, another College contemporary, Alfred Sohn-Rethel, whom Walter Benjamin had intense exchanges with, characterized this modern relation as 'the form of commodity and law of exchange of the commodities, which are the form and law of the *Verdinglichung* [reification]' and which 'become the *a priori* of the production in capitalism, hence, they are the constitutive fundamental law for the existence of society . . . .' (Sohn-Rethel, 1978, p. 33, my transl.)

Based on the readings of Mauss's 'Essay sur le don' and in particular his analysis of the Potlatch, the complex action of giving that Mauss observed among 'primitive societies', Bataille tried to identify the constitutive elements of expenditure on which social cohesion could be based. He identified the sacred as the momentum of this exchange. In accordance with Mauss, the phenomenon of the gift is a *fait social total* which is characterized by the fact that in the action of giving all sorts of institutions are realized, institutions such as the religious, the juridical, the moral, the aesthetic, the economic and the political. It encompasses all forms of consumption, production and distribution from family to politics. Bataille was particularly interested in this form of exchange, which he understood as expenditure, since it helped him to distinguish both unproductive consumption and production as moments that are bound together, something he understood as the irrational dimension of social cohesion. Modernity or rationality opposed expenditure as the accursed share which has always threatened rationality itself. Bataille instead understood this irrationality as a force on the basis of which a 'social rationality' becomes possible at all. In this relationship Bataille identified the experience of the sacred as the heterological which emerges out of this exchange economy and includes all human driving forces and irrational energies. The modern metropolis certainly manifests these diverse forces and energies.

In 1929 Georges Bataille and Carl Einstein founded the project of the journal *Documents*. This project and the discursive interventions it initiated outline some aspects of the College's sacred sociology. It describes particularly clearly the relationship between the sacred and the modern metropolis, the urban. I would like to refer to the section called Critical Dictionary which anticipates the journal's impact on the institutionalization of the College's theoretical work. The cultural criticism of modern space, proposed by the Critical Dictionary and performed throughout the journal, shows most clearly Bataille's preoccupation with the urban and in particular with modern life in the metropolis of Paris. The Critical Dictionary practices space-thinking from within the perspective of a playful constellation of concepts and images, when referring to concrete urban practices and places such as the *terrains vagues* of public abattoirs or, among other monumental and symbolic architectures, to the Bastille of Paris. By introducing images of the practices of everyday life which are invisible, peripheral, and tied to ephemeral urban spaces, like the practice of slaughtering cows, a heterological – or sacred – is conceived. Indeed, the experience of the fragmentation of modern urban space is one of the dimensions that define the conception of the Critical Dictionary. The dictionary, which in a traditional sense certainly excludes, has here become a critical tool that instead includes such things as urban 'experiences' of the dimension of the *mysterium tremendum*. An epistemological correlation is evidenced between the urban or the experience of the modern metropolis and the Critical Dictionary: the concepts no longer represent any use value because their value of knowledge has been annulated. The analysis of use value, proposed by Bataille with *Documents*, unfolds a critical dimension of cruelty which oscillates between the experience of the *mysterium tremendum* and *mysterium fascinans*, both inscribed in the sacred and in the space of the modern metropolis.

Let me explore this idea a little bit more. From within the perspective of reading the economic exchange system, use value does not refer to 'useful' or 'lucrative' but to 'expenditure', that is, the unproductive production or the sacred, which Bataille proposed in contrast to the ethnographers of *Documents* who re-affirmed use value in its relation to the profane by admitting a polarity between the sacred and the profane. This early reading of economics in its forms of expenditure and the sacred unfolds in Bataille's thinking as an irrational jump which leads to an irrational rationality, practiced with *Documents* as (anti)aesthetics. Following Bataille's conception, cruelty represents an intrinsic relationship between economics and language: the 'definitions' celebrated with the Critical Dictionary (Fig. 2.1) introduce the dark side of language while de-centring themselves from within the margins taboo. They display the ambivalence of the sacred which transgresses any possible language. It is this experience which remains irreducible, incommensurable and, hence, irrational. In this sense, its moments

CHRONIQUE

DICTIONNAIRE

ABATTOIR. — L'abattoir relève de la religion en ce sens que des temples des époques reculées, (sans parler de nos jours de ceux des hindous) étaient à double usage, servant en même temps aux implorations et aux tueries. Il en résultait sans aucun doute (on peut en juger d'après l'aspect de chaos des abattoirs actuels) une coïncidence bouleversante entre les mystères mythologiques et la grandeur lugubre caractéristique des lieux où le sang coule. Il est curieux de voir s'exprimer en Amérique un regret lancinant : W. B. Seabrook (1) constatant que la vie orgiaque a subsisté, mais que le sang de sacrifices n'est pas mêlé aux cocktails, trouve insipide les mœurs actuelles. Cependant de nos jours l'abattoir est maudit et mis en quarantaine comme un bateau portant le choléra. Or les victimes de cette malédiction ne sont pas les bouchers ou les animaux, mais les braves gens eux-mêmes qui en sont arrivés à ne pouvoir supporter que leur propre laideur, laideur répondant en effet à un besoin maladif de propreté, de petitesse bilieuse et d'ennui: la malédiction (qui ne terrifie que ceux qui la profèrent) les amène à végéter aussi loin que possible des abattoirs, à s'exiler par correction dans un monde amorphe, où il n'y a plus rien d'horrible et où, subissant l'obsession indélébile de l'ignominie, ils sont réduits à manger du fromage. — G. BATAILLE.

(1) *L'Ile magique*, Firmin-Didot, 1929 (cf. plus loin, p. 334).

CHEMINÉE D'USINE. — Si je tiens compte de mes souvenirs personnels, il semble que, dès l'apparition des diverses choses du monde, au cours de la première enfance, pour notre génération, les formes d'architecture terrifiantes étaient beaucoup moins les églises, même les plus monstrueuses, que certaines grandes cheminées d'usine, véritables tuyaux de communication entre le ciel sinistrement sale et la terre boueuse empuantie des quartiers de filatures et de teintureries.

Aujourd'hui, alors que de très misérables esthètes, en quête de placer leur chlorotique admiration, inventent platement la *beauté* des usines, la lugubre saleté de ces énormes tentacules m'apparaît d'autant plus écœurante, les flaques d'eau sous la pluie, à leur pied, dans les terrains vagues, la fumée noire à moitié

Photo Keystone
Chute d'une cheminée haute de 60 mètres
Banlieue de Londres.

rabattue par le vent, les monceaux de scories et de mâchefer sont bien les seuls attributs possibles de ces dieux d'un Olympe d'égout et je n'étais pas halluciné lorsque j'étais enfant et que ma terreur me faisait discerner dans mes épouvantails géants, qui m'attiraient jusqu'à l'angoisse et aussi parfois me faisaient fuir en courant à toutes jambes, la présence d'une effrayante colère, colère qui, pouvais-je m'en douter, allait devenir plus tard ma propre colère, donner un sens à tout ce qui se salissait dans ma tête, et en même temps à tout ce qui, dans des états civilisés, surgit comme la charogne dans un cauchemar. Sans doute je n'ignore pas que la plupart des gens, quand

FIGURE 2.1 Critical Dictionary 'Abattoir'. *Documents*, 6 (1929). Courtesy of the Staatsbibliothek zu Berlin - Preußischer Kulturbesitz

of violence or cruelty refer to the displacement of the referent, or language itself, while being a critique of the homogeneous rationality of the modern world. The sacred is understood here as a force for a kind of social formation, which helps to decipher those irrational dimensions, according to Bataille and the College, which bind together any social community. The

Critical Dictionary *plays* with the language of 'non-sense' or the 'useless' to find its answer in the expenditure of language, in an economics related to the experience of the sacred.

After the closure of the College, Caillois published 'Man and the Sacred' in 1939 as a more systematic answer to the College's theoretical programme and in particular to sacred sociology. Here Caillois focused on the ambivalent character of the sacred which he took up from Otto, Mauss, Durkheim and Bataille, when he observed that '[. . .] the cohesive quality of the sacred is opposed to its quality of dissolution. The first sustains the profane universe and causes it to endure and the second threatens and shakes it, but renews it, and saves it from a slow death' (Caillois, 2001, p. 128). Caillois concludes further that 'in its basic form, the sacred represents a dangerous force, incomprehensible, intractable but eminently efficacious'. (Caillois, 2001, p. 22) and that:

> On the contrary, those who rule their conduct by complete devotion to some principle tend to re-establish about them a kind of sacred environment, which excites violent emotions of a special kind that are capable of assuming a characteristically religious, ecstatic, fanatical, or mystical quality. On the social level, these emotions give rise directly or indirectly to dogmas and ritual, to mythology and worship. If contemporary examples must be cited, it would be sufficient to point out as a type of secular liturgy, the ceremony of the eternal light at the tomb of the Unknown Soldier under the Arc de Triomphe, and as a model of secular mysticism, the characteristic attitudes of party militants, which demand unqualified obedience of their members. (Caillois, 2001, pp. 133–4)

With the history of Western civilization, and in particular its secularization, Caillois argues, a process of internalization of the sacred has begun that finds its correspondence in the transitions of sacred emotions and behaviours to the 'profane' part of life and explicitly in ethics, politics and the emergence of 'civil liturgies' in the political space (Baxmann, 1995, p. 286). The experience of the modern metropolis gives shape to thinking contradictions by searching for a revision of categories of thinking: the urban space of the modern metropolis *is* contradiction. In this respect, the College focused on the experience of the lived – 'le vécu' – of society which is opposed to the fragmentation of the modern (urban) world. The ritual, myth, festivity, liturgy and play – once introduced by an ethnographic analysis of the 'sacred' in the tradition of Émile Durkheim and Marcel Mauss – here became objects of a novel ethnographic study and a certain Leitmotiv for a new reflection on man and society which exploded the traditional humanities and reclaimed the aesthetics (of the experience) as a point of departure (Baxmann, 1995, pp. 279–80). Both the College and the short-lived journal, *Document*, were at the centre of this postulate and, hence, of the programmatic redefinitions of the 'sacred' and 'magic' in modern life.

The Everyday Life and the Urbanization of Society

Following my initial questions, it might be fruitful to look for a moment at the theoretical coincidences between the French sociologist Henri Lefèbvre and the College of Sociology. These coincidences make clear the College's theoretical programme and some aspects of Lefèbvre's conceptualization of everyday life. First, both the College and Lefèbvre looked for a 'new sociology' which could explore the 'realities' of the changing world while delimiting sociology as a discipline and bringing together ethnographical and philosophical approaches, as well as those from art history, archaeology and literary theory, all of which could challenge the classical relationship of author/subject and the proper object of study. Secondly, they all practised a de-centring (theoretical) movement, positioning themselves in the everyday life in order to participate in the irrational dimensions of the modern world. They assumed that the sacred gives form to the mythical in this changing modern world; hence, they postulated the rediscovery of the 'magical universe'.

A first, the theoretical coincidence between Henri Lefèbvre and the College is made visible by re-reading the inaugural and programmatic lecture 'Le sacré dans la vie quotidienne' which Michel Leiris presented in 1938. Leiris noted there that the sacred is manifested as something integral to everyday life while it delimits the borders between the spheres of the sacred and the profane, traditionally opposed. He experimented – as the College later did programmatically – with the experience of the secret and the collective, with the everyday life as the experience of the sacred. Leiris looked in particular at the experience of the urban spaces of the modern world, such as gardens, the vague zones and shady worlds, in order to decipher those heterological and mythical spaces of the sacred that are lived with and perceived through the everyday life. The modern world, Leiris observed, is characterized by the confrontation and re-emergence of the sacred in everyday life and urban spaces between order and wilderness, between taboo and subversion; an experience which gives shape to our everyday itineraries through the modern city. The modern city is the analytical scenery through which Leiris could reclaim the sacred as a concept for the understanding of modernity itself. This somewhat shared theoretical coincidence between the College's sacred sociology and Henri Lefèbvre's conception of everyday life can be characterized by what Lefèbvre tried to think of as *life*, which he understood as space production in its tri-dimensionality of *espace vécu-espace conçu-espace perçu* (lived space-conceived space-perceived space) which he rationalized through the everyday life. At the centre of this conceptualization are the complexities and contradictions of (everyday) life. No wonder that Lefèbvre dedicated half of his life to the project: 'Critique de la vie quotidienne', published in three volumes between 1947 and 1981. Indeed, this project can best be characterized by his interest in the systematization of conceptualizing 'everyday life' to the extent of reclaiming it from the capitalist production of the modern city.

In the dynamics of the redefinition of 'reality' and 'truth' at the turn of the nineteenth century, which first opened up the conception of everyday life, a change of relation between the world of objects and man as observer was effected: since then the emergence of the concept 'everyday life' has operated nothing less than an epistemological shift. In this new relationship these two instances, 'reality' and 'truth', could no longer be articulated from a distance. Therefore the conception of objectivity of knowledge was radically changed. With the introduction of the concepts *Alltagswelt* and *Lebenswelt* the *Seinsgewissheit*, given previously by 'reality' and 'truth', was being reclaimed philosophically (Gumbrecht, 1995, p. 81). In this respect, Lefèbvre's 'Critique de la vie quotidienne' made this emerging epistemological shift visible by putting the modern world at the centre of his reflections. Consequently, Lefèbvre offered a new conception of the modern metropolis which he thought of in its intrinsic relation to and within the everyday life by proposing a new theoretical framework to comprehend the modern world through the hypothesis of the complete urbanization of society. The modern city here represented a crucial object for a social and philosophical analysis, as it constituted, par excellence, the space in which the new relationships of the modern could be observed.

I will therefore have a more detailed look at the concept 'everyday life'. Without doubt 'everyday life' is a philosophical concept with which Lefèbvre tried to resolve the confrontation between two opposing fields: philosophy and everyday life. The question 'How to exit from the everyday?' (Hess, 1988, pp. 51–2) marks that shared moment between Henri Lefèbvre and the College. The College took that question as a point of departure to decipher the marginal phenomena of the modern world, while assuming that modernity is not characterized by the disappearance of the sacred, but instead by the transformation of it. Lefèbvre approached the everyday from within the perspective of the production of everyday life, while he tried to respond to that problem by proposing a dialectical approach, one that had been dissolved by the union of everyday life and philosophy. While Lefèbvre therewith formulated a critique of the everyday life, he referred to a kind of radical negativity by assuming that knowledge of everyday life does not realize itself without its negation and, hence, with the desire to change it. It becomes clear that through the concept 'everyday life', in both projects, Lefèbvre and the College tried to redefine the irrational dimensions of modernity. In Lefèbvre's elaboration of the 'Critique de la vie quotidienne' one point returning again and again became relevant, that is, when the everyday loses its revolutionary power, the one it has when embedded in the sacred as an experience, and is instead incorporated and controlled by the logic of commodification which defines a new dynamic of appropriation and disappropriation of the imaginary space and, hence, reduces the everyday life's complexity in the modern metropolis to a homogenous experience. This is the crucial moment, Lefèbvre argues, which shapes the historical process of modernization as a process of complete urbanization of society.

Lefèbvre's observation of the crisis of the city as a crisis of the modern world concretizes the theory of space production that Bataille, in a certain sense, articulated with the Critical Dictionary almost two decades earlier, when trying to reclaim the sacred as a heterogeneous concept to describe the modern world. In this vein, I would like to decipher another theoretical moment shared by the College and Henri Lefèbvre: while the College's theoretical programme endeavoured to decipher the various collective energies which unite society's actions, the 'sacred' became the key concept with which to identify modernity's irrational dimensions and, hence, also defined a new concept of knowledge. Sacralization is understood as an imaginary and symbolic procedure that realizes itself in various 'objects'. An analysis of this procedure and of the constitution of the sacred allows us to decipher the significance of the mythical and the role of the cultural in modern societies:

> The sacred opposes the way of thinking and perception that make up the domains of production and consumption. Here the predominant principle of utility is defined by homogenization. It basically saturates all domains of culture and excludes the not immediately beneficial, heterogeneous elements. The sacred as an alternative form of social synthesis is therefore opposed to the abstraction of exchange. (Baxmann, 1995, p. 282, my transl.)

The conceptual coincidences between Lefèbvre and the College can be characterized by a shared preoccupation with modern man in relation to modern collective life. These coincidences describe a new social theory which includes the domains of human experience escaping a rational understanding while contextualizing the functioning of the concept of the sacred. While Lefèbvre reclaims an urban epistemology in which the human is at the centre of its conception, he includes irrational dimensions, such as the mythological, by delimiting the ideology of a programme for social change, of a theory for the production of space and a critique of everyday life that he opposes to the alienation of the economic rationality of capitalistic production; this is a Marxist legacy.

Towards a Cultural Analysis of the Sacred in the Modern Metropolis

Nothing much more than whistling in the dark. About which you have to first realize that Leiris had made the sacred an outcome of the adult's imagination of the child's imagination. He secularized the sacred, we might say, but preserved its magic in this way, allowing remembrance of the child's perceptions to enchant the things of the world. (Taussig, 2009, p. 33)

The sacred in the modern world is a heterogeneous and manifold experience while being understood – as the College reclaimed – as 'an alternative form of social synthesis' (Baxmann, 1995, p. 282). With respect to the urbanization of society as a process of cultural modernization, I would like to recall that '. . . the "sovereign *Dasein*" is a *Sein* of the affirmed expenditure and of the loss that even includes a self-loss. This loss of the "I" marks the subject not only in the moment of the sacred and immediate experience of expenditure, but also in the absolute knowledge that Bataille confronts with an "excessive" non-knowledge . . .' (Moebius, 2006, p. 345, my transl.). I would like to point out, following Bataille, that '"*general economics* demonstrates overwhelmingly that there is a production of excess energy that by definition will not be used. This excess energy can only be lost without the slightest purpose and hence without the slightest sense. This useless and non-sense lost is sovereignty"' (Bataille in Moebius, 2006, p. 345, my transl.), so that the sacred and magic might open up to a new conceptual understanding of both social rationality and the idea of sovereignty, related to the modern subject of the metropolis itself.

Finally, I want to point out that the College's postulates in a way propose a new research agenda of modern space and, hence, of the city as a field of knowledge that retroactively impacts the understanding of the very disciplines dealing with (urban) space as a phenomenon. In this sense, the College developed novel tools of decipherment of the urbanization of society and the sacred by proposing an alternative 'modernity' that rather includes and diversifies than excludes and homogenizes social and living forms, especially those given by an exclusive economic rationality. The College approached the modern transformations of the sacred and magic which are constitutive of our world in order to comprehend the irrational dimensions of our living world and everyday life and to rediscover the 'magical universe'. Hence, these novel approaches might help us in confronting the contradictions we live with in our urban spaces and, also, in avoiding totalitarian spaces of control. Both the College and Lefèbvre reclaimed the philosophical as a dimension with which to participate in the production of space by being engaged with it, and as a new knowledge which is no longer merged into divided disciplines but rather into the various and contradictory experiences of modern life and of social praxis. Thus, regarding these approaches, the 'sacred' may indeed be a key concept for the understanding of the cultural transformations of the city, even today.

Notes

[1] 'Dans une *épistème* où les signes et similitudes s'enroulent réciproquement selon une volute qui n'avait pas de terme, il fallait bien qu'on pensât dans le rapport du microcosme au macrocosme la garantie de ce savoir et le terme de son épanchement. Par la même nécessité, ce savoir devrait accueillir à la fois et sur le même plan magie et érudition' (Foucault, 1966, p. 47).

[2] 'Le projet des 'Magies naturelles', qui occupe une large place à la fin du XVIe siècle et s'avance tard encore en plein milieu du XVIIe, n'est pas un effet résiduel dans la conscience européenne; il a été ressuscité ... . La forme magique était inhérente à la manière de connaître' (Foucault, 1966, p. 48).

[3] '... le magicien est un fonctionnaire de la société, souvent institué par elle, et que ne trouve jamais en lui-même la source de son propre pouvoir. ... Enfin, ces pouvoirs, ces qualités ont tous un même caractère, procèdent tous d'une même idée générale. Cette notion nous lui avons donné le nom *mana* emprunté aux langues malayo-polynésiennes ... . Elle est à la fois celle d'un pouvoir, celle d'une cause, d'une force, celle d'une qualité et d'une substance, celle d'un milieu. Le mot mana est à la fois substantif, adjectif, verbe, désigne des attributs, des actions, des natures, des choses. Il s'applique aux rites, aux acteurs, aux matières, aux esprits de la magie, aussi bien qu'à ceux de la religion. Il en résulte que les rites et les représentations magiques ont le même caractère social que le sacrifice et qu'ils

dépendent d'une notion identique ou analogue à la notion du sacré' (Mauss and Hubert, 1929, pp. XVIII–XIX). (English translation by the author.)

[4] John D. Peel observed for example that: 'Judged from the standpoint of sociology no behaviour is properly speaking, irrational … . The term 'magic' is, I suggest, best expunged from our sociological vocabulary altogether' (Peel, 1969, p. 81).

[5] I refer here explicitly to two publications: Kamper and Wulf (1987) and Meyer and Pels (2003).

[6] 'La sociologie sacrée peut-être considérée comme l'étude non seulement des institutions religieuses mais de l'ensemble du mouvement communiel de la société: c'est ainsi qu'elle regarde entre autres comme son objet propre le pouvoir et l'armée et qu'elle envisage toutes les activités humaines – sciences, arts et technique – en tant qu'elles ont une valeur communielle au sens actif du mot, c'est-à-dire en tant qu'elles sont *créatrices* d'unité' (Bataille, 1995a, p. 36). (The French words not translated are put in italic by the author. English translation by the author.)

[7] 'C'était, je l'avoue, une entreprise vaguement antimarxiste. Je précise toutefois que cet antimarxisme n'impliquait nullement, au contraire, un engagement politique, disons à droite. Seulement voilà: nous ne supportions pas la réduction systématique de l'histoire à un déterminisme économique, c'est-à-dire à la lutte pour la vie et à des motivations étroitement utilitaires. Pour nous, il n'était pas question de contester la légitimité de ces motivations, mais elles nous semblaient singulièrement limitées par comparaison aux instincts de faste, de jeu, de vertige, de prestige qui ont une importance énorme, même au niveau collectif. Le Collège de Sociologie étudiait ces instincts et ces passions et travaillait à expliquer comment ils peuvent se composer en forces sociales' (Caillois in Baxmann, 1995, pp. 281–2). (English translation by the author.)

Bibliography

Bataille, G. (1929), 'Abattoir'. *Documents*, 6, 329.
—. (1967a), 'La notion de la dépense', in G. Bataille, *La part maudite*. Paris: Les Éditions de Minuit, pp. 24–45.
—. (1967b), *La part maudite*. Paris: Les Éditions de Minuit.
—. (1992). *Theory of Religion*. New York: Zone Books.
—. (1995), 'L'apprenti sorcier', in Hollier, D. (ed.), *Le Collège de Sociologie 1937–1939*. Paris: Gallimard, pp. 302–26.
Bataille, G. and Caillois, R. (1995a), 'La sociologie sacrée et les rapports entre 'société', 'organisme' et 'être'', in Hollier, D. (ed.), *Le Collège de Sociologie 1937–1939*. Paris: Gallimard, pp. 31–60.
—. (1995b), 'La sociologie sacrée du monde contemporain', in D. Hollier (ed.), *Le Collège de Sociologie 1937–1939*. Paris: Gallimard, pp. 245–51.
Baxmann, I. (1995), 'Das Sakrale im Rahmen einer Kulturanthropologie der Moderne: Das Collège de Sociologie', in Dotzler, B. (ed.), *Wahrnehmung und Geschichte. Markierungen zur Aisthesis materialis*. Berlin: Akademie-Verlag: pp. 279–98.

Caillois, R. (1938), *Le mythe et l'homme*. Paris: Gallimard.
—. (1983), *L'homme et le sacré*. Paris: Gallimard.
—. (1995a), 'L'ambigüité du sacré', in Hollier, D. (ed.), *Le Collège de Sociologie 1937–1939*. Paris: Gallimard, pp. 364–402.
—. (1995b), 'La fête', in Hollier, D. (ed.), *Le Collège de Sociologie 1937–1939*. Paris: Gallimard, pp. 641–93.
—. (2001), *Man and the Sacred*. Chicago: University of Illinois Press.
Cassirer, E. (2010), *Philosophie der symbolischen Formen. Teil II: Das mythische Denken*. Hamburg: Felix Meiner.
Durkheim, E. (1912), *Les formes élémentaires de la vie religieuse*. Paris: Alcan.
Eliade, M. (1959), *The Sacred and the Profane. The Nature of Religion*. New York: Harcourt Brace.
Foucault, M. (1966), *Les mots et les choses. Une archéologie des sciences humaines*. Paris: Gallimard.
Gumbrecht, H. (1995), '"Alltagswelt" und "Lebenswelt" aus genealogischer Perspektive', in Kniesche, T. (ed.), *Körper, Kultur: kalifornische Studien zur deutschen Moderne*. Würzburg: Könighausen & Neumann, pp. 76–99.
Habermas, J. (1984), 'The French Path to Postmodernity: Bataille Between Eroticism and General Economics'. *New German Critique*, 33, 79–102.
Hertz, R. (1928), *Mélanges de Sociologie Religieuse et Folklore*. Paris: Alcan.
Hess, R. (1988), *Henri Lefèbvre et l'aventure du siècle*. Paris: Métailié.
Kamper, D. and Wulf, C. (eds) (1987), *Das Heilige. Seine Spur in der Moderne*. Frankfurt am Main: Athenäum.
Lefèbvre, H. (1947), *Critique de la vie quotidienne. Introduction*. Paris: Gallimard.
—. (1961), *Critique de la vie quotidienne. Fondements d'une sociologie de la quotidiennité*. Paris: Gallimard.
—. (1968), *La vie quotidienne dans le monde moderne*. Paris: Gallimard.
—. (1970), *La révolution urbaine*. Paris: Gallimard.
Leiris, M. (1995), 'Le sacré dans la vie quotidienne', in Hollier, D. (ed.), *Le Collège de Sociologie 1937–1939*. Paris: Gallimard, pp. 94–119.
Lewis, Gilbert (1994), 'Magic, Religion and the Rationality of Belief', in Ingold, T. (ed.), *Companion Encyclopedia of Anthropology: Humanity, Culture and Social Life*. London: Routledge, pp. 563–90.
Maffesoli, M. (1991), 'Le rituel dans la vie sociale', in Lambert, J. (ed.), *Roger Caillois. Témoignage, études et analyses*. Paris: Édition de la Différence, pp. 366–72.
Marroquin, C. (2005), *Die Religionstheorie des Collège de Sociologie. Von den irrationalen Dimensions der Moderne*. Berlin: Parerga-Verlag.
Mauss, M. (1934). 'Fragment d'un plan de sociologie générale descriptive'. http://classiques.uqac.ca/classiques/mauss_marcel/essais_de_socio/T4_fragments_plan/fragments_plan.pdf (21.11.09).
—. (1967), *The Gift. Forms and Functions of Exchange in Archaic Societies*. New York: Norton.
—. (1968), *Les fonctions sociales du sacré*. Paris: Édition de Minuit.
Mauss, M. and Hubert, H. (1929), *Mélanges d'histoire des religions*. Paris: Librairie Félix Alcan.
Meyer, B. and Pels, P. (eds) (2003), *Magic and Modernity. Interfaces of Revelation and Concealment*. Stanford: Stanford University Press.

Moebius, S. (2006), *Die Zauberlehrlinge. Soziologiegeschichte des Collège de Sociologie (1937–1939)*. Konstanz: UVK-Verlag.
Moebius, S. and Papilloud, C. (eds) (2006), *Gift – Marcel Mauss' Kulturtheorie der Gabe*. Wiesbaden: Verlag für Sozialwissenschaften.
Otto, R. (1947), *Das Heilige. Über das Irrationale in der Idee des Göttlichen und sein Verhältnis zum Rationalen.* München: Biederstein Verlag.
Peel, J. (1969), 'Understanding alien belief-systems'. *The British Journal of Sociology*, 20(1), 69–84.
Rincón, C. (2001), 'Magisch/Magie', in Barck, K., et al. (eds), *Ästhetische Grundbegriffe. Historisches Wörterbuch in sieben Bänden.* Stuttgart: Metzler, pp. 724–59.
Sohn-Rethel, A. (1978), *Warenform und Denkform.* Frankfurt am Main: Suhrkamp.
Taussig, M. (2009), *What Color Is the Sacred?* Chicago: University of Chicago Press.

Chapter 3

The Lingering Smell of Incense: Exploring Post-secular Public Space

Pieter Dronkers

It was only in 1983 that the Dutch government lifted the constitutional ban on open air processions. The annulment put an end to the heated discussions that had accompanied the prohibition since its imposition in 1848 (Margry, 200, p. 423). Time and again, shifts in political power and changing social circumstances fuelled the debate on the legitimacy of the ban. In the years of post-World War II reconstruction the dispute was particularly fierce. At that time, there was no consensus on what direction the religiously divided Dutch society should be moving in. One of the pressing issues was the complaint of many Roman Catholics that they were often treated as second-class citizens. In this context, the procession ban turned out to be a mediagenic case to renegotiate the liberties of, and relationships between, the different religious and ideological communities in Dutch society. Roman-Catholic politicians argued that Protestants had dominated the public space for far too long. Since approximately forty per cent of the Dutch were Roman Catholic, it was about time to drop the ban. But Protestant opinion leader and theologian Oepke Noordmans wrote that lifting the ban would prove to be devastating for the freedom of all citizens (Noordmans, 1986). A passing procession would turn city squares into churches and the urban flâneur would feel obliged to kneel down for the intrusive presence of the sacred in the streets. The city air that was supposed to set human beings free would be driven off by the pervasive smell of incense. Noordmans emphasized that he did not want to deny civil rights to Roman Catholics; however, restrictions were necessary to secure the public quality of shared space. In the end, the Roman Catholics got the short end of the stick. It would take another thirty years before the situation changed.

The final annulment of the procession ban came as part of a comprehensive package of rules implemented in the 1980s to cut the last remaining ties between church and state. In that process of policy making, theories about the secularization of society had been directive. Secularization theorists predicted that the era of faith as a politically relevant factor was over. If faith was to survive at all, then it would only do so in the private sphere. However, the prognosis of these theorists turned out to be partly misguided. Although church membership is still falling, religion did not at all recede to the private sphere. To the contrary, the public presence of religious identities is once again a major cause of contention. As in other European countries, headscarves have become the focus of negotiations over freedom and identity in the Netherlands. In 2009, Dutch conservative-nationalist politician Geert Wilders proposed the introduction of a special tax for women who wanted to cover their heads. Wilders argued that the modern Dutch cityscape was 'polluted' by headscarves. Wearing this religious garb had to be discouraged by requiring an annual payment of 1000 Euros.[1]

Wilders' tax proposal was another chapter in the lingering discussions on the Islamic headscarf that has kept opinion leaders, politicians and scientists captivated since the turn of the century. I do not aim to contribute to the many interesting studies that have already been published on this particular issue.[2] In this chapter, I propose to explore in more general terms the consequences of the post-secular condition for our understanding of public space in liberal, western European societies.

I take post-secularity to be the observation that religion remains a relevant public phenomenon, although it may be in new forms. This post-secular framework brings a set of classical political questions that have been neglected under the secularization paradigm to the fore. Old problems gained new urgency: what sort of religious practices have a legitimate place in public space? Which rituals should be forbidden and on what grounds? Who has the power to define the boundaries of the public space and who or what is excluded? And how is the public/private dichotomy deployed to locate and relocate expressions and performances of identities and subcultures? The last question is probably the most pressing. The public/private distinction orchestrates the spaces we live in and influences how citizens can mediate between and express the various loyalties and memberships they have.[3] In this chapter, I examine how different political approaches evaluate the new visibility of religion. [4] Does post-secularity trigger dominant political theories to reconsider their conceptualizations of public space?

This theoretical question has practical implications. Although it often goes unnoticed, political reflections on public life build always on an interpretation of physical space (Stavrakakis, 2007, p. 143). Political rearrangements of public life are rooted in and have consequences for the spatial ordering of everyday life. The question I am exploring is not only spatial, but normative as well. Any interpretation of the public defines the freedom of citizens to express their identities and convictions. It influences the extent to which the common realm is open towards religious rituals and practices. Shifting boundaries between public and private change the cityscape and the design of urban squares. I shall focus on these normative—spatial implications of the way in which various political frameworks incorporate post-secularity.

The first section argues that the urban is the most appropriate level to analyse the political interaction between post-secularity and public space. In the second section, I shall take a closer look at post-secularity. What does it mean to study public space within this framework? After these preliminary explorations, I shall introduce a case study that helps to analyse how two political approaches redefine public space in light of post-secularity. In the last section, I will make a case for a third conception of the public space.

Urban Public Space

I have three reasons for taking the city as the central object of analysis in this chapter. First, arguing from an urban level helps to sidestep a problem that is inherent in many political theories. Often, philosophers reason as if public space is embedded in a well-defined nation-state (Bosniak, 2006, pp. 5–6). The work of the liberal theorist John Rawls is an example. Spelling out his definition of society, Rawls wrote: 'we are to regard it as self-contained and as having no relations with other societies. Its members enter it only by birth and leave it only by death' (Rawls, 2005, p. 12). However, in our globalizing and transnational era, boundaries between different groups and nations have become fluid and almost all contemporary political controversies are related to precisely these developments. Starting from the city as part of a global network that transcends national boundaries and that is increasingly multicultural makes it impossible to rely on assumptions about fixed national boundaries.

The second reason to focus on cities is that iconic metropolises like London, Paris and Istanbul help to imagine what abstract concepts like community, religious diversity and social cohesion might look like in practice. Post-secularity challenges theorists and politicians to reflect on how the transcendental fits into these urban imaginaries. Is the city a secular entity where the sacred only has a place in the private sphere (Sheldrake,

2007, p. 249)? Or does the built religious heritage help to foster a sense of place-identity facilitating the identification with the urban landscape?

Third, taking my starting point in the urban helps to keep in touch with the fast-changing realities of everyday public life. The public is fluid, always on the move and fundamentally contested (Göle, 2006, p. 27). It is the shared space, where citizens meet, perform their identities and seek recognition for their attachments and identities. A careful analysis of urban life leads to a clearer view on what is repressed and kept away from the public gaze. The city as the primal site for theoretical reflection puts diversity as a fundamental theme on the agenda of political philosophy.

The challenge of post-secularity and pluralism, then, is whether and how a political community is prepared to grant dissenters and minorities the right to be present and to participate in the city.[5] In this chapter I shall consider various answers to this challenge. I distinguish three options, following the illuminating taxonomy of public space developed by political theorist Jeff Weintraub.[6] The first conception of the public Weintraub points to is republican. It perceives the public as the domain of the polity and the citizens. Moral values and social expectations structure the civic community. The private, as the antipode, is the realm of the household and the necessities of everyday life. The second definition has a liberal breeding ground. Here, the public is the domain of the state and individual rights and freedoms. The private is first and foremost the economic sphere. The third and last model takes its starting point in practices of sociability. The shared domain is the space for symbolic display and self-representation. Within the chaotic web of everyday encounters a common sphere develops. The private is any aspect of the self that people choose to hide.

In the next sections, I analyse the republican and liberal approach, respectively, and I shall introduce an agonistic interpretation of the public as the sphere of sociability. Before I do so, however, I will first elaborate the idea of the post-secular city.

The Post-secular City

In the late 1950s, Mircea Eliade wrote that he feared that the sacred would not survive the hastiness, turmoil and superficiality of the modern city. Once the *polis* had represented the best human beings could achieve. The early urban settlements, the European medieval towns and cities in the East were and are engrafted onto a concept of a sacred ordering (Sennett, 1990, pp. 10–19). However, according to Eliade the modern city was different. It was nothing but chaos distracting its inhabitants from what was good and holy. Eliade described urban life as 'the second fall of man' (Eliade, 1965, p. 17, p. 180).

Only a few years later Harvey Cox published a far more positive account of the urban, summarized in the programmatic title 'The Secular City'. Cox contended that the secularization of the cityscape had been an essential condition for making room for a great variety of lifestyles, cultures and traditions. Only cities that no longer tried to realize the New Jerusalem could guarantee free living space to everyone. Therefore, the urban had to draw on pragmatic and profane principles devoid of any reference to the sacred (Cox, 1966, pp. 60–2). The secularization of the city would result in more liberty for all city-dwellers. However, this and similar accounts of secularization obscured for too long that religion in fact remained present in the urban. It was only in the 1990s that it was widely acknowledged that the secularization hypothesis had to be revised. Although the theory had rightly predicted the fall of church attendance for the western European context, it could not account for the observation that in other respects faith remained an important public issue. Even Peter Berger, one of the founding fathers of the secularization theory, agreed that it would be more adequate to define secularization as 'a shift in the location of religion' (Berger, 1999, p. 10; cf. Casanova, 1994). Indeed, faith found a new place in the public and globalization processes help to explain this renewed presence.

Migration, to start with, increased the cultural and religious diversity of cities. Migrants introduced new practices and rituals and sought public recognition. In some cases, the new traditions awoke curiosity and enriched the lifestyles and moral outlooks of the city-dwellers. Often, however, the new practices met with fierce resistance and resulted in alienation and discontent. Moreover, globalization resulted in a multiplication of options and possibilities. The growing cultural diversity in the streets, as well as exploring new worlds through travelling and mass media, turned individual identities into difficult reflexive projects. Charles Taylor has analysed the consequences of these new epistemological conditions for religion. Faith had become 'one option amongst others' (Taylor, 2007, p. 3). Religion is now one of the many competitors on the free market of identities and this has changed its character fundamentally. Faith lost its authority and turned into a lifestyle. Since the dominant discourse of globalization is self-realization through the adoption of self-selected ways of living, religion is nowadays for some an important medium for self-expression and for others a strange relic from bygone times (Spybey, 2001). Indigenous religious practices are no longer embedded in fixed traditional interpretations.

Faith-based rituals are reinterpreted and take on new meaning. Globalization resulted in the deconstruction of traditional power-structures. Religious institutions, once the sole authority to interpret the dogmas and the primary authority responsible for the correct performance of rituals, lost their public role. Religion is de-institutionalized and takes on new forms within society (Hermans, 2003, pp. 75–82).

The relocation of religion within a globalizing context marked the cityscape in European countries. On one hand, faith is provokingly visible. Religious garb is a topic for continuing dispute as are the construction of mosques and, especially, minarets (Maussen, 2004). On the other hand, faith disappears from the stage. New urban districts are planned without leaving space for prayer houses and derelict churches are turned into art galleries and supermarkets. These developments have various paces in different neighbourhoods. Sociologist Schmuel Eisenstadt has coined the concept 'multiple modernities' to indicate that every society develops in its own way a specific form of modernity that is tailored to the context (Katzenstein, 2006, pp. 4–6). Although the framework was primarily designed to analyse macro-historical processes, the concept of multiple modernities is also helpful to describe developments in urban districts. Inhabitants and users of the same public space express different worldviews in divergent ways. Religious, cultural and other transnational attachments are exposed and performed.

The growing complexity and richness of the urban texture is a social challenge. The diversity renders traditional patterns of feeling at home in the city useless. It alienates people from the neighbourhoods they once felt familiar with. At the same time the diversity makes new ways of identifying with a fundamentally pluralist city possible (Vidler, 1992, p. 177). Richard Sennett (Sennett, 1990, pp. xii–xiv) summarized this challenge as the dialectic relationship between fear and the art of exposure. The multiplicity of the city can be threatening, but is also a source of inspiration and creativity. The complexity is subservient to discovering other worldviews, trying new lifestyles and changing attachments to different communities (cf. Luther, 1992, pp. 199–211). This, once more, underlines the importance of the question of whether and how religion can be present in the public domain.

Atheist Buses in the Streets of London

In the next sections, I shall discuss how major strands of political philosophy reconceptualize public space in a post-secular era. I will use the 2009 atheist bus campaign in London as a case study. This section introduces this initiative.

In June 2008, journalist and comedy writer Ariane Sherine published a column on the blog site of British newspaper *The Guardian*. Sherine criticized a campaign run by the association 'Proclaiming Truth in London'. The group advertised on buses with slogans like: 'Jesus said: I am the resurrection, and the life, whoever believes in me will never die' and 'When the Son of Man comes, will he find faith on the earth?'. Sherine mocked this kind of religious propaganda since it predicted hell for all non-believes without providing any convincing proof for the existence of God. The slogans suggested that 'a man with a beardy face is going to be upset with you, for ever, because you've refused to acknowledge his existence, despite the fact that he's too antisocial to come down here and say hi'.[7] In another column, Sherine elaborated that these kinds of religious advertisements frightened people into believing. At first as a joke, she proposed to organize a pro-atheism campaign, since it was time for a 'publicly visible counter-view to refute . . . threats of eternal damnation'. Such an initiative would 'give atheism a more visible presence in the UK, generate debate, brighten people's day on the way to work, and hopefully encourage more people to come out as atheists'.[8] Sherine's columns drew a wide response from the internet community.[9] News websites paid attention to the campaign, a Facebook group was created, and many blogs discussed Sherine's suggestions. When well-known atheist Richard Dawkins and the British Humanist Association voiced their support for the initiative, Sherine decided to suit the action to the word. When she started raising funds, the internet proved once again to be essential for the success of the campaign.[10] Through the website JustGiving.com she raised over £153,000 in a very short time.[11] This was enough to have 200 buses running in the streets of London as of 6 January 2009, stickered with the message 'There's probably no God. Now stop worrying and enjoy your life'. Another 600 buses outside the capital carried the same slogan. Sherine's idea that had started out in virtual reality was materialized in the urban reality and made the headlines in many countries.

The British initiative inspired sympathizers and humanist organizations to launch similar campaigns in countries like Finland, the Netherlands, Germany, Switzerland, Austria, Italy, Spain, Croatia, Australia, Canada and the Unites States.[12] Most of these initiatives met opposition. Outdoor advertising and public transport companies were often reluctant to get involved and public reactions were mixed. Due to complaints, a public transport company in Zagreb decided after just one day to remove the bus posters of the Women's Network of Croatia. The slogan 'Without God, without a master' was said to conflict with national ethical and religious traditions.[13]

For the organizers these controversies proved that it is easier to run a religious advertisement campaign than an atheist one. It at least illustrates the urgency of questions about the place of religion and other worldviews in the public space. How do normative political theories define public space in view of this type of post-secular conflict?

Republican and Communitarian Conceptions of the Public

I take the writings of the French historian Marcel Gauchet as a paradigmatic example of the republican approach to post-secular public space. In his essay 'La religion dans la démocratie' Gauchet evaluates the public role of religion. His work is informed by the French context, but his insights are nevertheless relevant to the theoretical discussion of this chapter. Gauchet (Gauchet, 1998, p. 14) reconstructs that until the French Revolution, faith represented a domain outside and in competition with the political. However, already during the seventeenth and eighteenth century, religion lost most of its sovereignty and became an instrument to support and legitimate absolutist rule. The French Revolution marked the final break with the past. The introduction of the Cults of Reason and the Supreme Being aimed to replace traditional religiosity with creeds that helped to legitimize the Revolution. However, the Revolution also opened the path to a reconfiguration of the relationship between religion and society. The Revolution's pulse towards democratization sparked the development of a public sphere where, in the best Rousseauist tradition, people convened to deliberate about public affairs. This common domain was supposed to transcend personal interests and to enable citizens to free themselves from expediency, day-to-day worries and the galling bonds of religious communities. Gauchet calls the public therefore the 'sacred' space of the Republic (Gauchet, 1998, p. 102). Since the republican community now has transcendental quality itself, it no longer needs religion as legitimating power. Faith has even become an uninvited guest in the public sphere of common deliberation since religious hair splitting too easily hampers the free and autonomous character of public discussions.

The emergence of the civil society, however, also encouraged the self-organization of citizens along shared interests or convictions. Religious institutions lost political power, but won social influence. In the French context, this paradoxical situation is illustrated by the 1905 law on the separation of churches and state. This hotly contested piece of legislation explicitly defined churches as private institutions aiming at the organization of religious services. This very act, however, implied also the legal recognition of the social significance of churches. Religion and state were separated, but faith did not disappear from the public domain.

Since the 1970s, Gauchet argues, the relationship between the public and religion has profoundly changed once again. As secularization theorists had predicted, many traditional churchgoers withdrew their membership. However, faith remained publicly present. Gauchet links this visibility of religion to the observation that over the last four decades the market has taken over civil society's role as the central mechanism for ordering civic life. Relationships between people are no longer established through the transcending power of the public realm but they are now regulated through the individualizing force of consumerism.

Like Charles Taylor, Gauchet concludes that faith is today nothing but one of the many elements that people can take up in their search for identity (Gauchet, 1998, p. 121). Gauchet argues that this new function of religion explains why it seeks public recognition. Since faith expresses the believers' identity, she wants to bring it out into the open.[14] The public realm transformed from a site for deliberation over and representation of the common good to a stage for the performance of personal belonging and group identities (Gauchet, 1998, p. 101, p. 134). The nation-state, seeking ways to prove its legitimacy in a globalizing age, presented itself as the champion of the right of the free and unhindered exhibition of these identities. Gauchet fears that these developments will in the end result in social fragmentation and destroy social peace. Therefore, the French historian calls on his fellow-citizens to restore the sacredness of the public sphere and to confine expressions of religious attachment to the private realm. For Gauchet, post-secularity makes it necessary to reinforce the republican character of public space.

In the French physical public space, the Republic is indeed visibly present. State institutions like schools, courts and town halls represent the republican identity. The big open squares in Paris are archetypical places where citizens can meet and deliberate about politics (van Melik, 2008, pp. 34–5). The argument of visibly representing republican ideals was also used to justify the 2004 ban on wearing headscarves and other ostensive religious symbols at public schools. The initiators of the ban argued that performances of religious identities did not belong at public schools. A similar way of reasoning might also explain why the example of the atheist campaign was not followed in the Hexagon. The republican squares are not the right places to express personal convictions about the (non-)existence of God. Nevertheless, there are exceptions that prove this republican rule. Once a year, the group Marche pour Jesus France (MPJF) organizes a prayer procession through the streets of Paris. In the flyers the MPJF distributes, the unique character of the march is emphasized. The permission to make the Church visible at the Place de République lasts only for a few hours per year and the MPJF calls on all believers to seize this opportunity with both hands.[15]

To sum up, in republican theory, the public is the space of shared values and a common identity. Communitarian theorists working in the line of Alisdair MacIntyre have a similar definition of public space. In his groundbreaking 'After Virtue', MacIntyre stated that the modern society is in a state of grave disorder (MacIntyre, 1984, p. 2). Like Gauchet, the British philosopher argued that living together peacefully has become complicated since citizens no longer share a conception of the common good. Contrary to the French historian, MacIntyre does not blame the regulative power of the market and individualization. MacIntyre traces the roots of this social disarray back to the Reformation period. By preaching that the human soul is so corrupted that it can never realize its potential, Calvinists prepared the seedbed for a type of political theory that has given up on the idea that a shared concept of what is good and holy can tie citizens together. Instead, the post-Reformation project has come to find reasonable principles that can manage an increasingly pluralistic society. This shift from a teleological to a deliberative approach resulted in continuing disagreement about the best way to live together peacefully. To solve the moral and social fragmentation resulting from this, MacIntyre advocates a return to the societal model of the Athenian polis as the only chance to escape civil war (MacIntyre, 1984, p. 133). All citizens should reorient their life projects towards a common concept of what is good and holy.

Since MacIntyre assumes that such a major social reorientation might take some time, to say the least, he proposes as an 'in between' solution the constitution of 'communities whose central bond is a shared vision of and understanding of goods' (MacIntyre, 1984, p. 258). This communitarian strategy pushes the public space for the time being into the background. Since the public is the domain of moral breakdown, the communitarian interest lies in the association of like-minded people. The sacred is not to be found in the chaotic metropolis, but in the possibly even gated communities that the city contains. Only these nodes of moral survival can be the bulwarks of the struggle for moral and spiritual renewal of the public. From a communitarian point of view, then, it is legitimate to bring a specific conception of the common good to the attention of all citizens. Running a bus campaign to promote a specific world view can be welcomed from a communitarian viewpoint. Such an initiative might be considered as just adding another voice to the unstructured polyphony of the public domain. However, if this is an effective instrument to reorient society towards a common *telos*, communitarians would not hesitate to make use of it.

Liberal Approaches

Contrary to republican theorists, liberal thinkers do not conceptualize the public as the sphere of shared ideals of the good life. John Rawls, the most prominent liberal philosopher of the last century, made a distinction between a political public realm and a non-political public realm. The former is the domain of political deliberation. Since this is the space where political decisions are taken that affect all citizens, it is unreasonable to use religious and ideological arguments in justifying the decisions, since these are only plausible for people who share that particular moral outlook. In the political public space only those rational and reasonable arguments should count that every citizen can understand. However, in the non-political public sphere – or background culture as Rawls calls this domain – everybody has the freedom to live according to the religious and cultural traditions he or she identifies with (Rawls, 2005, pp. 382–3). Implicitly, Rawls conceptualizes the physical public space as an easy accessible field that should be open to all kinds of individual expressions of ideological, religious and cultural allegiances. There can be no restriction to advertisement campaigns on buses, except if they can be justified by rules that all citizens can adopt on reasonable grounds.

Scholars of multiculturalism have argued that the Rawlsian formulation of liberalism has significant flaws. The main objection is that Rawls developed an idealist and moral theory of liberalism and does not really engage with the power struggles and negotiations that are part of everyday life and politics. Will Kymlicka, for instance, has argued that the non-political public sphere is not as open and pluralist as Rawls hopes it to be. In practice, the liberty of dissenters and minorities is often constrained by a dominant societal culture that functions as the cultural horizon of public life. For Kymlicka a societal culture is a territorially-concentrated set of a shared language and common practices and rituals (Kymlicka, 2007, p. 34). All Western democracies, liberal as they might be, pursue a nation-building project to foster civic attachment and social cohesion. Although he admits that no state can do without integration policies, Kymlicka calls for attention to the discriminatory effects of these projects. The protection of the dominant societal culture can easily be used as an argument to limit the freedom of dissenters and minorities. An example of the kind of concerns multicultural theorists have in mind is the ban on the Croatian 'Without God, without a master' campaign since it was said to conflict with national, religious traditions. To prevent dissenters and members of minority communities from becoming second-class citizens, multiculturalists are in favour of state policies that protect the cultures and identities of minorities, in order to guarantee that everybody can live the life of her or his choosing (Kymlicka, 2001, pp. 47–8). Kymlicka even goes as far as to argue that a state has to grant specific group rights to minorities to protect their cultural freedom. These rights compensate for the dominant presence of a nationalistic societal culture.

Like the multiculturalists, Jürgen Habermas has critically analysed and reviewed the central principles of liberal theory. In his early work 'Strukturwandel der Öffentlichkeit' Habermas offered a genealogy of the public domain. Like Gauchet, Habermas presented his reconstruction of the emergence of the public as a universally valid model of the public, but his historical focus is on central Europe. Habermas contends that the roots of the public domain are to be traced back to the coffeehouses of the European eighteenth century metropolises. Sipping their coffee, merchants mutually agreed that they needed a state with fixed and reliable rules to safeguard their long-term capital investments. The arbitrariness of royal rule had turned the state into an unreliable partner. It was time for a new political order that would guarantee individual liberty and stimulate free trade. According to Habermas, these capitalist incentives were at the basis of the public sphere that would finally develop into a countervailing power to state authority. The primary objective of this public deliberation was the protection of the private sphere where citizens pursued their own life plans and visions of the good life.

Habermas argued that from the nineteenth century onwards, the boundaries between the public and private domain increasingly blurred. The public sphere turned into a battlefield where the divergent interests of the social classes clashed. Arguments lost out to power struggles and private companies and mass media increasingly got a grip on what was left of the deliberative processes. In fact, Habermas argues, the public no longer functions as a countervailing power to the state. What is more, the commercialized public space increasingly penetrates the private realm of citizens and determines the lifestyles and conceptions of the good that people endorse.[16] Since deliberation no longer structures the public, it is now a chaotic space where people demonstrate their group attachments and commodified identities.[17] The Christian and atheist bus campaigns illustrate Habermas's thesis that the public is a realm of manifestation instead of deliberation. Propaganda and manipulation are put to work to influence the moral outlook and lifestyles of citizens. Habermas's political project, then, is to try to restore the communicative function of the public. Once again, it should become the domain of civic deliberation.

For a long time, Habermas has been of the opinion that religion had no role to play in his communicative project. He assumed that faith was irrelevant for public argumentations. Recently, he has revised his ideas in the light of the continued public presence of religion. He now argues that the civic debate should be 'epistemically adjusted' to post-secularity (Habermas, 2006, p. 15). Religious traditions have a special power to articulate moral intuitions and as such can provide arguments that are relevant for political deliberation.

Post-secular Public Space

So far, I have reconstructed republican and liberal approaches to public space in a post-secular era. The concept of the post-secular city has been central to my analysis. This city is fundamentally secular in the sense that it is no longer structured along religious principles, although some traces of a once dominant religious tradition might still be present in the urban landscape. This city is post-secular, however, in that a constantly growing diversity of worldviews, affiliations and identities claim a right to public space. The normative political approaches that I have explored evaluate this claim to public space differently. Gauchet and Habermas regret that the public has progressively changed into a showcase of self-selected identities. While Gauchet sketches how citizens can regain shared space if they all decide to adopt the same republican values, Habermas advocates the restoration of the deliberative function of the public. The projects of MacIntyre and Kymlicka go in a different direction. The former is in favour of the establishment of tradition-based communities amidst the chaos of the metropolis. The latter criticizes political theories that prioritize social cohesion over the rights of minority groups. Gauchet's republicanism is more vulnerable to Kymlicka's criticism than Habermas's communicative project. Indeed, Habermas has argued that the rules of deliberation should be epistemically adjusted to the deep pluralism that is characteristic for the post-secular society. However, like Gauchet, Habermas cherishes the idea that the public can once again become the central instrument for the integration of all political viewpoints.

I think that Kymlicka is methodologically right in starting his political reasoning with the everyday tensions and problems of the deep pluralism in society. He observes that in every society there are many nation-building mechanisms at work that aim to foster social cohesion and a common identity. For Kymlicka, then, the problem is not that there is too much plurality, but, to the contrary, that in some situations there is not enough freedom for divergent lifestyles. However, Kymlicka's multicultural alternative of minority rights is, at least in a western-European context not convincing. Like communitarians, Kymlicka assumes that the various cultural and religious traditions in society are embodied in communities that can be delineated from other social groups. However, I would like to argue that this is a too static view of how people construct their identity in a globalizing age (cf. Phillips, 2007). People pick out their own lifestyle and often only partially identify with a particular group. Citizens borrow from different sources: from what they find in the public realm as well as from the subcultures of the communities they belong to. A multicultural account of public space has to be based, then, on a more dynamic and multiple understanding of individual identity-construction. Therefore, it is not the religious or cultural traditions themselves that need special protection, but the individual freedom to identify with these traditions.

In the early 1990s, Iris Marion Young suggested that perhaps the diversity of the modern city itself best protects the freedom of citizens to live in accordance with their individual understanding of the good life. For Young, the diversity and complexity of the urban landscape is not so much a problem to be solved as a breeding ground for a more just society (Young, 1990, pp. 236–41). For Young, city life offered an inspiring imaginary towards this ideal. The American philosopher defined living in the urban as the being together of strangers. 'In the city persons and groups interact within spaces and institutions they all experience themselves as belonging to, but without those interactions dissolving into unity or commonness' (Young, 1990, p. 237). Young prepared the ground for contemporary agonistic visions of the public. In this approach, urban public space is in the first place a site marked by the shared practice of negotiating diversity. Citizens take responsibility for the living space they share and they participate in a process of ongoing deliberation about how much commonness is required and how various identity expressions can have a place in the public realm. According to Doreen Massey the throwntogetherness and the power inequalities of the modern city necessitate but also inspire a struggle for freedom and equality. Public space is not created through the acceptance of whatever is deemed to be a public value. It is participation in the social practice of negotiating the common good that makes the shared living space genuinely public (Massey, 2005, p. 153; cf. Göle, 2006, p. 37).

At times, the diversity of urban public space is a confusing experience. Nevertheless, I do not agree with Mircea Eliade that city life is the second fall of humankind. I think that the urban experience of plurality is a necessary characteristic of a public space that tries to guarantee freedom to all citizens under post-secular and multicultural conditions. The public then is the space of ongoing negotiation on the complex balance between expressions of dominant cultures and alternative identities (Hajer and Reijndorp, 2001, p. 104). The concept of the post-secular city helps to bring into focus how, in some cases, religious identities seek recognition but are denied access to the public. Sometimes for good reasons, but often their exclusions curtail the liberties of citizens without justification. The post-secular city is a place where you walk past women wearing headscarves, breathe in the pervasive smell of incense and catch an atheist bus in less than a few minutes.[18]

Notes

[1] Geert Wilders, Speech to the Dutch House of Representatives, 16 September 2009. http://www.pvv.nl/index.php/component/content/article/12-spreekteksten/2360-algemene-politieke-beschouwingen-2009-inbreng.html, accessed 15 January 2011.

[2] For instructive analyses of the headscarf debate see Göle (2003), Bowen (2007) and Joppke (2009).

[3] In this chapter I focus on the public/private dichotomy and I do not consider the possibility that the sacred or the religious represents a realm in its own right. Roman law, for instance, was constructed on the triangle of a public, a private and a sacred sphere (Geuss 2001, p. 7). Since Roman times, however, our worldview has become irrevocably secular in the sense that it is today impossible to perceive the sacred as representing an unquestioned absolute and authoritative order. Post-secularity acknowledges the disappearance of an independent sacred realm, but recognizes that religion at least for the time being remains an important factor in public space.

[4] This public visibility of religion is not the re-emergence of traditional forms of faith. Religion has taken on new forms that differ fundamentally from its past appearances (for this distinction see Hoelzl and Ward 2008).

[5] I take the expression 'right to the city' from Henri Lefebvre. Here, I follow Engin Isin's (2002, p. 13) interpretation of this term.

[6] Weintraub 1997. Cf. Staeheli and Mitchell 2007. Rianne van Melik (2008, pp. 18–19) gives an overview of definitions of public space from a socio-geographic point of view.

[7] http://www.guardian.co.uk/commentisfree/2008/jun/20/transport.religion, accessed 15 January 2011.
[8] http://www.guardian.co.uk/commentisfree/2008/oct/21/religion-advertising, accessed 15 January 2011.
[9] http://www.guardian.co.uk/commentisfree/2008/aug/06/richarddawkins.religion, accessed 15 January 2011.
[10] http://www.guardian.co.uk/commentisfree/2008/oct/23/atheist-bus-campaign-ariane-sherine/print, accessed 15 January 2011.
[11] http://www.justgiving.com/atheistbus/, accessed 15 January 2011.
[12] http://www.atheistcampaign.org/, accessed 15 January 2011.
[13] http://www.delo.si/clanek/77241, accessed 15 January 2011.
[14] Religion represents a choice: 'Mais un choix dont je suis moi-même, en fait, l'objet: son enjeu n'est pas du côté de la vérité du message auquel je me rallie, mais du côté de la définition subjective qu'il me procure' (Gauchet, 1998, p. 131).
[15] 'La Marche pour Jésus est la seule manifestation chrétienne publique reconnue par les autorités, qui nous permette de chanter et danser dans la rue avec l'accord de la Préfecture de Police de Paris ... Elle est un moment fort dans la capitale où une proclamation de masse est réalisée. C'est un moyen qui nous permet de rendre l'Eglise visible dans la rue, en contraste avec d'autres manifestations, reflet de notre société actuelle'. Extracts from the brochure 'Christ est ma vie' distributed by the MPJF during the Marche Pour Jésus from Place de la République to Place de la Nation on 21 May 2005.
[16] '[D]ie publizitätsbezogene Innerlichkeit weicht tendenziell einer intimitätsbezogenen Verdinglichung' (Habermas, 1969, p. 189).
[17] Habermas illustrates this development by quoting approvingly sociologist Hans Paul Bahrdt: 'Das Wechselverhältnis von öffentlicher und privater Sphäre ist gestört. Es ist nicht deshalb gestört, weil der Großstadtmensch per se Massenmensch ist und deshalb keinen Sinn mehr für die Kultivierung der Privatsphäre hat, sondern weil es ihm nicht mehr gelingt, das immer komplizierter werdende Leben der Gesamtstadt in der Weise zu überblicken, daß es für ihn öffentlich ist' (Habermas, 1969, p. 175).
[18] I want to thank Prof. Dr. Frits de Lange and the participants of the expert seminar 'The Sacred in the Metropolis' for their helpful comments on earlier versions of this chapter.

Bibliography

Berger, P. L. (1999), 'The Desecularisation of the World: A Global Overview', in Berger, P. (ed.), *The Desecularisation of the World: Resurgent Religion and World Politics*. Washington: The Ethics and Public Policy Centre, pp. 15–32.

Bosniak, L. (2006), *The Citizen and the Alien: Dilemmas of Contemporary Membership*. Princeton: Princeton University Press.

Bowen, J. R. (2007), *Why the French Don't Like Headscarves: Islam, the State and Public Space*. Princeton: Princeton University Press.

Casanova, J. (1994), *Public Religions in the Modern World*. Chicago: University of Chicago Press.
Cox, H. (1966), *The Secular City: Secularisation and Urbanization in Theological Perspective*. New York: SCM.
Eliade, M. (1965), *Le Sacré et le Profane*. Paris: Gallimard.
Gauchet, M. (1998), *La Religion dans la Démocratie: Parcours de la Laïcité*. Paris: Gallimard.
Geuss, R. (2001), *Public Goods, Private Goods*. Princeton: Princeton University Press.
Göle, N. (2003), *Musulmanes et Modernes: Voile et Civilisation en Turquie*. Paris: La Découverte.
—. (2006), 'Islamic visibilities and Public Sphere', in Göle, N. and Ammann, L. (eds), *Islam in Public: Turkey, Iran and Europe*. Istanbul: Istanbul Bilgi University Press, pp. 3–43.
Habermas, J. (1969), *Strukturwandel der Öffentlichkeit: Untersuchungen zu einer Kategorie der bürgerlichen Gesellschaft* (4th edn). Neuwied: Hermann Luchterhand.
—. (2006), 'Religion in the Public Sphere'. *European Journal of Philosophy*, 14(1), 1–25.
Hajer, M. and Reijndorp, A. (2001), *In Search of New Public Domain*. Rotterdam: NAi.
Hermans, C. A. M. (2003), *Participatory Learning: Religious Education in a Globalizing Society*. Leyden: Brill.
Hoelzl, M. and Ward, G. (2008), 'Introduction', in Ward, G. and Hoelzl, M. (eds), *The New Visibility of Religion: Studies in Religion and Cultural Hermeneutics*. London: Continuum, pp. 1–11.
Isin, E. F. (2002), 'City, Democracy and Citizenship: Historical Images, Contemporary Practices', in Isin, E. F. and Turner, B. S. (eds), *Handbook of Citizenship Studies*. London: SAGE, pp. 305–16.
Joppke, C. (2009), *Veil: Mirror of Identity*. Cambridge: Polity.
Katzenstein, P. J. (2006), 'Multiple Modernities as Limits to Secular Europeanization?', in Byrnes, T. A. and Katzenstein, P. J. (eds), *Religion in an Expanding Europe*. Cambridge: Cambridge University Press, pp. 1–33.
Kymlicka, W. (2001), *Politics in the Vernacular: Nationalism, Multiculturalism and Citizenship*. Oxford: Oxford University Press.
—. (2007), 'The New Debate on Minority Rights (and Postscript)', in Laden, A. S. and Owen, S. (eds), *Multiculturalism and Political Theory*. Cambridge: Cambridge University Press, pp. 25–59.
Luther, H. (1992), *Religion und Alltag: Bausteine zu einer Praktische Theologie des Subjekts*. Stuttgart: Radius.
MacIntyre, A. (1984), *After Virtue: A Study in Moral Theory* (2nd edn). Notre Dame: University of Notre Dame Press.
Margry, P. J. (2000), *Teedere quaesties: Religieuze rituelen in conflict; Confrontaties tussen katholieken en protestanten rond de processiecultuur in 19e-eeuws Nederland*. Hilversum: Verloren.
Massey, D. (2005), *For Space*. London: SAGE.
Maussen, M. (2004), 'Policy Discourses on Mosques in the Netherlands 1980–2002: Contested Constructions'. *Ethical Theory and Moral Practice*, 7(2), 147–62.

Noordmans, O. (1986), 'God op straat?', in Noordmans, O. (ed.), *Verzamelde werken: De kerk en het leven.* Kampen: Kok, pp. 563–5.
Phillips, A. (2007), *Multiculturalism without Culture.* Princeton: Princeton University Press.
Rawls, J. (2005), *Political Liberalism: Expanded Edition* (3rd edn). New York: Columbia University Press.
Sennett, R. (1990), *The Conscience of the Eye: The Design and Social Life of Cities.* New York: Norton.
Sheldrake, P. (2007), 'Placing the Sacred: Transcendence and the City'. *Literature & Theology,* 21(3), 243–58.
Spybey, T. (2001), 'The Constitution of Global Society', in Bryant, C. G. A. and Jary, D. (eds), *The Contemporary Giddens: Social Theory in a Globalizing Age.* Hampshire: Palgrave.
Staeheli, L. A. and Mitchell, D. (2007), 'Locating the Public in Research and Practice'. *Progress in Human Geography,* 31(6), 792–811.
Stavrakakis, Y. (2007), 'Antinomies of Space: From the Representation of Politics to a Topology of the Political', in BAVO (ed.), *Urban Politics Now: Re-Imagining Democracy.* Rotterdam: NAi.
Taylor, C. (2007), *A Secular Age.* Cambridge, MA: Harvard University Press.
van Melik, R. G. (2008), *Changing Public Space: The Recent Redevelopment of Dutch City Squares.* Utrecht: Koninklijk Nederlands Aardrijkskundig Genootschap.
Vidler, A. (1992), *The Architectural Uncanny: Essays in the Modern Unhomely.* Cambridge, MA: MIT.
Weintraub, J. (1997), 'The Theory and Politics of the Public/Private Distinction', in Weintraub, J. and Kumar, J. (eds), *Public and Private in Thought and Practice: Perspectives on a Grand Dichotomy.* Chicago: University of Chicago Press, pp. 1–42.
Young, I. M. (1990), *Justice and the Politics of Difference.* Princeton: Princeton University Press.

Part Two

Religion, Built Environments and Urban Societies

Chapter 4

Religion in the Built Environment: Aesth/Ethics, Ritual and Memory in Lived Urban Space

Sigurd Bergmann

The Sacred *in* the Non-sacred

Most societies distinguish places that are especially important, sacred and powerful for them (Ivahkiv, 2001, p. 44). The design and shaping of built environments for human settlement has been embedded in religious worldviews and practices through the whole history of humanity.

In Asia, geomantic wisdom and traditional procedures, where the flow of energy dictates the location of a building, are still at work in the selection of a place for settling from time to time. One can find many examples where economic interests, for example in a multinational company planning for a skyscraper in Seoul, are combined with older geomantic practices, not only in the countryside but also in urban architecture.[1] The shape of a traditional African village mirrors the human body and its diverse interrelations and it locates the human settlement in a reciprocal analogy to the spiritual cosmos. The shape of the house and the village refers to the body; the centre is the 'stomach space', the cooking place, and the whole looks like a man lying on his right side. The shape of the houses and the village is designed according to anthropomorphic and cosmological images.[2] Cities of the classical Maya in Yucatan have been located at the intersection of the subterranean water streams, where the most powerful gods dwell, and the complex sky filled with divine stars/planets (Bergmann, 2009b). Premodern villages and cities in Europe have applied the form of the *circle* in their design in order to mirror and come closer to the horizon and to locate the city in the circle of the world, while they have used the *square* to symbolically connect to the divine. The images of nature and the cosmos have been crucial for the design of built environments.[3] Settlements have been cosmo-sized spaces. Also the image of the human body has, as Richard Sennett has shown in detail, influenced the shape of urban space (Sennett, 1994). Images of

God have been built in stone, and buildings have affected religious imagination and practice.

One can wonder if and how urban spaces today still follow this foundational code about the image of the body *in* the spatial design. The negotiation of power takes place in religious semiotics, where architecture materializes religious codes such as the encounter between above and below, heaven and earth, the interplay of centre and periphery, inside and outside, hierarchies of height (represented in plateaus, thresholds and stairs), territorializations of exclusion where only the initiated are permitted to enter sacred areas, and much more. The medieval northern European Hansa city, for example, uses its cathedrals, councils, built masses and towers as a symbol for the 'Concordia' (unity) of the city and its history, as a tool for maritime navigation, and as an expression of power in a transregional economic competition. Towers have, as we know from the story of Babylon, been built in order to bridge the distance between heaven and the earth (Woschitz, 2005), and the skyscraper of the modern metropolis still applies the same ideology, where elites are supposed to rule from above, even if the older religious belief system no longer works according to the new norms and values of capitalism.

So-called secularization has in fact changed the identity and function of religion in the last centuries, but it has not really de-sacralized urban space. One might try the opposite hypothesis and claim that urban space has become an even more complex and experimental arena for spiritual spatiality, and that this freedom is catalysed by secularization, which has set traditional religious institutions free from earlier identities as power regimes and now allows them to find their new ways. In short, secularization has accelerated resacralization, even if we should not regard the 'return of the sacred' (Daniel Bell) automatically as evidence of the strength of the secularization theory. The sacred, if it really exists, is no longer what is has been, but returns, in well-known as well as in unknown spatial appearances.[4] Resacralization does not simply mean the return of religion but an amalgamation of reconstructed older and invented new traditions. While premodern and modern cultures could still be analysed by seeking some kind of analogy and integration of built space and religion, late modern urban space is characterized by much more diffuse borders between the sacred and the profane. Christianity has obviously catalysed this development if one, for example, follows Harvey Cox (Cox, 1965). This makes the reflexive task much more difficult as the border between sacred and non-sacred architecture no longer makes any sense in an urban context where religious communities both wax and wane, and where architecture and urban planning operate consciously and unconsciously with religious tools and codes.

For the theme of this book such a complexity is challenging where the sacred can hide *in* the non-sacred, and where confessional religious places and buildings are not necessarily in continuity with their own tradition. It makes the analytical task difficult but also much more exciting. The historical lack of reflecting about the relation of space and religion makes it even more difficult and even more necessary to catalyse such research. Foucault has rightly stated that while the nineteenth century has been obsessed with time – development and standstill, crisis and cycles, etc. – our century represents the age of space, where other questions are at core: simultaneity, juxtaposition, the near and the far, the side-by-side and dispersions (Foucault, 2006, p. 317).

Religious studies and theology have lately discovered the spatial turn and the need to follow it, but as far as I can see such a turn has been initiated and will scarcely stop, but rather accelerate and change our perspectives, maybe it will even transform the theory of religion in general (Bergmann, 2007). The wideness of the field can be approached from many angles. In the following I will concentrate on three: aesth/ethics, ritual and memory. Before we go ahead I will present my own theoretical preferences. As the discourse is still open and creative it seems necessary for every scholar to clarify his/her understanding of what is meant by 'space' and 'religion', in my case summarized as 'lived religion' in 'lived space'.

Lived Religion in Lived Space

Following Henri Lefèbvre, Edward Soja has developed the field of critical urban studies that he describes as Thirdspace study (Soja, 1996). His approach also offers an exciting challenge to religious studies and theology. Religion does not work without or beyond space; therefore, a study of religion and contextual theology must develop qualitative interpretations of the spatiality of God, the believers, their worldviews and values and their cultural and spiritual practices. Urbanization and the dynamics of synekism should therefore be approached as essential religious processes.

According to Soja, the 'trialectics of being' relates spatiality, historicity and sociality, while the 'trialectics of spatiality' relates the lived, the perceived and the conceived (Soja, 1996, p. 71, p. 74). A Firstspace perspective investigates cityspace with regard to its materialized spatial practices while a Secondspace analysis explores it as a mental and ideational field, where the conceived space of imagination is at its core. A Thirdspace study examines urbanism as fully lived space, a simultaneously real and imagined, actual and virtual, locus of structured individual and collective experience and agency (Soja, 2000, p. 11). 'Synekism' is defined as 'the stimulus of urban agglomeration' and in particular, the economic and ecological interdependencies and the creative – as well as occasionally destructive – synergisms that arise from the purposeful clustering and collective cohabitation of people in space, in a 'home' habitat (Soja, 2000, p. 12).

As valuable as Soja's theory is to enlighten the study of religion about the dynamics of social spatiality, it lacks an insight into the depth of the human dimension. Certainly sociocultural and spatial environments always affect human behaviour and imagination, but human subjectivity also impacts the spatial formation of social life. Georg Simmel states rightly that the relationship between spatial design and social forms follows a double direction (Simmel, 2006, p. 304). Spatiality affects social life, and social life affects spatiality. Social life is not just a system but a complex interplay of subjective, cultural, historical and ecological processes. Humanities in general and religious studies and theology in particular can therefore contribute valuable insights into the understanding of lived space. If we regard urbanization and synekism as deeply religious processes, Soja's approach is not profound enough. Urban processes cannot be fully understood as a 'locus of structured individual and collective experience and agency' in the frames of cultural studies and social sciences, assisted by selected technical and historical disciplines. Invoking the spirits and the Spirit is a crucial challenge for urban theory if it does not want to run the risk of falling back from Third- into Secondspace analysis.

In order to catalyse space studies one needs to clarify the concept of religion. The well-known conflict between substantive (essentialist) and functionalist concepts, where some scholars try to run the debate as a kind of confessional dispute, seems in my view hardly helpful for a cooperation of space and religion studies. Rather than to follow either one or the other doctrine, I would prefer to regard religion as a sociocultural process as well as an individual belief in the reality of the sacred or divine. Both substantive and functionalist dimensions must be respected and balanced, and both internal and external perspectives should be combined.[5] A study of religion as a Thirdspace discipline should especially try to grasp both the subjective and cultural dimensions of religion in lived space. If it were to only go for a totalitarian functionalist method it would lose sight of the creative power that religious visions generate for the spatial design of social life. If it were to only go for a substantive method it would not be able to understand the contextual interplay of culture and belief. One could debate the notions and ask whether we should prefer 'religion', 'spirituality', 'the sacred' or 'faith' as central terms, but at this open stage of the discourse I would prefer to approach the field with many different tools.

The concept of 'lived religion' (*gelebte Religion*) is inspired by phenomenology, and it emerged in German practical theology in the 1990s. It can be connected to Soja's concept of lived space in a fruitful way. Lived religion focuses on 'the religiosity of the people, of individuals and groups as embedded in the *contexts* of life-worlds and biographies' (Streib, 2008, p. 53). In such a view religion is no longer regarded as an institutionalized form of belief but it can appear both inside and outside of traditional spheres. Other modes of expressing such an understanding are to talk about explicit and implicit religion or visible and 'invisible religion' (Thomas Luckmann). Also Clifford Geertz' anthropology of religion can be useful to understand lived religion as a reciprocal confirmation of worldview and ethos, that is religion as something that takes place in between ideology and practice (Geertz, 1973). The concept of lived religion is, however, not a theory or really a concept but rather emancipation from the bonds of reductionist and limited conceptualizations of religion. It integrates different elements and impulses from phenomenology, cultural studies, aesthetics and pedagogics.

If lived space represents the 'real-and-imagined, actual-and-virtual, locus of structured individual and collective experience and agency' (Soja, 2000, p. 11), lived religion would represent both the practical and the imagined experience and encounter with the sacred. Lived religion takes place in lived space. Both interact in a double direction (Fig. 4.1): lived space includes and affects lived religion, and lived religion affects the spatiality of faith and social life.

CITYSPACE
lived, perceived and conceived space

RELIGION
lived (believed, practised and materialised) faith

The circle of function (Funktionskreis) between lived space and lived religion

FIGURE 4.1   The circle of function (Funktionskreis) between lived space and lived religion

The challenge for research would then be to interpret this exchange of space and religion. It might even turn religious studies itself into a Third-space discipline. Christian theologians could then study built environments and urban processes not only as challenges for ethics, but as religious phenomena and expressions of experiences with God. Non-sacred architecture could then be studied in light of sacred architecture in order to explore the exchange of both. Allegedly secular places, such as museums, art halls and public squares, could then be perceived as arenas for the spatialization of worldviews, values and images of nature and the sacred. The global sacred, as Bron Szerszynski has called it (Szerszynski, 2005, p. 159ff), could then be identified in a broad range of phenonomena in lived space, where the idolatry of technification but also the vision of a flourishing ecojustice is at stake.

For the scholar of religion such an approach would make it necessary to question the priority of normative sources, such as in dogmatics, sacred scriptures and confessional hierarchies, and to include and emancipate the believers themselves as sources for so-called religiosity. Synekism, that is the co-habitation of people in a built urban environment, represents in itself a religious process, which we could – in continuity with Hegel's understanding of architecture – circumscribe as a 'highway toward the adequate realization of the Godhead' (Hegel, 1971, p. 143).[6] Religion would in such a perspective not only be at work in the designing, perceiving and conceiving of urban space, but it would function as an invisible and visible force in the whole of Soja's trialectics.

How can we interpret lived religion in lived space? In the following I will explore three different themes – aesth/ethics, ritual and memory – and discuss different theoretical tools for an analysis. The first is inspired by phenomenology and the ecological aesthetics of the German philosopher Gernot Böhme.

Aesth/ethics

The discipline of aesthetics has dwelt in the margins of the history of philosophy, while, for example, epistemology and ethics have been regarded as central topics. Moral philosophy is characterized by a poor integration with other discourses and it treats normativity and human images of the good and right as if it lacks body. Such an isolation of ethical thinking on the one hand, and its extensive power over decision-making discourses on the other, makes it necessary to re-contextualize and embed ethical thinking and acting in man/woman's bodily being. This is especially important with regard to our understanding of space and built environments as these affect our bodily life directly and without any rational detours. As Le Corbusier's gigantic project has shown, it seems problematic to root urban planning dominantly in ideational principles. The dominance of utilitarianism is evidence of the destructiveness of ethical models which are brutally pulled over reality.[7] It is therefore common today to regard architecture as a practice that deals with 'existential place' as Juhani Pallasmaa has expressed it and to develop it as a process of building for human bodily being where the 'senses of the skin' are included in a qualitative synaesthetics, that is the cooperation of all human senses.[8]

In order to counteract the asymmetry between the human skills of bodily perception and awareness on one side and the reflexiveness about values and norms on the other, I have coined the programmatic term of 'aesth/ ethics' (Bergmann 2005b, 2006). 'Aesthetics' is here understood not as a theory of beauty in the narrow sense, but as a discursive and artistic production and reflection of practices and discourses on synaesthetic perception, creation and reception. An ecological aesthetics is a self-aware human reflection on one's living-in-particular-surroundings (Böhme, 1989, p. 8f; Böhme, 1995). The slash between aesthetics and ethics has been invented to signal the intention not to leave moral philosophy and ethics to itself but to embed it continuously in perceptions. If ethics is defined as a discursive reflection on moral problems, it becomes difficult to exclude people's mental capacities and to separate aesthetic competence from moral competence. Ethics must necessarily be embraced by aesthetics. The perception of moral problems must be prior to their reflection and solution. It takes both a sharp mind and the capacity of the senses to see our neighbour's misery, to answer Cain's question: 'Lord, am I my brother's keeper?' The experience of space not only as a physically perceived space or an ideationally conceived space, but as a truly plastic lived space is at the core of such a trialectic 'aisthesis' embedding 'ethos'.

The notion of atmosphere can serve as a central term in such an aesth/ ethics of space. It dissolves the dichotomy of subject and object and can therefore be useful for an analysis of lived religion in lived space. An atmosphere is characterized by what it does not merge as a causal consequence of human actions. An atmosphere surrounds something. It is shining from a living creature, a thing, a place or an artefact. We can experience atmospheres both intuitively and reflexively. Atmospheres emerge, they can endure, and they can disappear in the spaces *between* something and us. Obviously humans cannot create atmospheres but they can create artefacts which themselves are capable of producing and mediating atmospheres. I do not simply inhabit a city but a city and its atmosphere inhabit me.[9]

Atmospheres are characterized through their being both human and physical, both subjective and objective. It is no longer the distinction of subject and object but the encounter of both in a common phenomenon that is at the focus of reflection. Men and women perceive themselves in the mirror of their natural surrounding and their artistically and technically designed surroundings. We can, as Goethe rightly states, only understand ourselves through and in the world.[10] That turns the atmosphere also into a screen for the emergence of our human identity.

An atmosphere emerges in the interspaces between outer human surrounding and inner bodily soul spiritual being. It is not at all diffuse and uncertain, shallow or subjective but it offers a notion, which in an exciting way treatises the interrelatedness of the outer and inner, the bodily and spiritual, the surrounding and the internalized. In cooperation with related terms such as aura, chord and charisma, atmosphere is fruitful as a central notion for an aesth/ethical interpretation of built environments. It can also inspire theology to deepen its pneumatology and to reflect the Holy Spirit who takes place on diverse atmospheres and surroundings. For a theologian it would be more appropriate to talk about the Spirit rather than the sacred. This must not necessarily happen in a limited confessional sense but can take place in an open-minded discourse. Eckhard Lessing's definition of the Spirit as 'the being of the one at or with the other' (Lessing 1992; Bergmann, 2005a, p. 9f.), allows a creative language about experience of the Holy Spirit's work in space and place. The question '*how does the Spirit take place?*' would be a central one for such an urban pneumatology. We can also break through the limits of rational theology and talk about atmospheres as guides, traces and links that connect the Creation to the life-giving Spirit. Atmospheres are in such a theology *vestigia Dei* (God's traces on earth). With the help of these spherical traces in the spaces-between believers can navigate in God's horizon and follow the Spirit into a transfigured creation. It remains to work out such a theology for the late modern postmetropolis.

Atmospheres must, however, not necessarily be interpreted in the horizon of Christian pneumatology, they can also be perceived and reflected in different religious traditions. The term in itself and its foundation in our bodily being and our perception and awareness about the environment, which we are a part of, allows discussion of spiritual atmospheres in built atmospheres. The sacred can then no longer be misunderstood as something transcendent above, but appears in the space in between built artefacts and human perceptions, practices and images within them. A notion like atmosphere overcomes the dialectics of transcendence and immanence, it replaces this dialectics so to speak with transparency. Atmospheres come and go, they are connected to persons, artefacts and environments. Atmospheres make places transparent; they become diaphane for emotions, ideas, revelations and vibes. Spatiality is in such a view not simply an arena or theatre where religious drama can take place, but urban space becomes itself a player in the drama of encounters of the human and divine. 'Houses can fly',[11] streets can move, and cathedrals and temples can dance.

Ritualization

Another way of approaching the connection of the sacred and the urban departs from ritual theory. Social processes can be studied in light of this quite new field in cultural and religious studies. The lens of looking at social life as rites, rituals and ritualizations offers exciting possibilities to combine the analysis of actions and ideas. As far as I know, ritual theory has not been applied to the analysis of built environments, and I would therefore like to collect some pieces and see what we can do with them. Even if a ritual represents a form of social action that is deeply dependant on the context where it takes place, ritual theory itself is characterized by the same lack of spatial reflexiveness that characterizes most of the social sciences. Markus Schroer has shown in detail how the dominant models of social sciences still include a Newtonian understanding of space and how most of them are not able to turn to the new understanding of lived space as an essential dynamic element of social life itself (Schroer, 2006). This is, unfortunately, also true for ritual theory, but it should not hinder us from using it further with regard to the sacred in the city.

Rituals are sociocultural mediums constructed of 'tradition, exigency, and self-expression'. According to Catherine Bell, a ritual invokes the ordered relationships between human beings and non-immediate sources of power, authority and value. A ritual enables people to embody assumptions about their place in a larger order of things (Bell, 1997, p. xi). Ritualizations are those actions that transform a practice into a ritual. The older assumption that religion and ritual would decline in the process of modernization has, as we know, not come true. With regard to rituals we can, however, see a development where ritual practices themselves are regarded as objects for belief, rather than ideologies or images. Scholars have furthermore developed a perspective where processes of ritualization have been analysed in different social spheres. One can even wonder if the skill to ritualize represents an essential human skill in social life.

Reflecting on rituals of the sacred in the modern city, one would need to follow a double direction of impacts. How does urban space affect ritualization, and what do rituals mean for lived space? It seems obvious that the choice of place is essential for the development of a ritual. Actions create some kind of a 'ritual place' and decisions about the choice of place are part of a broader negotiation. A procession, for example, moves from one (sacred) place to the other, or it carries the charisma of the sacred from the inner to the outer. A procession also changes the surroundings it travels through. As long as the ritual endures, a place can no longer be used for transport or trading; and also the remembrance of a ritual affects the character and atmosphere of a place, even if the ritual is not executed any longer. The relationship of ritual and place seems to be intimate, complex and somehow reciprocal. Place and ritual affect each other. The specific attributes of place and context offer necessary conditions for ritualization, and the ritual practice includes and transforms the atmosphere and identity of a place where it takes place.

The classical Mayan city of Mayapán in Yucatan represents a deep interconnectedness of ritual and place. The city was built in the interface of subterranean (water based) and heavenly gods and powers and offers a complex symbolic space with integrated religious, political, economic and ecological dimensions. The cenote offers an entrance for the water gods to Earth and a channel of communication between humans and gods, while the pyramid and observatory connects the city to the sky. In Europe, the Gothic cathedral offers an interior that mirrors the image of God in a way that the Creator's revelation and incarnation continues in a spatial inhabitation of the Spirit who gives life to the church and its believers.

Another interesting capacity of ritual lies in its normative power. Roy R. Rappaport has shown in his famous ecology of religion how rituals work as 'homoeostatic', that is as aesthetically normative regulations of social interactions with nature (Rappaport, 1968; 1999, p. 411; Grimes, 2003). Due to ritual practices, humans preserve images and norms about how to interact with hunting, farming and modes of survival. Rituals can work as normative practices that regulate human ecology. In his later book, Rappaport regards ritualization as the essential way of fabricating meaning; the ritual fabrication is in contradiction with the scientific rational production of knowledge (or the 'epistemologies of discovery' as he calls them). Rappaport argues against the dominant power of rational knowledge and pleas for a synthesis of both (Rappaport, 1999, p. 451ff). He also emphasizes the significance of 'ultimate sacred postulates'. No matter how much these are constructed, humans experience and regard them as real and sacrosanct.

Could we regard also the modern 'postmetropolis' as a scenery where lived space emerges from both of these sources, ritual and rational fabrication of meaning? It is obvious that a city is built on rational knowledge, but how does it interact with ritual practises and what are its ultimate sacred postulates? How are ritual practices regulating social and environmental processes, and how should they? What kinds of images of the sacred determine the development of urban space today?

A third interesting observation is about movement. Bodily movement as well as emotional motion seems to be crucial in every ritual practice. Rituals of birth and death accompany the newborn and the dead neighbour. While the first moves into existence, the other moves out of this world and into another one, and rituals mirror both these movements. Movement in itself is central in, for example, rites of passage or pilgrimages, while other rituals connect to the rhythm and circle of natural seasons. A ritual turns space into symbolic space and time into symbolic time. Movements according to specific spiritual references sacralize space and time. While some initiated are allowed to move into specific spatial spheres, others have to stay outside or in limited spheres. While some places are open for all, others have to be avoided in order to keep the order alive. The ritual that connects the community to invisible powers achieves spatial order. Such a relation is central for social harmony, spatial order and the meaningfulness of a community. How is ritual practice as movement linked to the mobility of urban space? Could we regard 'the ethics of mobilities' (Bergmann and Sager, 2008) as some kind of a ritualizing practice, where ritualized movement regulates urban mobility? The pattern of centre and periphery still continues, even if modern urban centres are mainly organized as markets. The hierarchy of places that an ordinary citizen: a) should either avoid, or b) could visit for purposes, or c) could access freely can also be found in the postmetropolis.

Stairs and terraces still work very well to visualize a difference between the profane and that which claims to be accessed with a specific attitude. Frank Lloyd Wright's (recently restored) villa in Buffalo creates a symbolic space (of shelter) through its stairs and terraces where the visitor enters and leaves the building. The steep stairs up to the Roman temple entrance can only be treated with a feeling of dignity, *Erhabenheit* and respect for the powers.

Finally, I would like to sum up my observations and try to merge them into an agenda for religious urban studies. A ritual fabricates meaning. It connects the community to invisible powers and connects the human being and the environment to these in order to preserve their well-being. How can we study lived urban space as an environment through the lens of ritualized meaning? Can the city itself be regarded as a producer of meaning? What would happen if were to regard architecture and urban planning as a partly ritualized activity? How are rational productions and ritual fabrications of meaning interlinked in city planning?

Or is it a characteristic of the modern city that it does not produce any meaning at all, as its inhabitants do not share a common cosmology and ritual practice? Several attempts to create such a common ritual practice have been initiated in the last few years. For example in Malmö, a cultural association arranged a successful 'festival of the dead' in 2006 in order to counteract the asymmetry of life and death in modern culture.

The *Festival of the Dead* was arranged by the cultural association *Rárika* in Malmö in 2006, one week after Halloween. The altar of the dead was installed in a central park without any signs referring to a specific religious confession. (For a more detailed discussion see Petersson's essay [2009] on the altar.) Rituals regulate social behaviour and imagination in a normative way. How is this true in late modern urban space today? Even if the discourse about democracy persuades us that all places are open for everyone, reality does not provide evidence. In a similar way that temples in premodern times have had a hierarchy of spheres, which were more or less open to all or strictly limited to religious elites, the late modern city offers what we could call maps of avoidance. Some areas will be avoided or only accessed for very specific purposes, such as banks, embassies or business buildings. Others are only approached for purposes such as schools, hospitals, shops and theatres. Only a few buildings are truly open public places such as squares, botanic gardens, museums and railway stations. An exciting example of a strongly ritualized space is the modern airport, where rites of passages take place several times and where a strict regime of surveillance and control is surveying all movements in the sharply drawn map's territory.[12]

Rituals, as we see, regulate human movements and as urban space offers a complex potential for many kinds of movements which are interlinked in a sublime way, an analysis of ritual practises and their ability to regulate movements in urban space would generate a lot of new insights. Again, it seems as if I have left our theme and the sacred, but my point is that rituals represent a form of social practice which takes place in the city both as visible and as invisible religion. Rituals are not necessarily embedded in religion. They can fabricate meaning but can also be meaningless. They are nevertheless able to create and carry a community and they produce specific ritual places which also affect a broader surrounding. Rituals transform places into sacred places either for a short or a long time.

We can, for example, compare the spiritual pilgrimage with modern sport, even if sport events are both similar to and different from rituals. The pilgrim doesn't understand his walk as mere transportation. Pilgrims experience their walking as a tool for contemplation and for mental and bodily regeneration, which we could easily compare to the modern city marathons. Even if the runner wants to achieve a goal, it is the process of running together with many others that gives meaning to the run and the whole modern marathon. Most of the participants are not professional athletes but ordinary people who have spent a lot of time preparing and training. They are sweating, they are limping, they are faltering, but the experience of partaking in a common exertion makes their pain meaningful and even sensual. The marathon appears as a deeply ritualized form of common movement in urban space. No doubt it changes the city itself, and it transforms the economy of the modern urban space for trading, transport and symbolic encounters into something else. Like a carnival, a religious festival or a course for celebrating the winning football team, the urban lived space radically changes its atmosphere when the mass just runs.

Furthermore the ritual approach to architecture and urban studies offers a promising potential to connect to the aesth/ethical study of atmospheres. A ritual generates atmospheres. It transforms them, and it can create an atmosphere that is only present as long as it endures, or create a preserving atmosphere that forms an alliance of ritual and place and affects our memory in a specific way. But environments can also generate an atmosphere that affects the ritual practice that takes place there. The relationship between place, ritual and atmosphere, therefore, needs to be imagined as a threefold one where place, ritual and atmosphere can influence each other in complex ways. Rituals are designed in order to be repeated, which gives them a special capacity to affect our memory. All together, place, ritual and atmosphere contribute to create our sociocultural collective memory of a built environment and its sacredness.

Remembrance versus Urban Amnesia

The third path that I want to run follows the traces of remembrance. A city is an artefact that to a high degree draws on history; its own history as well as the history of the world system that sustains it. Events of the past have left their marks in and between the buildings. Some traces are preserved while others are destroyed. Built environments should themselves be understood as built memories as they preserve complex information about the time of their origin as well as about change through the ages. Buildings can resist time and decay, and they can mirror continuity and discontinuity in time. No matter how much urban space represents the dynamics of the present, it remains always dependant on its past. The mode of remembering the past is crucial for processes of imaging the future; the visions that run the urban planning should therefore be embedded in the history of the place.[13]

The way of integrating remembrance in architecture and urban planning can therefore tell us a lot about a city's atmosphere. It's handling of the past reveals how lived space grows out of a synthesis of remembrance and envisioning. In the same way as our human consciousness mostly consists of processes of remembering, urban space also develops in time and stores fragments of the past. Lived space is remembered space. The city consists of a diversity of 'Erinnerungsräume' as Aleida Assmann has called it (Assmann, 2006). Specific places serve as 'sites of memory'.[14] Urban space cannot, of course, build a neurological memory such as animals and human beings need in order to navigate their surroundings and survive. But we can without doubt regard a city as an agglomeration of the past, the present and also the visions of the future. Urban studies do not usually acknowledge the past in the satisfying way that it deserves. Therefore, I would like to draw our attention to the relation of remembrance and the sacred in the city.

Looking back to antiquity, memory was not just a human skill, but a divine power of first rank. Mnemosyne was a Greek goddess and after her copulation with Zeus she gave birth to the nine muses, among them Clio, the muse of history. Following antiquity's worldview, and one must not believe in the Greek gods for that sake, we could say that our ancestors lived in and by memory. Their history was carried by a divine memory. The process of keeping alive the sociocultural memory of a group has been essential for all premodern oral cultures, and it is still significant in the late modern present. Museums, libraries and computer-based archives assist us today as institutional tools but architecture and urban space also represent a gigantic warehouse filled with traces of the past. No search machine can find its way on its own through such an archive, even if computer companies want to convince us with their credo 'Everything is on the net!'. As the unsustainable economic world order and turbo capitalism drains the physical substances of our collective memory brutally and rapidly, and as modern communication media draw most of our awareness to transient and glamorous constructions of the present, the need for keeping histories alive increases radically. No wonder, therefore, that museums, libraries and places of remembrance have been emphasized by wise architects and have become more important in the last decades of urban development.

Built memory also always includes a remembrance of the sacred; it preserves inhabitants' values, visions and experiences with a Spirit who gives life. As the theme of memory and urban space would need a whole book to unfold, I will finally focus on the specific need to remember the suffering of our foregone generations and the challenge to visualize and integrate painful memories in urban space. Religious buildings, churches and cemeteries have in earlier times filled this task, but as society and religion change in the late modern era, the spatial figuration of memory must also take new shape.

One of the finest physical and spiritual qualities of space is its limitedness. Also the most attractive open horizon works through a line at the edge, which is expressing the end of something, maybe the beginning of something else. The city can, in analogy to the organism, be regarded as a process of giving birth, evolving life and fading away. Even if the postmetropolis succeeded in covering the whole planet it would still remain a part of limited space in analogy to the limitedness of our human body. Regarding the city in such a horizon, it becomes obvious how amnesia represents a necessary capacity for the development of the postmetropolis which wants to renew itself in new constructions in a limited space. 'Amnesia' aims, in accordance with its connotation in medicine, at the process where the intention to build something at a specific place extrudes what is already there and violates the memories which are carried by this place.

Violating buildings as artefacts of the sociocultural memory of a population, and violating the memory of the suffering of foregone generations appears as one of the characteristics of late modern urban space. The nearly total exclusion of death characterizes it, as well as a continuous disturbance of processes of individual and sociocultural remembrance, in order to give room to new processes of construction.

How does urban space destroy or enhance the skills of the citizens' memory? Does it enhance 'memorability'? (Bloomer and Moore, 1977). How could the remembrance of the past and the sufferings of foregone generations be spatially expressed? Might city planning brush its history against the grain, not only to find war memorials, museums or nationalist sites but to integrate built elements for the remembrance of the homeless, poor, weak and those citizens who do not become visible in the stories of success? (Matthew, ch. 25).

Walter Benjamin proposes in a famous essay entitled On the Concept of History (Benjamin 2006) that we take the 'tradition of the oppressed' as our presupposition for a new understanding of history that runs counter to the notion of progress within history. The German liberation theologian Johann Baptist Metz has claimed that the remembrance of suffering is not just a task but that it is necessary in order to find and apply the processes of true liberation from powers of teleological and technological thinking.

The Christological foundation of such a hermeneutics of suffering is the remembrance of Christ's sufferings. The subject is the Holy Spirit that makes this remembrance possible in the first place. Metz formulates an essential principle in Christian understanding of salvation and liberation through his emphasis on the tradition of the oppressed. The tradition of the oppressed is found only among those who are poor and despairing right now and only at the places where they suffer – only near to them (Metz, 1972). The challenge to rebuild the city into a habitable place must, in such a perspective, acknowledge and design spatiality in a way that benefits both the sociocultural and ecological memory of those who are usually blocked off from writing and reading our common history on the pages of built environments. The central question for urban planning as well as for a Thirdspace aesth/ethics is: what does the remembrance of the pain of the past mean for the design, planning and development of urban space? (Bergmann, 2008).

Remembering the past for the sake of the present and the future represents one of the strongest human skills to make oneself at home. Making oneself at home, or in German 'Beheimatung', belongs to the crucial skills for humans to live (Bergmann, 2010). Dependant on our vulnerable bodies the need for shelter, as well as the need to socialize, was necessary for survival in Stone Age environments as well as in late modern cities. Anthropogenic climate change today deepens this often forgotten insight even more as it challenges humans to accommodate to changing planetary conditions for survival. The tricky, radically new ethical question, however, with regard to climate change is how to afford to a surrounding affected by global change, which in itself is socially produced by humans who are not aware and conscious about what they did and do, how to make oneself at home at 'Earth, our home'[15] which we ourselves are spoiling? What would such a built remembrance look like? Three examples could, as I hope, offer inspiration for urban planning to come. In Berlin, the 'garden of exile' at Daniel Libeskind's Jewish Museum offers a painful experience of a space that disorientates and displaces the visitor by capturing and destroying efficiently the human memory, consciousness and belonging.

It confronts the visitors with a spatiality that confuses and dislocates them. The displacement of strangers is materialized in a way that becomes nearly unbearable as the building totally encaptures the visitor's body, mind and soul. An experience like this will not stay connected only to the Jewish people's history but will trans-contextualize. After such a visit one can recognize and identify similar spaces of constriction in different contexts.

In Hannover, one of the three medieval old churches in the heart of the city was not rebuilt after the war but restored as a ruin. The church is open for visitors all night and all day. It is used for liturgies sometimes, but also as a hall for cultural events and exhibitions. With such manifold functions it can serve also as a creative metaphor of the late modern church in the city today. It offers a space that, due to its lack of a roof, is highly dependant on heaven and rooted on earth. It preserves the history of the sufferings in the war in a way that can still be bodily felt if one touches the walls marked by bullets. And it offers a space for shelter as well as for contemplation and social encounters. The atmospheres that come and go at this place cannot just simply be interpreted as spiritual or sacred; this space works more like a screen on which citizens can throw many kinds of feelings, images and stories. The atmosphere of this sacred place does not feel like anything else in the city. A wonderfully simple way of answering the question of whether I would like to live in a city or not, is found in the location of the cemetery. Dieter Hoffmann-Axthelm has rightly pointed this out and asks: 'How could I trust a city which evacuates its dead as far out of its centre as its logistics office or its sewage works? Obviously, in such a city nothing is arranged to abide and stay, why would I want to stay there?' (Hoffmann-Axthelm, 1998, p. 73).

Who would like to move to a city where the dead do not have a place at all? What happens to the city's atmosphere if its cemeteries are located in the central parts, where citizens can walk, contemplate, rest and take a breath, and where ancestors nurture us – as is common in both African and Asian traditional modes of religion – while we respond with sorrow and care to give them a good place to rest? Cemeteries remind us of the close and intimate relationship between the past and the present. The old 'Judenfriedhof' (Jewish cemetery) in Hannover has been protected by the city and its layers of graves have grown in height through the ages. Even if the visitor is not allowed to walk on it, the location of the graves so close to the houses creates a unique place.

The Jewish cemetery (the oldest in northern Germany) was opened in 1654 and used until 1864. It includes more than 700 graves, among them Heinrich Heine's grandparents and Felix Mendelssohn Bartholdy's ancestors. Since 1671 it has been protected by the Duke's writ of protection on two stone tables at its entrance. One can wonder why we have nowadays moved the suffering, and also our own dead ancestors so far out of the city that we do not need to perceive them at all. Ars moriendi, the art of dying, is not precisely a characteristic of late modernity. An even closer relation of ancestors and the living can be found in Korea where graves and tombs in the countryside are traditionally located directly in the field for agricultural production. Due to geomantical criteria the location of graves and acres has been executed with great care. The complex geo-wisdom system of geomancy operates with experiences and images of energy flows in the landscape. A similar religious system of locating buildings, graves and settlements is totally lacking in the history of Europe (Bergmann, 2009a).

'In a land that I will show you'

To sum up: the theme of this article can be approached from many angles; here I have chosen to reformulate it as 'lived religion *in* lived space'. By departing from Soja's influential concept of 'lived space/Thirdspace' in critical urban studies and connecting it to the concept of 'lived religion', as elaborated in a phenomenologically inspired practical theology, we could envision a dynamic flow of differentiated impacts between religion and urban space. By following the three paths of aesth/ethics, ritual and memory I could focus more closely on this flow of impacts. The invented concept of aesth/ethics could help us not to separate the ethical from the aesthetical in this flow but to embed ethics in aesthetics, and the phenomenological notion of atmosphere made it possible to overcome conventional dichotomies that hinder us from perceiving and interpreting the rich complexity of qualities in this exchange.

Approaching urban space through the lens of rituals could make us aware of another perspective. Rituals, regarded as regulating human movements, represent a form of social practice which takes place in the city both as visible and as invisible religion. Rituals, although not necessarily embedded in religion, can fabricate meaning and carry a community; they can produce specific ritual places which affect broader surroundings. Rituals, such as pilgrimages or marathons, can transform places into sacred places either for a short or a long time.

Urban space was finally approached as a 'built remembrance'. Built environments can be understood as built memories as they preserve complex information about the time of their origin as well as about change through the ages. No matter how much urban space represents the dynamics of the present, it remains always dependant on its past. The mode of remembering the past is therefore crucial for processes of imaging the future, which is of high relevance to approach the Sacred in the City; the specific metropolitan forms of urban amnesia should hereby especially be explored with a critical eye.

For an exploration of the Sacred in the allegedly non-sacred modern city, my reflection might have helped to inspire the reader to approach the theme of the book with new tools and to open his/her eyes to the rich complexity and manifold flows between lived religion in lived space. The Sacred might, in such a frame, appear in both expected and unexpected places, and it might run across both as that which we regard as sacred and as that which we experience as a living place inhabiting us. The question as to what extent the Creator of space and time dwells and reveals in this Sacred has not been dealt with in this chapter, which one should definitively regard as a challenging lack to be adjusted by others (and the author) in the future.

Let me end by almost pointing to such a theological direction in open questions. How would an urban landscape look where vegetables can be grown in permaculture urban environments, where ancestors can stay at home after they have left us and where the remembrance of suffering is an essential part of our lived space? What rituals would fertilize and preserve such a lived space and what kind of atmospheres would emerge in it? How are atmospheres and our memory interconnected? (Zumthor, 2006). How would the inhabitation of the Holy Spirit take place in such a city that no-one has visited yet, even if it appears in the horizon, 'in a land that I will show you' as God had promised Abraham (Gen. 12:1). With Gerhard Hauptmann's enchanting image of our peaceful and enjoyable future of salvation *as* a beautiful city: 'Die Seligkeit ist eine wunderschöne Stadt, wo Friede und Freude kein Ende mehr hat'.

Notes

[1] For a short introduction into geomancy and fengshui see Field (2005). For a differentiated discussion see Bergmann (2009a).

[2] Cf. in detail Sundermeier's intepretation of 'The anthropomorphic dwelling in the village of the Dogon in Mali' (according to Forde, 1954, p. 98), in Sundermeier (1988).

[3] Eck distinguishes between 'orthogenetic' and 'heterogenetic' cities, which either 'create and sustain the ethos and order of a whole culture' or 'reveal the tensions and conflicts of a society'. Of course, this is not an either/or, but most cities do both, even if some cities have developed a prominent orthogenetic position, such as Jerusalem, Istanbul, Rome, Kyoto and Beijing (Eck, 1987, p. 2).

[4] Berleant rightly says that sacredness does not lie in the physical place alone but 'in the significance that people assign to it' (Berleant, 2003, p. 47). He quotes

R. Hepburn, who interprets the sacred with aesthetic experience by reflecting the strong perceptual focus 'where we can find ... modes of being *other than our own*'. Speed shows how the perception of an environment as sacred represents an emotional construction that affects our attitudes and behavior towards it (Speed, 2003).

[5] For a substantial discussion and an argument for an understanding of religion where both substantive and functionalist dimensions are respected and balanced, and where it is necessary to combine both internal and external perspectives (see Sundermeier, 1999, pp. 25–7, 238–42).

[6] I am aware of the problems that will arise if one fully follows a Hegelian path. For our purpose it is enough to learn from his understanding of architecture as 'paving the way' and designing the sacred: 'Denn die Architektur bahnt der adäquaten Wirklichkeit des Gottes erst den Weg und müht sich in seinem Dienst mit der objektiven Natur ab, um sie aus dem Gestrüppe der Endlichkeit und der Mißgestalt des Zufalls herauszuarbeiten' (Hegel, 1971, p. 143).

[7] For a study of different ethical models in the discourse about ecological urban planning see Kjellberg (1998).

[8] Pallasmaa elaborates the concept of 'existential place', and discusses in detail the significance of existential situations, the architect´s existential sense, and existential encounters (Pallasmaa, 2005, p. 129). His book '*The Eyes of the Skin*' (1996) has been widely adapted and turned architecture into a synaesthetical practice.

[9] Cf. Isasi-Díaz' wonderful essay about Havana 'that inhabits me', and the immigrant's double-sided emotional geography, which she describes as 'displaced/multi-sited', between Havana and New York (Isasi-Díaz, 2004).

[10] 'Der Mensch kennt nur sich selbst, insofern er die Welt kennt, die er nur in sich und sich nur in ihr gewahr wird' (the human being only knows herself as far as she knows the world, which she only becomes aware of in herself, and only in the world she becomes aware of herself) (Goethe, 1989, p. 306).

[11] Zaha Hadid – according to Kasa – departs from the body as a foundational place for architecture and characterizes architecture as 'the movement itself between different places' (Kasa, 2000, p. 276).

[12] For an analysis of the built space of Frankfurt airport and its visitors and employees' movements, territories and feelings in a phenomenological and practical-theological perspective see Söderblom (2008).

[13] Cf. M. Taylor, who distinguishes between 'degenerative' and 'regenerative' utopias in Philadelphia and elsewhere.

[14] Nora defines 'lieux de mémoire' (sites of memory) as sites 'where [cultural] memory crystallizes and secretes itself' (quoted in Taylor, 2008, p. 149).

[15] http://www.earthcharter.org/, 18 September 2006.

Bibliography

Assmann, A. (2006), *Erinnerungsräume: Formen und Wandlungen des kulturellen Gedächtnisses*. Munich: Beck.

Bell, C. (1997), *Ritual: Perspectives and Dimensions*. New York/Oxford: Oxford University Press.

Bell, D. (1978), The Return of the Sacred. The Argument from the Future of Religion, in *Zygon*, Vol. 13, pp. 187–208.
Benjamin, W. (2006), *Selected Writings. Vol. 4:* 1938–1940. Cambridge Ms.: Belknap Press.
Bergmann, S. (2005a), *Creation Set Free: The Spirit as Liberator of Nature* (Sacra Doctrina: Christian Theology for a Postmodern Age 4). Grand Rapids, MI: Eerdmans.
—. (ed.) (2005b), *Architecture, Aesth/Ethics and Religion*. Frankfurt: IKO-Verlag für interkulturelle Kommunikation.
—. (2006), 'Atmospheres of Synergy: Towards an Eco-Theological Aesth/Ethics of Space'. *Ecotheology: The Journal of Religion, Nature and the Environment*, 11(3), 326–56.
—. (2007), 'Theology in its Spatial Turn: Space, Place and Built Environments Challenging and Changing the Images of God', *Religion Compass*, 1(3), 353–79.
—. (2008), 'Making Oneself at Home in Environments of Urban Amnesia: Religion and Theology in City Space', *International Journal of Public Theology*, 2, 70–97.
—. (2009a), 'Ecological Geomancy: Earth Energy and the Wisdom of Spatial Design', in Bergmann, S. and Yong-Bock, K. (eds), *Religion, Ecology & Gender: East-West Perspectives*, Berlin: LIT, pp. 147–74.
—. (2009b), 'Cities on the Stream of Gods: Mayan Sacred Geography', (unpubl.) (German version in: Bergmann, 2010).
—. (2009c), *In the Beginning Is the Icon: A Liberative Theology of Images, Visual Arts and Culture*. London: Equinox.
—. (2009d), *Så främmande det lika: Samisk konst i ljuset av religion och globalisering*, Trondheim: Tapir [So Strange The Similar: Religion and Globalization in Sami Art].
—. (ed.) (2009e), *Theology in Built Environments: Exploring Religion, Architecture, and Design*. New Brunswick NJ/London: Transaction.
—. (2010), *Raum und Geist: Zur Erdung und Beheimatung der Religion – eine theologische Ästh/Ethik des Raumes*. Göttingen: Vandenhoeck & Ruprecht.
Bergmann, S. and Sager, T. (eds), (2008), *The Ethics of Mobilities: Rethinking Place, Exclusion, Freedom and Environment*. Farnham, UK and Burlington, VT: Ashgate.
Bergmann, S., Scott, P., Jansdotter, M. and Bedford Strohm, H. (eds) (2009), *Nature, Space and the Sacred: Transdisciplinary Perspectives*. Farnham, UK and Burlington, VT: Ashgate.
Berleant, A. (2003), 'The Aesthetic in Place', in Menin, S. (ed.), *Constructing Place: Mind and Matter*. London: Routledge, pp. 41–54.
Bloomer, K. and Moore, C. W. (1977), *Body, Memory, and Architecture*. New Haven/London: Yale University Press.
Böhme, G. (1989), *Für eine ökologische Naturästhetik*. Frankfurt/M.: Suhrkamp.
—. (1995), *Atmosphäre: Essays zur neuen Ästhetik*. Frankfurt/M.: Suhrkamp.
Cox, H. (1965), *The Secular City: Secularization and Urbanization in Theological Perspective*. New York: MacMillan.
Eck, D. L. (1987), 'The City as a Sacred Center', in Smith, B. and Baker Reyolds, H. (eds), *The City as a Sacred Center: Essays on Six Asian Contexts*. Leiden: Brill, pp. 1–11.
Field, S. L. (2005), 'Fengshui', in *Encyclopedia of Religion and Nature*. New York: Continuum, pp. 649–50.

Forde, D. (ed.) (1954), *African Worlds: Studies in the Cosmological Ideas and Social Values of African Worlds.* London: Oxford University Press.
Foucault, M. (2006), 'Von anderen Räumen', in Dünne, J. and Günzel, S. (eds), *Raumtheorie: Grundlagentexte aus Philosophie und Kulturwissenschaften.* Frankfurt/M.: Suhrkamp, pp. 317–29.
Geertz, C., (1973), 'Religion as a Cultural System', in Geertz, C. (ed.), *The Interpretation of Cultures.* New York: Basic Books, pp. 87–125.
Goethe, J. W. (1989), 'Bedeutende Fördernis durch ein einziges geistreiches Wort', in Goethe, J. W. (ed.), *Zur Naturwissenschaft überhaupt, besonders zur Morphologie: Erfahrung, Betrachtung, Folgerung, durch Lebensereignisse verbunden.* Hanser: München, pp. 306–9.
Grimes, R. (2003), 'Ritual Theory and the Environment', *The Sociological Review,* 51(2), 31–45.
Hegel, G. W. F. (1971), 'Vorlesungen über die Ästhetik', in Hegel, G. W. F. (ed.), *Ästhetik I/II.* Stuttgart: Reclam, pp. 35–682.
Hoffmann-Axthelm, D. (1998), 'Ist der Tod mitgedacht? Zentralität der Stadt', in Dannowski, H. W. (ed.), *Gott in der Stadt: Analysen-Konkretionen-Träume,* Hamburg: EB-Verlag, pp. 67–73.
Isasi-Díaz, A. W. (2004), 'La Habana – The City That Inhabits Me', in Tanner, K. (ed.), *Spirit in the Cities: Searching for Soul in the Urban Landscape.* Minneapolis, MN: Fortress Press, pp. 98–124.
Ivahkiv, A. (2001), *Claiming Sacred Ground: Pilgrims and Politics at Glastonbury and Sedona.* Bloomington, IN: Indiana University Press.
Jackson Rushing, W. (1995), *Native American Art and the New York Avant-Garde, 1910–1950.* Austin, TX: University of Texas Press.
Kasa, E (2000), *Arkitekturen som kunst.* Trondheim: NTNU.
Kjellberg, S. (1998), *Urban Ecotheology.* Utrecht: International Books.
Larcher, G. and Woschitz, K. M. (ed.) (2005), *Religion – Utopie – Kunst: Die Stadt als Fokus.* Wien: LIT.
Lessing, E. (1992), 'Geist V. Dogmatisch und ethisch', in *TRE 12.* Berlin, pp. 218–37.
Luckmann, T. (1967), *The Invisible Religion.* New York: MacMillan.
Metz, J. B. (1972), 'Erinnerung des Leidens als Kritik eines teleologisch-technologischen Zukunftsbegriffs', *Evangelische Theologie,* 32, 338–52.
Nora, P. (1989), 'Between Memory and History: Les Lieux de Memoire', *Representations,* 26, 7–24.
Pallasmaa, J. (1996), *The Eyes of the Skin: Architecture and the Senses.* London: Academy Editions.
—. (2005), *Encounters: Architectural Essays* (ed. P. MacKeith). Helsinki: Rakennustieto Oy.
—. (2009), 'Artistic Generosity, Humility and Expression: Architecture as Lived Metaphor, Collaboration, Faith and Compassion', in Bergmann, S. *Theology in Built Environments: Exploring Religion, Architecture, and Design.* New Brunswick, NJ/London: Transaction, pp. 23–38.
Petersson, A. (2009), 'The Altar of the Dead: A Temporal Space for Memory and Meaning in the Contemporary Urban Landscape', in Bergmann, S., Scott, P., Jansdotter, M. and Bedford Strohm, H. (eds), *Nature, Space and the*

Sacred: Transdisciplinary Perspectives, Farnham, UK and Burlington, VT: Ashgate, pp. 131–44.
Rappaport, R. (1968), *Pigs for the Ancestors: Ritual in the Ecology of a New Guinea People*. New Haven: Yale University Press.
—. (1999), *Ritual and Religion in the Making of Humanity*. Cambridge: Cambridge University Press.
Schmied, W. (ed.) (1980), *Zeichen des Glaubens, Geist der Avantgarde: Religiöse Tendenzen in der Kunst des 20. Jahrhunderts*. Stuttgart: Klett Cotta.
Schroer, M. (2006), *Räume, Orte, Grenzen: Auf dem Weg zu einer Soziologie des Raums*. Frankfurt: Suhrkamp.
Sennett, R. (1994), *Flesh and Stone: The Body and the City in Western Civilization*. London: Faber and Faber.
Simmel, G. (2006), 'Über räumliche Projektionen sozialer Formen', in Dünne, J. and Günzel, S. (eds), *Raumtheorie: Grundlagentexte aus Philosophie und Kulturwissenschaften*. Frankfurt: Suhrkamp, pp. 304–16.
Smith, B. and Baker Reynolds, H. (eds) (1987), *The City as a Sacred Center: Essays on Six Asian Contexts*. Leiden: Brill.
Söderblom, K. (2008), 'The Phenomenon of Mobility at the Frankfurt International Airport: Challenges from a Theological Perspective', in Bergmann, S. and Sager, T. (eds), *The Ethics of Mobilities: Rethinking Place, Exclusion, Freedom and Environment*. Burlington, VT: Ashgate, pp. 177–93.
Soja, E. (1996), *Thirdspace: Journeys to Los Angeles and Other Real-and-Imagined Places*. Malden, MA: Blackwell.
—. (2000), *Postmetropolis: Critical Studies of Cities and Regions*. Oxford: Blackwell. p. 11.
Speed, F. (2003), 'The Sacred Environment: An Investigation of the Sacred and Its Implications for Place-Making', in Menin, S. (ed.), *Constructing Place: Mind and Matter*. London: Routledge, pp. 55–65.
Streib, H. (2008), 'More Spiritual than Religious: Changes in the Religious Field Require New Approaches', in Streib, H., Dinter, A. and K. Söderblom, K. (eds), *Lived Religion: Conceptual, Empirical and Practical–Theological Approaches, Essays in Honor of Hans-Günter Heimbrock*. Leiden: Brill, pp. 53–67.
Sundermeier, T. (1988), *Nur gemeinsam können wir leben: Das Menschenbild schwarzafrikanischer Religionen*. Gütersloh: Gütersloher Verlagshaus Mohn.
—. (1999), *Was ist Religion? Religionswissenschaft im theologischen Kontext*. Gütersloh: Kaiser, Gütersloher Verlagshaus.
Szerszynski, B. (2005), *Nature, Technology and the Sacred*. Malden: Blackwell.
Tanner, K. (ed.) (2004), *Spirit in the Cities: Searching for Soul in the Urban Landscape*. Minneapolis, MN: Fortress Press.
Taylor, J. (2008), *Buddhism and Postmodern Imaginings in Thailand: The Religiosity of Urban Space*. Burlington, VT: Ashgate.
Taylor, M. L. (2004), 'Degenerative Utopia in Philadelphia', in Tanner, K. (ed.), *Spirit in the Cities: Searching for Soul in the Urban Landscape*. Minneapolis, MN: Fortress Press, pp. 69–97.
Woschitz, K. W. (2005), 'Peter Breugels "Der Turmbau von Babel" ', in Larcher, G. and Woschitz, K. M. (ed.), *Religion – Utopie – Kunst: Die Stadt als Fokus*. Wien: LIT, pp. 46–66.
Zumthor, P., Oberli-Turner, M. and Schelbert, C. (2006), *Thinking Architecture*. Basel: Birkhäuser.

Chapter 5

Kinhin in a Megacity – Implicit Meanings of the 'Walking-in-the-Park'-Movement in São Paulo

Frank Usarski

Preliminary Remarks

According to Stark and Finke the number and frequency of public reports of a religious group is often reciprocal to the latter's conventionality and statistic strength (Stark and Finke, 2000, pp. 18–19). The 'Walking-in-the-Park'-movement, the focus of this chapter, represents a religious circle that fits well to this description. Nevertheless, the movement is worth a closer look since its origin, its underlying ideas, as well as the nature and the circumstances of its activities are open for an interpretation that satisfies the heuristic impulse of this publication indicated by the motto 'the sacred in the city'.

After a general introduction to the 'Walking-in-the-Park'-movement the latter will be submitted to a fourfold interpretation. First, due to its underlying Buddhist aspirations, the movement has a spiritual character and should be recognized as such. Secondly, it will be argued that the movement reflects certain elements of the biography of its founder. Thirdly, there is the question of the relation between the walking meditations and the overall metropolitan surroundings in which they are realized. Finally, it will be asked to what degree the movement is a particular expression of the general situation and evolution of Buddhism in Brazil as a whole.

The 'Walking-in-the-Park'-Movement – A Short Introduction

The 'Walking-in-the-Park'-movement is composed of Brazilian Buddhists who regularly gather in public parks of São Paulo to practice the Zen walking meditation (*kinhin*) in public areas. Generally, the meetings start with a conventional zazen meditation followed by a walking meditation of about one hour. The movement was founded in April 2001 by the Brazilian Claudia Souza de Murayama, better known by her religious name Monja Coen, a reminder of her monastic training between 1983 and 1995 at the Aichi Senmon Niso-do, a temple for Soto Zen nuns in Nagoya, Japan.

At first the group met every Sunday at 10 a.m. alternatively in five parks. While two are located a considerable distance from the city (the Vila dos Remédios Park and the 'Horto Florestal') and have served only sporadically as a meeting place, the weekend activities of the movement have been concentrated in three parks located in different neighbourhoods of São Paulo, that is the 'Parque da Aclimação' in the neighbourhood of Liberdade [1], the 'Parque da Luz' in the neighbourhood of Bom Retiro [2], and especially in the Água Branca Park in the neighbourhood of Perdizes [3], which is the closest to Monja Coen's the Zen-Dojo.

According to Monja Coen, twelve practitioners joined the first public Walking Meditation. One week later the group had grown to twenty people. In the third week, fifty participants met in the Água Branca Park.[1] In the second half of 2001 the movement had grown to over 100 practitioners.[2] Since then, this number has never been reached again. Instead, the initial enthusiasm decreased gradually with the consequence that the frequency of the meetings was reduced to one public Walking Meditation per month.[3] Today it is still an item of the Zen-Dojo's agenda[4] although it currently attracts only a handful of Monja Coen's followers.

On the other hand, Claudia Souza de Murayama's initiative in São Paulo served as a model for analogous activities in other parts of Brazil. There is, for instance, the *Associação Meditar* in Cuiabá, capital of the Federal State of Mato Grosso, which organizes walking meditations regularly in the Mãe Bonifácia Park. One can also take part in the 'meditative walks' in the Botanic Garden of Rio de Janeiro sporadically promoted by the *Sangha Viver Consciente*.[5] Another example is the event 'Zen no Parque' promoted by the Soto Zen Temple in Curitiba in the Federal State of Paraná.[6]

The 'Walking-in-the-Park'-Movement and its Buddhist Spirit

Although there is no convincing proof of the hypothesis that the technique of walking meditation was taught by the Buddha himself (Silananda, 1995; Tepvisuddhikavi, 2000), it is without doubt an ancient spiritual technique and an important Zen method propagated both by the Soto and by the

Rinzai School. From this standpoint the 'Walking-in-the-Park'-movement is an expression of the effort to maintain the authenticity of the Buddhist religion in a cultural environment strongly influenced by Roman Catholicism. The group's affinity with historical Buddhism is also given by the choice of the green surroundings in which the meditations take place. About 2,500 years ago, Buddhism came to light in the midst of profound socio-historical changes, including urbanization, that contributed to the formation of opposite tendencies, such as wandering recluses and the establishment of small spiritual circles a distance from the cities favouring an introspective religiosity in opposition to the technocratic religiosity of 'official' Brahmanism (Schneider, 1992, p. 16ff). In this sense it is symptomatic that Siddhartha Gautama discovered the element of suffering as the basic constituent of existence while he exposed himself to the conditions of life of the normal citizen in the streets that surrounded his palace. As a consequence of his shocking insights, and convinced of the possibility of liberation from the painful wheel of reincarnation, the Shakyamuni left his noble residence to assume the 'alternative' lifestyle characterized by the search for silence, simplicity, intimacy with nature and religious exercises under the open sky, in caves or at the feet of big trees (Schmithausen, 1997). Soon he joined a group of five ascetics dwelling in a forest and practising at the banks of a river. Finally, as a result of extensive and profound meditations under a giant peepal tree, Siddhartha Gautama reached Nirvana. His first walk as a Buddha led him to Sarnath, a village near the city of Varanasi, where he delivered his first sermon in the local deer park and stayed during the first rainy season after his illumination.

Besides these allusions to remote, calm and pleasant places the Pali Canon is full of similar metaphors when referring to the Buddha's walks through a rural area of about 400 km^2 that in contemporary geopolitical terms corresponds to a territory covering parts of the north-eastern Indian Federal State of Bihar and of Nepal. There are, for instance, sutras that detail a speech of Buddha at the hill of Gayashira, a retreat close to Kaushambi at the margins of the Yamuna River or of a meditation under a tree in the Parileyyaka forest. Other texts tell us that the Buddha's favourite place was the monastery in the Jeta Forest. He was also fond of a piece of land known as Venuvana, which means 'Bamboo woods' and is remembered as a beautiful place far from any city and because of its quietness it was convenient for the monks who preferred to practise in undisturbed, silent surroundings (Bercholz and Kohn, 1994, p. 31ff).

According to the above scenery, the choice for a park as a place for the walking meditation seems appropriate as far as it expresses the concern for authenticity of an ancient method that has emancipated itself from its original background and is now applied under completely different historical, cultural, geographical and social circumstances. Furthermore, one should remember the emphasis that nature enjoys within certain East Asian Buddhist traditions. During the process of its transplantation to China, Korea and Japan, Buddhism incorporated a series of elements of the native religions encountered in these respective countries. One of the impacts was that of Taoism, known for its attempts to harmonize man with the cosmos. Later, Buddhism came in contact with Shintoism, known for its profound intimacy with nature and the veneration of objects such as rocks and trees as dwelling places of sacred powers (kami). It was especially Zen that took over the admiration of nature and inspired the development of sophisticated branches of Japanese art such as the cultivation of bonsai trees, ikebana or the arrangement of stone gardens as well as other methods which promote a sense of harmony, pureness and silence since they are 'intimately associated with the contemplative intuition of fundamental truth vibrating in the deeper levels of man's consciousness' (Merton, 1993, p. 108–11).

Seen from this standpoint, Monja Coen's option for a calm, green and arborous environment as the setting for the walking meditation reflects the preferences of the Japanese Buddhist School in which she was trained and to which she is committed.

The 'Walking-in-the-Park'-Movement and Its Implicit References to Monja Coen's Biography

Due to her religious merits as well as to her readiness to appear in the media and at public events such as inter-religious dialogues,[7] humanitarian campaigns,[8] congresses[9] and university meetings,[10] Monja Coen is currently not only considered one of the main representatives of Zen[11] or the 'strong voice' of the Soto school,[12] but as the central symbolic figure of Brazilian Buddhism. One of Monja Coen's virtues as a contemporary Brazilian Zen teacher consists of her transcultural rhetoric resulting from her studies and spiritual experiences both in classic Japanese Soto-Zen settings and in the alternative religious cultural environment of the American West Coast. Seen from this angle, it becomes plausible why the walking meditation not only reflects Claudia Souza de Murayama's twisted biographical paths but also her Occidentalized interpretation of a spiritual heritage of Asian Buddhism.

Before moving to Japan, Claudia Souza de Murayama, born in 1947 and in the 1970s affected by the Eastern spiritual aspirations of the counter-culture, had spent some years in the Zen Center of Los Angeles. It was in this institution that Claudia Souza de Murayama first learned what it means to practice *kinhin* in the public since the local Zen instructors led their disciples to the streets in order to maintain inner silence in the midst of the urban noise and despite the curiousness of the neighbours.[13]

However, it was not the classical version of *kinhin* that was on the agenda of the Zen Center of Los Angeles but an already modified form suggested by Thich Nhat Hanh, a Vietnamese master known for a modernist Buddhist approach in terms of the efforts to overcome a one-sided 'otherworldly' approach through the emphasis of a socially engaged Buddhism in search of the solutions to concrete social and political problems. Thich Nhat Hanh belongs to a group of contemporary Asian teachers whose Buddhist approach shows great sympathy for the concerns and interests of the former counter-cultural movement from which a considerable portion of contemporary Western converts to Buddhism have inherited their values, attitudes and religious aspirations.

According to Alan Watts, one of the main reasons that made Zen interesting for a Western audience was the latter's intimacy with nature (Watts, 1996). The idea of rebalancing the disturbed relationship between man and nature has been particularly articulated from the second half of the twentieth century onwards, initially by representatives of a younger stratum of the urban population who also showed the tendency to leave their homes in the bigger cities for idyllic, religiously more auspicious places. Although for many the distance from urban surroundings was only a temporary solution, the concern for ecology including the valorization of green and healthy conditions as a propitious background for a religious lifestyle is still an important issue for circles inspired by the counter-cultural spirit of the late 1950s and the 1960s. This includes practitioners of the so-called New Age spirituality which is characterized by a wide spectrum of approaches in favour of the synchronization of man and cosmos and an affinity with certain landscapes and spots outside big cities charged with a special energy which can be shared by those who visit these places (Adrian, 2003).

Seen from this angle and bearing in mind the counter-cultural roots of Claudia Souza de Murayama's passion for Zen, one can assume that nature is for her a source of vital energy which nourishes the human being. When she was asked why the embracing of trees is a constituent of her movement's walks she answered: 'We embrace them because of their age and their height. Trees irradiate stability and are very strong.'[14] Statements of this kind indicate that the choice of a park for the setting of the walking meditation is in tune with an 'alternative' spiritual attitude characteristic of Monja Coen's approach to Zen.

Besides Claudia Souza de Murayama's latent counter-cultural ambitions, there is a second biographical element that sheds additional light on the 'Walking-in-the-Park'-movement. It has to do with Monja Coen's ambiguous situation as a mediator between two segments of Brazilian Buddhism and the necessity to reconfirm her status in the relevant field. As the following paragraph indicates, the 'Walking-in-the-Park'-movement turned out to be an important strategy in the given context.

In 1995, the year of her return to Brazil, Claudia Souza de Murayama assumed the leadership of the *Busshinji* Temple, a traditional Zen institution with a Japanese ethnic background localized in Liberdade, a neighbourhood of São Paulo the Asian character of which testifies to the local presence of a large number of Japanese and more recently Korean immigrants. Later Monja Coen became a member of the South American Soto Zen Council and was elected president (1997–8) of the 'Brazilian Federation of Buddhists Sects' [sic], an umbrella organization of the major Japanese Buddhist branches active in Brazil. However, being a Buddhist modernist who sympathized with the inclusion of converts into the *Busshinji* community, Muruyama came more and more in conflict with the order's conservative fraction. She finally left the *Busshinji* Temple and founded the *Tenzui Zen Dojo* as a more convenient spiritual home for Buddhist converts (Rocha, 2006, p. 50–4). The first meeting of the movement in April 2001 fell exactly at the time when the crisis in the Busshinji Temple in the neighbourhood of Liberdade reached its peak and Monja Coen decided to abandon the institution in order to found her independent Zen Center in the neighbourhood of Pinheiros. At least in the beginning of the post-Busshinji period, the reunions of the movement were the highlights in Monja Coen's agenda and contributed to the growing visibility of Claudia Souza de Murayama. Seen from this standpoint the 'Walking-in-the-Park'-movement can be interpreted as a means of preparing and underlining Monja Coen's position as an independent dharma teacher.

The 'Walking-in-the-Park'-Movement against the Hostile Conditions of a Megacity

Milton Santos, one of Brazil's foremost geographers, characterizes an urban centre as an inseparable conjunction of interrelated objects and actions (Santos, 1996, p. 51) and as 'an artificial geographic environment that consists of residues of primitive nature that are progressively covered by human products'. In other words an urban centre is a place in which 'real nature' has been transformed into 'entirely humanized nature' (Santos, 1997, p. 42). While this description fits the conditions of almost any major town in the world, it is more than adequate for São Paulo, South America's economic centre and biggest city of about 1530 km^2 and approximately 11 million inhabitants. The overall hostile conditions in terms of the omnipresence of pavements and concrete, intense traffic, noise and lack of fresh air in the metropolis not only represent a daily physiological and psychological burden for the *paulistanos*, but are immediately noticed by any visitor who sets foot on this ecologically highly alienated spot of the earth. As Berryman puts it:

> Few find the city physically attractive. The sea is only an hour away, but there is no sign of its presence. The Tietê river winding its way through town is a polluted canal. The city's colonial past is only a memory, since most of the oldest buildings are factories and warehouses dating from the early decades of this century. . . . No grand design is evident in the city layout, as the various districts run into each other at angles, reflecting the chaotic, unregulated way the population has expanded during this century. (Berryman, 1996, p. 9)

This is not an exaggeration but corresponds both to the inhabitants' daily experience of, and official statements of, the city's government. According to the latter, 48 per cent of the city's territory officially qualifies as a dense urbanized area suffering from a considerable lack of vegetation. Only 9 per cent is considered intensely arborous.[15] This is a poor situation: São Paulo's green areas are few.[16]

What do Buddhists do in the face of these circumstances, especially when they follow the principle that whenever it is possible one should meditate under conditions that – according to a recommendation of the Zen master Thich Nhat Hanh (Hanh, 2002, p. 47) – allow the practitioner to enjoy the purest air in order to let the inner being be penetrated by the energy inherent in the element? They try to avoid – as much as possible and against all odds – the external perturbations, searching for 'islands of tranquillity' [17] that could bring some relief from the disadvantages of metropolitan life. An obvious counter-means is to generate a physical distance from the pollution, hectic pace and noise of the busy streets and chaotic crowds. This strategy is not only applied by the 'Walking-in-the-Park'-movement but also by a handful of *zazen* practitioners associated with the Busshinji Temple who meet once a month for a 90 minute sitting meditation on the roof of the Copan Building, a skyscraper with 37 floors in the heart of São Paulo city.[18]

While the Busshinji group favours a 'vertical' solution to the problem of noise and super-population, Monja Coen contents herself with the invitation to join her movement in a horizontal distance to the hustle and bustle of the streets. At least slightly out of the way of the immediate urban stress, she instructs the *kinhin* practitioners that it is auspicious when 'at every step one feels ones breath, and is continuously conscious of the air, the noises and the smells that surround us'. [19] This recommendation is given despite the remaining negative environmental influences in geographical limited green spots that probably would be considered inappropriate for a meditation technique based on silence if one could find more spacious and similarly accessible green areas in the city. However, toughened up by the metropolis' inhuman conditions, participants of the movement are willing to make the best of their given circumstances.

Joshin, one of the most active of the group, for example, answered when asked about the significance of a park as a place for the meditation:

> In a city, the individual is surrounded by a totally disorientated, disturbing and confusing social environment. People raise their voices and cars blow their horns. But it seems nobody realizes how deconstructed life is. When we practice the walking meditation in a park we notice that we are capable of bringing harmony into the disharmony. One notices a tiny animal that has fallen onto ones shirt, or the presence of a much smaller one. One becomes aware of the infinity of the cosmos, the universe. There are things even bigger than that and at the same time smaller than the smallest animal. All this can be the result of a Walking Meditation when it is practiced in a natural setting.[20]

The 'Walking-in-the-Park'-Movement as a Symbolic Expression of Contemporary Brazilian Buddhism

From the start the Walking Meditations have frequently been an issue in the Brazilian media. Since then countless, without exception, friendly articles, websites, TV reports and radio interviews have contributed to the extremely positive image of the movement and its founder. As already mentioned, the reason for this intense public interest has nothing to do with the quantitative relevance of the movement. Rather, the media support is foremost a reflection of Monja Coen's excellent national reputation as an authentic, competent and endearing dharma-teacher Buddhist. The latter's fame, however, is itself a reflection of two more general, interrelated tendencies.

First and most importantly, Brazil is in many respects a tolerant country. Although it is officially one of the world's biggest Catholic countries, religious liberalism is, for the most part and the majority of the population, a living reality. One indicator of the spectrum of religious alternatives and their generally peaceful coexistence is the system of 142 sub-categories to which the Brazilian Institute for Geography and Statistics (IBGE) refers when it analyses the National Census questionnaires in terms of the religious affiliations of the population.

The second explanation for the presence of the 'Walking-in-the-Park'-movement in the media is that Buddhism in general is often not only tolerated, but welcomed by many Brazilians as a highly respectable manifestation of legitimate spirituality. In the last decades this positive opinion has been constantly reconfirmed by a considerable number of press releases. More than that, reports under headlines such as 'The Success of Zen',[21] 'Buddhism conquers Brazil'[22] or 'The Rise of Buddhism in Brazil'[23] have also contributed to the conviction that Buddhism is a trendy and booming religion in Brazil. Under these circumstances it is not a surprise that the visibility of Monja Coen and her circle of meditators in public parks appear as one of many signs of the growing impact of Buddhism upon Brazilian society.

However, both eye-witnesses to the activities of Monja Coen's circle in general and official statistics of the actual numerical relevance of Brazilian Buddhism in general indicate that the public image of the 'Walking-in-the-Park'-movement is based on erroneous assumptions. Rather, data stemming from the last two National Censuses tell us that Buddhism not only represents a very small religious minority but is also in decline. In 2000 only 214,873 Brazilians declared themselves Buddhists. This is approximately 0.14 per cent of the country's population and obviously represents a relatively insignificant percentage for a religion frequently and enthusiastically mentioned by the Brazilian media. The statistical irrelevance becomes even more evident when one compares the numerical situation of Buddhism to that of two religious minorities publicly almost ignored: in 2000 0.6 per cent of Brazilians declared themselves Jehovah's Witnesses; 0.73 per cent were Seventh Day Adventists. More than that, if one compares the figures for 2000 with those raised by the National Census in 1991 (236,405 Buddhists), it becomes evident that Buddhism, instead of benefiting from a boom, suffered from a significant decline. Taking these figures for granted, one can come to the conclusion that the quantitative negative evolution in the last years and actual numerical status of the 'Walking-in-the-Park'-movement represent, on a minor scale, an analogous dynamics characteristic for Brazilian Buddhism in general.

Concluding Remarks

Perhaps the most remarkable characteristic of the 'Walking-in-the-Park'-movement is the long staying power of its founder who, after ten years of maintaining the respective activities on her schedule, does not show any sign of demotivation or frustration but continues to invite Zen practitioners to *kinhin* sessions in the public parks of São Paulo whether a considerable number of participants appear at the meetings or not. Depending on what side of her personality and aspects of her biography is taken into account, there are different explanations for this persistence. Those who consider the split from the Busshinji Temple a key moment of Monja Coen's religious career might argue that holding on to the walking meditations is a question of prestige and a self-confirmation of her independence and autonomy as a dharma-teacher. If the emphasis lies on her talent to make use of the media in order to promote her image as a spokeswoman and national symbol of Brazilian Buddhism, the 'Walking-in-a-Park'-movement is open to the interpretation that even a small circle committed to an unconventional and somehow exotic practice is capable of maintaining the public interest in Zen Buddhism the way Monja Coen teaches it. For those who are of the opinion that the walking meditation is primarily a result of Claudia Souza de Murayama's affinity with the aspirations of the counter-culture the main message behind her perseverance could be the following: Paulistanos! Don't let the hostile conditions of this city get you down! Keep on resisting! At least we, the *kinhin* meditators, will continue to show up, since we believe in the supremacy of spirit over matter!

Notes

[1] See Monja ensina meditação nos parques. *Folha de São Paulo*, 28 June 2001, caderno equilíbrio, p. 7.
[2] See Meditação em movimento. *Correio Braziliense*, 21 August 2001.
[3] See Mensageira da paz, *Isto é Gente*, 28 April 2003.
[4] See http://www.zendobrasil.org.br/si/site/0300, accessed 28 February 2011.
[5] See http://www.viverconsciente.com/eventos.html, accessed 25 January 2011.

⁶ See http://zennoparque.wordpress.com/, accessed 25 January 2011.
⁷ See for instance, Ato multirreligioso celebra 80 anos da Folha. *Folha de São Paulo*, 18 February 2001, A 17.
⁸ One example is Monja Coen's engagement for the International Campaign for a Culture of Peace and Non-violence of the UNESCO inaugurated on 15 July 2000 at the Plenário Juscelino Kubitschek da Assembléia Legislativa do Estado de São Paulo.
⁹ Among other events, Monja Coen gave talks at the first Brazilian Meditation Congress, 19–21 March 2004, in Curitiba and at the second annual meeting of the Brazilian Association for the History of Religions (ABHR), 23 May 2000, in Ouro Preto.
¹⁰ One example is Monja Coen's at the Ato Ecumênico pela Paz Mundial e Capacidade de Resistência, 10 October at the Pontificial Catholic University in São Paulo.
¹¹ See Templos revestem budistas de novas visões de mundo, *Estado de São Paulo*, 27 October 1998.
¹² See Monja Coen, a voz forte do Zen-Budismo, *Jornal da Tarde*, 28 March 1999.
¹³ See http://www.terra.com.br/planetaweb/351/matérias/351_entrevista_monja_3.htm, accessed 30 September 2002.
¹⁴ Monja ensina meditação nos parques. *Folha de São Paulo*, 28 June 2001, caderno equilíbrio, p. 7.
¹⁵ See *Atlas Ambiental do Município de São Paulo*, São Paulo: Prefeitura do Município de São Paulo, 2002, pp. 63–4.
¹⁶ For a map showing the distribution of green areas of the city of São Paulo according to the official São Paulo Municipality Environment Atlas, see: http://atlasambiental.prefeitura.sp.gov.br/mapas/102.jpg, accessed 15 February 2011. For a map of the division of neighbourhoods of São Paulo according to the city's tourist website, see http://saopaulosp.com/bairros-de-sao-paulo, accessed 25 January 2011.
¹⁷ See Templos revestem budistas de novas visões de mundo. *Estado de São Paulo*, 27 October 1998.
¹⁸ Entre o céu e o inferno, *Revista TRIP*. 190, 8 July 2010, http://revistatrip.uol.com.br/revista/190/salada/entre-o-ceu-e-o-inferno.html, accessed 28 February 2011.
¹⁹ See Meditação em movimento. *Correio Braziliense*, 21 August 2001.
²⁰ Quote from two interviews realized by my student Bruno Simões Gonçalves at 10 October and 14 November 2003 at the Tanzui Zen Dojo, São Paulo.
²¹ See Onda Zen, *Elle*, June 1998.
²² See O Budismo conquista o Brasil, *Corpo & Mente*, October 2000.
²³ See A ascensão do Budismo no Brasil, *Época*, June 2003.

Bibliography

Adrian, I. (2003), 'Nature and Self in New Age Pilgrimage'. *Culture and Religion*, 4(1), 93–118.
Bercholz, S. and Kohn, S. C. (1994), *O Pequeno Buda: entrando na correnteza*. São Paulo: Siciliano.

Berryman, P. (1996), *Religion in the Megacity. Catholic and Protestant Portraits from Latin America*. Maryknoll, NY: Orbis Books.
Hanh, T. N. (2002), *Meditação andando. Guia para a paz interior*. Petrópolis: Vozes.
Inoue, N. (2000), 'From Religious Conformity to Innovation. New Ideas of Religious Journey and Holy Places'. *Social Compass*, 47(1), 21–32.
Merton, T. (1993), *Zen e as Aves de Rapina*. São Paulo: Cultrix.
Norohna, F. A. (2000), *Cultivando Bonsai no Brasil*. São Paulo: Escrituras.
Prefeitura do Município de São Paulo (2002), *Atlas Ambiental do Município de São Paulo*. São Paulo: Prefeitura do Município de São Paulo.
Rocha, C. (2006), *Zen in Brazil. The Quest for Cosmopolitan Modernity*. Honululu: University of Hawai'i Press.
Santos, M. (1996), *A Natureza do Espaço: Técnica e Tempo. Razão e Emoção*. São Paulo: Hucitec.
—. (1997), *Metamorfoses do Espaço Habitado*. São Paulo: Hucitec.
Schmithausen, L. (1997), 'The Early Buddhist Tradition and Ecological Ethics'. *Journal of Buddhist Ethics*, 4, 1–74.
Schneider, U. (1992), *Einführung in den Buddhismus*. Darmstadt: Wissenschaftliche Buchgesellschaft.
Silananda, S. U. (1995), *The Benefits of Walking Meditation*. Kandy: Buddhist Publication Society.
Stark, R. and Finke, R. (2000), *Acts of Faith. Explaining the Human Side of Religion*. Berkeley, CA: University of California Press.
Tepvisuddhikavi, P. (2000), *A Buddhist Way of Mental Training*. Bangkok: Mahamakut Buddhist University.
Watts, A. (1996), 'Beat Zen, Square Zen, and Zen'.*Chicago Review*, 42(3–4), 49–56.

Chapter 6

Life Stance and Religious Identity in an Urbanized World: The Meaning of Life as a Modern Predicament

Rik Pinxten & Lisa Dikomitis

> A moral culture is one in which decisions take into account considerations of good and bad, right and wrong, just and unjust. Without the support of such a culture, which helps to assess the behaviour of ourselves, other people and institutions, enhanced civic participation is inadequate.
>
> (Lasch-Quinn, 2003, p. 33).

This citation puts great emphasis on sense and the meaning of life for a good life, both for individuals and for societies. The quote comes from a text that, as so many analyses today, deplores the decline of life stance and moral-religious rules and values triggering the shrinking of civil society. The question we address in the present contribution is: what can be understood by the impact of the urban way of living for a growing majority of humanity on the meaning of life and on the ways life stances and religions are transferred? More poignantly, do the loosening grip and the decrease of control by kin and/or small community in the urban context produce freedom, anxiety, creative potential or other reactions in the generations who grow up in larger urban areas? It may not be a moral or existential loss, but it certainly makes for new formats to deal with the meaning of life (see Geertz, 1973).

The urbanization of the world seems an irreversible fact (with over 60 per cent of the world's population already living in urban contexts in 2005 [Castells, 2002]). In that sense, the trend is a universal one, going hand in hand with a rapidly deploying globalization of services, communication and trade. At the same time nationalism is far from dying out, and transnational relationships and ditto travel and trade are becoming part of the daily life of millions of people. The growth of urban contexts and of urban living conditions happens in a globalizing world, with a rise in demography and a sharp growth in the battle for natural resources (e.g., water, oil, gas, uranium, etc.). In that historical context the new information technologies (mobile phone, PC, etc.), the communication explosion (the internet and the search programmes) and tourism and trade are gradually having a deeper impact on lifestyle, on knowledge and on the religious and cultural taste and value systems. At the least, that is what we all experience in our private life, when looking at the younger generation and comparing their use of media and IT facilities with that of only two decades ago. The 1990s will certainly be remembered as the decade of the breakthrough of the mobile phone and the PC in a large segment of the world's population. The so-called 'peace dividend' of that time allowed for an unforeseen and sudden expansion of this technology. We are now trying to assess the impact on the traditional domains of anthropological inquiry: kinship ties, beliefs, values, tastes, material products and religion. While the globalization processes involve a great percentage of humanity and in some cases (like natural resources or the market economy) the whole of the world's population, it is important to keep in mind that it does not intrinsically entail equal opportunities or equal health and wealth for all. We need to reflect on the uneven interconnectedness of people as well. As Friedman puts it: 'We are told that the world is one place, but for whom, one might ask!' (Friedman, 1997, p. 70). Unfortunately globalization, which by its very name seems to imply the inclusion of everybody, in actual fact produces new exclusions and continues some of the old inequalities (see Allen and Hamnett, 1995).

With this contribution we offer at the very least some insights in this research area. There is prolific writing on these in each of the sub-disciplines involved. Although we obviously appreciate this work, it will hardly be referred to in a systematic way. Indeed, we do not want to assess the field nor bring a state of the art contribution, but rather feel free to develop a theoretical angle to the whole field and try to come up with sharp and relevant questions where possible. Some aspects of the problematic we sketch were dealt with elsewhere (Castells, 2002; Pinxten et al., 2004).

We all have a sort of idiosyncratic attitude, at least when compared to researchers in religious studies. That is to say, anthropologists tend to be especially knowledgeable in one particular field, and hence to sometimes approach questions under an almost casuistic angle. As authors guilty of this vice we have come to appreciate the tremendous importance of the deep analysis of a case and will not in any way try to deny the strength of fiercely detailed empirical studies. However, we also have come to learn that comparison is of the essence if casuistics is to be avoided and allow for a scientific model or theory (Geertz, 1983). On top of that, we personally side with the emphasis on the importance of the conscious and scrupulous contextualization of anthropological knowledge (Nader, 1993; Pinxten, 1997). So, the general tendency of this chapter will be one of broad comparative analysis with an acute awareness of the contextual constraints of cultural and religious phenomena (including these thoughts themselves) in the present world, instead of arguing in minute detail on the basis of available ethnographic data.

Making Sense in the City[1]

The basic philosophical question of our focus needs some explanation. When we try to combine knowledge of religious studies with that of anthropology a most intriguing problem materializes. In the perspective of our identity dynamics model the learning processes in religions can be characterized as identity forming paths, where religion is a vehicle for identity construction (see Pinxten and Verstraete, 2004). That is to say, either in the education of mythological meanings or in ritualistic practices, every new generation is socialized in a tradition or in an identity group by means of religious markers: one is raised from childhood to adulthood in age groups undergoing a series of rituals together, one is initiated in the holy lore of the tradition through becoming knowledgeable in the sacred stories, and so on. Religious beliefs and/or practices can be analysed as vehicles for identity dynamics. This need not imply that they are the only ones, or that this is their sole use or function. It only states that it gives us an insight (which has comparative potential) of how religious traditional practices and/or beliefs work in the socialization process. Continuing a local identity may safely be regarded as a role of religion (Pinxten, 2010).

From that axiom we then move on to the generalization that in the relatively recent non-colonial analyses in religious studies it appears that religions do constitute identity for a group primarily by using one or two types of basic referents: the small group (village, lineage group, clan, age groups, etc.) or the genealogy.

In several myths of origin (e.g., Long, 1964) a genealogy of the people is described: this allows for the contemporary clans or for the kinship groups to situate themselves vis-à-vis one another within the great stream of the people. In some instances (most notably in the Old Testament) it explains for everybody of the present generation how and why they are related with each other through belonging to one people. Where the blood tie and the descent from the first days till the present time are crucial for the religious identity of Judaism and hence of the Jewish people, some other traditions adopt a mixed genealogical model. Navajo Indians of the USA, for example, give a primary identifier role to clan membership, but the genealogical reasoning is more open than in a tradition where blood ties are dominant and exclusive markers: new clans emerge every so often in the history of the people through intercultural marriages, expanding the range of the people occasionally (Witherspoon, 1977).

A second referent, which possibly allows for even more variation and fuzzy borders is that of the small group. This could either be the household, the family (especially the extended family), the neighbourhood or the village. The very model of democracy was founded in what today would be regarded as a village context: the ancient Greek 'polis' was usually a community of twenty or thirty thousand free citizens. Athens at its highest moment of glory counted not more than one hundred thousand citizens (Dutoit, 1989). In terms of our present day world, these are villages or at best little towns. Sociologically speaking these concentrations of people are controllable: in principle, all contacts within such a context can at some point or other in life become face-to-face contacts. Put differently, within the constraints of this kind of magnitude (i.e., the village) all people can be known and treated as persons one has encountered 'in the flesh' or heard about as neighbours or relatives. In technical terms the 'polis' has mainly group characteristics: face-to-face contact is the primary characteristic interaction between people (Pinxten and Verstraete, 2004). In contemporary cities, and most certainly in the vast and mixed complexes of multi-million metropolitan areas like Mexico City, Tokyo or even Brussels, this character is not retained. They harbour communities where face-to-face contact is a minority phenomenon (happening in small groups within the complex), but is unattainable at the level of extension of the city as such. One cannot communicate in a direct way with a million people, not even in a lifespan. One can only invest in virtual interactions when one wants to reach the community inhabiting a large city: through advertisements, media, papers and books, and the like.

The general thesis in thinking about sense making in the city (meaning especially the contemporary type of large concentrations of people) then becomes: to the extent that religions and other types of *Weltanschauungen* stick to the old referents of descent lineages and (small) groups, they cannot offer an adequate answer on the meaning of life at the level of the larger cities. Or, alternatively, it is relevant to look at the ways the modern urban context impacts on the communication and interaction formats and even on the themes of different traditions of 'making sense', even more so when the urban context is worldwide, becoming the main and dominant one.

Our general proposal is to try and 'unpack' what the term 'making sense' or 'meaning of life' could mean in a thoroughly and irreversibly urban context. Do the rules of conduct of the kinship group hold, or is individualism an inevitable and 'natural' attitude of the city dweller? Is networking in the present era and in the urbanized context yielding a world filled with individualists, and does that mean egoists? Or will it enhance despair and a steep rise in suicides or low thresholds for euthanasia? On the other hand, the rise of different sorts of community identities might be appreciated as a quite different response to the same trends of globalization and individualization.

Augustine on the Human Predicament

Whatever else, Augustine of Hippo (CE 354–430) is, unlike some of the later theologians, respected by a wide variety of Christian denominations, both Catholic and Protestant. His view is illustrative of the way Westerners have been dealing with sense making. Admittedly, modernity has introduced important shifts in the Western outlook, but we claim that some of the parameters of the primary attitude have not changed.

In 'The City of God' Augustine presented a powerful view on the meaning of life, according to Christian heritage. He analysed the downfall of the Roman Empire and pointed to the causes of the decline. The barbarians were not the main protagonists: they only finished a process of decay with intrinsic dynamics. According to Augustine, the fact that the Romans had it all wrong is the main cause: they worshipped the wrong gods, and lived with the wrong moral rules. In Augustine's interpretation, they did not follow God's will. In a remarkable proposal Augustine tries to 'prove' in 'The City of God' why the Romans and the heathens in general ran themselves into the ground by disregarding God's plan, and how the Christians can come to know the latter. Creation, the death and resurrection of Christ and the meaning of life for every single Christian are explained in one integral 'theory' about the principles and workings of the 'city of heaven'.

Human beings will be saved to the extent that they live as much as possible according to these divine principles and workings in their miserable and mortal life on earth. Otherwise, according to the rules of the common 'city of earth' (i.e., that of the Romans and other heathens) their life will yield eternal misery, making it all pointless or devoid of meaning. The important point is not so much the concrete proposal of what people have to do in order to gain eternal bliss, but rather the frame of mind where an integral and integrated sense or meaning for life is thought out and expressed.

Moreover, Augustine presents this frame on the basis of an argumentation that shows where and why other proposals (in this case those of the heathens) had to fail and how God's plan takes care of it all by bestowing a keen and thorough deeper sense on human life. Moreover, this major shift in thinking about the meaning of life is versed in a metaphor about two cities: the city of evil, despair and futile senseless life in the 'city of the earth' and the 'city of heaven' as an ideal of rules of conduct and beliefs. According to our interpretation, the deep message here is that life and everything human beings encounter in their world of experience holds a place in one grand encompassing ideology which gives meaning to it all.

We can point to other Church fathers (Paul, for certain) or theologians as well, but the point is made and that should suffice. What we emphasize with this short digression on Augustine is that the Christian heritage with its emphasis on meaning and sense making, understood as an encompassing or integral (cognitive) interpretation of the lived reality, has been so pervasive in the history of the West that it gained the status of reality or obviousness in the mind of the lay person and the researcher alike. Moreover, this interpretation has a normative aspect as well: it yields certain unmistakable rules of conduct and the attached values. In other words, according to this tradition life has to have a meaning and sense making is an important activity of humankind. Over the centuries the latter emphasis has become deeply engrained in Western culture. We adopt the view that 'there has to be a sense' in it all and that human beings are only fully human when the dimension of 'making sense' or 'meaning of life' is present in their culture. Maybe it even serves as a normative foundation for the culture one belongs to.

In the very notions of 'primitive culture' versus 'civilization' of the nineteenth century and that of 'development' in the later era, this emphasis became crucial: if anything, the 'primitive' lacks the meaning of life or at the very least holds faulty attitudes here, pretty much in the way Augustine analysed the 'mistaken' position of Romans and heathens. Development, in order to catch on, implies the adoption of the normative programme of the meaning of life. At the same time, and not surprisingly, anthropologists have detailed the lack of this dimension in numerous traditions (probably somewhat similar to oral Christianity of the pre-Reformation era). For example, when asked about the lack of myths and of meaning in their elaborate ritual life the Nepalese Jains told anthropologist Humphreys that they did not care about that at all. They even advised her, in case she would be in need of myth or meaning, to borrow some from other traditions: the Jains had no need for them (Humphreys, 1996).

Similarly, large development programmes of the past decades shipped a normative programme on sense making along with the material project and the discussion on the failures often turned on this issue again. This led some critics of the development attitude very recently to break away from the attitude and plead for the right to be different (Verhelst, 2003).

Augustine used the image of the city in his time. Obviously, that image will be hard to compare with contemporary urban realities. As mentioned before, the city in those days counted limited numbers of people (thousands, tens of thousand, but never even a million, Dutoit, 1989). Probably the image of the city had to stand in his mind for that of a certain type of order: the wrong order (although not really chaos) of the city of the world versus the divine order of the city of God. It is clear from the reading of Augustine's book that the author imagines to be able to have an overview of the 'city', which in itself guarantees this notion of order. Given the fact that the author spoke and wrote at the time of the downfall of the western Roman Empire (i.e., the fifth century CE), the proposal can be appreciated indeed as an attempt to plead for a concrete and manageable type of order for a relatively small amount of people in a context that can be overseen and managed with the proper means. It is clear that in the present era, with over six billion people we know of (compared to the few million Augustine was aware of) and the concentration of more than half of them in poorly structured and fast growing urban contexts which can not be genuinely managed by any central ruler or council most of the time, and with impact on large areas and ultimately on the life conditions of the whole of humanity, the projection of an ideal order for the world in the image of a well ordered city is unlikely. The very notion of the meaning of life in Augustine's understanding of the order emanating from God could be advanced in a context of promise for a strong monocultural Christian world in the making as pitched against the multitudes of semi-orders of the barbarians all around. However, in the present world at the very least eight strong religious orders are recognized as competing forces to rule large areas of the world by rightist thinkers such as Huntington (Huntington, 1996), whereas less opinionated social scientists would rather speak about several thousand cultural traditions, which continuously loan and adopt traits and practices between each other in an endless chain of lesser or greater transformations

(Hannerz, 2003). The very idea of the one good and holy format for all is less likely now than at the time of Augustine, since our knowledge of the diversity in the world is so much greater.

In terms of the focus of this chapter we question whether the universalized urban living conditions of humanity will change the relevance or lack of the sense making or meaning producing processes, which were so dominant in the Western tradition, and to what extent and in what way. Will Westerners dilute or even lose their urgency vis-à-vis the meaning of life questions, or will the rest of the world adopt this basically religious emphasis in the course of the process of urbanization?

The Old and the New Worlds

The situation in Europe may be different from that in other parts of the world: in 1800 a rough 3 per cent of the world population lived in urban contexts, mainly in the so-called 'old world' (from the point of view of Europe, that is, definitely not that of China). By 2000 this percentage has risen to half the population, and the so-called Third World cities are the fastest growing urban complexes. In terms of religious expansion through and in cities, Europe is cited in recent studies as the sole region in the world where secularism is holding out (Martin, 2005). Everywhere else in the world, according to Martin, religion is on the way up. So, only Europe constitutes a 'problem' from the point of view of churches. We are not convinced that this is a 'problem', but will not go into this here. We are not convinced either that the concepts used (secularism and religion) apply without misunderstandings or potentially dangerous abuses throughout the world. We go into the effects of the urban condition here, because it might be leading us to a crucial question about 'making sense in the urbanized world'.

We take as a given that presently three generations are living in a shared context around the world. On that basis we can speculate on the different experiences and perspectives in each of them on the issue at hand. The learning processes of each of the generations have shifted rapidly and possibly irreversibly: the present grandparents were raised in religious schooling and followed all the regular procedures in their youth and later life (baptism, puberty ritual/holy communion, marriage in a church, etc.), but their children who are now parents themselves had to engage in a hectic survival struggle as double wage-earners. For them, the traditional institutions were gradually less frequented, except for the grand occasions (like marriages and funerals, for example). Family ties and traditions became less important for this generation, where individualism sets in together with a generalized consumerism. The youth of today breaks away drastically from former patterns: they develop their personal network of relationships and peer groups, partly through school and leisure circles and increasingly through virtual contacts and networks (Castells, 1996; Bateson, 2000). For the first time, from the 1990s on the world of experience expands tremendously by means of the availability of mobile phones and PCs for a large segment of the present generation of youngsters. Over these three generations, urbanization has been increasing tremendously all over the world, triggering a deep change in experiential opportunities and at the same time heightening a contradictory way of living in cities. The opposition in life experiences and expectations in rural and in urban areas is rapidly dissolving, since on the one hand the physical and the informational boundaries between both are blurring (Smart and Smart, 2003), and on the other hand information technology in the past two decades has made it possible for people to share life experiences, regardless of their lack of kinship ties or their differences in religious background. Paraphrasing Appadurai (Appadurai, 1996) one can say that the 'imagination combines with new media technology to allow us to affiliate in ways that bring us closer to someone around the globe than to our next-door neighbour' (Smart and Smart, 2003, p. 267).

In an attempt to assess what such globalization processes yield in terms of cultural (and religious) shifts Hannerz (Hannerz, 2003) offers a very useful model of three scenarios. He presents an insight into the three types of 'theories' which are around to explain the impact on cultural processes and formats of economic globalization. One scenario projects that the world is 'Westernizing' uniformly (e.g., Wallerstein, Klein and others in Hannerz, 2003). A second one, which is extremely powerful in the political arena today, professes that a small amount of 'civilizations' (re)emerges in the present era and is due to yield clashes between them in the future (Huntington, 1996). Hannerz claims that anthropologists do not find empirical data to support either of these scenarios. At the micro-level what appears to be happening looks like continuous streams of small transformations, adaptations and reshufflings of cultural structures and processes. Hence, anthropologists doubt that the geopolitical trends which are proposed by the ideologists and the colleagues of international politics yield uniform patterns of living experiences and sense making processes in the local communities. Rather, what we observe at the micro-level are continuous small shifts and changes, often captured by such notions as 'creolization' or 'glocalization'. Hannerz speaks about the 'transformationalist' view. A better term is needed than any of these three, but we lack a good candidate so far. The important point is that the third view looks at the many ongoing little adaptations, lending and importing, exchanging and transforming processes going on all over the world in a myriad of ways, and yielding numerous new forms of 'change-in-continuity'. There is no general 'take-over' by one or more cultures.

Moreover, such processes can be witnessed around the world. That is to say, granting that Fordism has reached its limit as an economic system in Western or other contexts (with increased specialization of production, Keynesian fiscal policies, union-capitalist treaties for the benefit of all, etc.) and globalization is moving up worldwide (with corporate power, delocalization, and so on), the cultural processes and structures do not simply obey these economic trends. Rather, culturally speaking one witnesses most of all two concurrent trends: worldwide one sees an increase in complexity of societal and cultural processes and an increase in diversity of tastes and patterns. The latter two trends manifest themselves in a variety of ways and a plurality of smaller or more encompassing processes, indicated in the following paragraphs.

Through urbanization one sees at the same time an 'increased connectivity' (Smart and Smart, 2003) as expressed in the worldwide web and a continuation or even a growth in local identity. The latter is visible in ever more festivities, but also vigilance activities in neighbourhoods, 'wars' between regions or cities, and the like. Cities especially (smaller ones and of course metropolitan areas) face a sudden and encompassing growth in diversity of cultures, languages and religions. One of the features pointed at by researchers in this regard is that of transnationalism (Glick Schiller et al., 1992a). That is to say, more citizens detach themselves from the local ties and customs they run into when settling in a city as a foreigner. Rather, they obey the local rules and do business with the establishment, but at the same time they strengthen the ties with their region or country of origin, for which they now became successful migrants. Even small cities illustrate this trend in an incontestable way. For example, a city like Ghent (Belgium) with some 300,000 inhabitants is now confronted with refugees from over 150 non-European countries, while Brussels or Amsterdam have migration groups from almost 300 different countries.

A slightly different perspective points to the growth of so-called 'double loyalties' in migrant leaders and communities: Smith studied in depth the remarkable engagements in political mandates of migrants and former residents from Chicano descent (Smith, 2004). Typically, several of them took up offices in their former country (e.g., Mexico, the Caribbean Islands) while staying loyal to the USA. Similar developments can be witnessed with North African and Turkish migrants in Europe. In both of these phenomena the link between citizenship and nationality is cut, and engagements and loyalties can hence be detached from belonging to one nation only.

Another important line of research is offered by political scientists, social geographers and urban sociologists. A leading thinker here is Manuel Castells, who was able to sketch a theoretical frame combining the analysis of the impact of information and communication technologies, urbanization and worldwide political trends after the Cold War. In his magnum opus Castells presents this frame of reference (Castells, 1996): the rapid deployment of ICT in the world (starting in the 1980s) triggered a new division of wealth, those regions which have excellent higher education, a climate of freedom and new high tech facilities take the lead worldwide and yield rapid and distinctive new wealth for the population. Most commonly these regions are dense urban areas, since the richer urbanized parts of the world prove to fulfil all the conditions of excellent higher education, a high degree of creativity and room for innovation. With the globalization of the capital markets and of some types of trade and industry the power of the nation state is quickly eroded. The combination of all these trends have landed us presently in a world where traditional labour conditions and the concomitant national government power dwindle, insecurity on the labour market rises and with these all sorts of identity movements flourish. In the latter category we also find all sorts of religious identity movements. When their profile and action procedures fit nicely in the urban conditions we predict that their success (temporary or not) will be greater. The Evangelical and the Pentacostal churches are the better known examples from recent studies on these issues (see Smart and Smart, 2003). We claim that not all is understood on these matters, but that it is at the very least likely that the generalized urban context for human populations seems to 'select out' certain types of religious presences. Taking Castells's theory as a point of departure for further research promises to be very fruitful to contextualize processes and structures of 'making sense in the city' (Castells, 2002). Obviously we do not make a value choice here, saying that developments such as urbanization or globalization are good or bad in a moral or a political sense. We cannot possibly make such judgments.

New Themes and Engagements

The impact of a series of parameters, which will need to be analysed and thought through more thoroughly to be sure, can be assessed more fruitfully with the younger generation. In a rather generalized way the old churches, but also the traditional non-religious sense making organizations (the humanist federations, the Masonic lodges, and so on) are said to be losing appeal for the younger generation (e.g., Verté et al., 2006). On the other hand Buddhism is a booming phenomenon in the West and in the East, and a variety of New Age, neo-pagan, fundamentalist or exotic sense making groups and activities are offered on an ever more varied market: sweat lodges from the North American Indian denomination are a success in Europe, and Wiccas and Satanists are attractive throughout the West. On the other hand, the tremendous rise of television preachers and congregations in the Americas as well the birth of city shamanism in very diverse places on the globe are only countered by a spread of spirituality in many places and the reappearance of traditional churches (Catholic, Protestant, Orthodox) in international politics. Finally, all sorts of eclectic products are offered: Catholic Buddhists, Anglican Buddhists vision seekers inside and outside of established churches, peyote cults, Santeria initiates, Capoiera Christian scouts, and so on.

One way of appreciating this variety of religious and life stance forms is by describing and eventually assessing them by means of the standards from our past. That is to say, by looking at and thinking about them in the religionistic terms outlined at the start of this chapter: do they qualify as 'meaning of life' perspectives such as we came to understand these in the religious traditions that were developed in the small communities of the past? The answer will undoubtedly be that most often they do not. Indeed, people in the urbanized world of today increasingly build their own networks in which a variety of sense making perspectives can hold their places within one lifetime. More often than before, people pick and choose what they like without bothering about a fixed neighbourhood or a binding tradition. The city context offers the opportunities and allows for sufficient anonymity to carry this through. Some examples illustrate what we mean by this: the North American Indians (i.e., the Navajo) were members of a medicine tradition and became peyotists in the span of two generations: they picked up the peyote cult during weekend trips in the cities of Oklahoma, from where it spread over all Indian reservations in half a century. In Europe, so-called perennially Catholic countries such as France and Belgium (especially Flanders) witness a boom of Eastern denominations (Buddhist and other traditions). Again, the proliferation happens through urban networks. Further examples can be found in abundance in 'non-Western' places: the shaman tradition of Central Asia surfaced again after seventy years of Soviet domination and persecution, taking the form of city shamanism now (Denaeghel, 1998); China witnessed a rather sudden growth of the so-called

Falung Gong sect in the metropolises and reacted with a fierce persecution (the Tien an Min tragedy). Examples could be multiplied.

Research questions which emanate from this synthesis are:

a. One fact we want to stress is that it is clear that urbanization is an irreducible trend for the world population. This is a completely new human predicament: for the first time the (larger) urban context will be the predominant one for a growing majority of the human population, and hence for formal and informal education of this and the next generations. In order to survive and flourish in this new predicament, human creativity will be an essential asset. However, forces of inertia may be presupposed to be at work. We know, as anthropologists, that linguistic structures are relatively stubborn and conservative. May we presuppose that the same is true of sense giving and making processes and their products? If we can speak of tradition in the old sense of the term (the immovable, stable 'core of a culture') it might be in these domains of the cultural field. Do the formats of belonging and of learning about particular traditions yield forces of inertia, which pull to continuation or even conservatism?
b. How can we begin to unwrap the impact of generalized urbanization in the particular way it is taking place: in an economic globalization context, with growing availability of new information technologies, and fast development of partially structured metropolizes in the poorer parts of the world? What processes of learning and adaptation, of individualization and of belonging take shape there, and what will be their impact on the structures and contents of life stances and religions of the younger generation who are rapidly picking up the opportunities offered by context and means and developing individualized networks or 'shopping around for values' in a variety of traditions on the market? Does this entail that the older and established churches are hence bound to withdraw in a hopelessly conservative or even reactionary doctrine and practice, which Taylor (Taylor, 2006) seems to imply when looking at the ruling of the new Catholic Pope? Or, put differently, how can such institutes adapt to this new predicament? Not only in terms of doctrine (which may be the easier part), but also in terms of interpersonal relationships and learning styles.
c. If we thought about meaning producing and transferring traditions such as life stance systems or religions in terms of continuity and stability (and dearly fought changes) in the past, then by doing so we clearly presupposed that uniformity, training new generations to become the same as past generations was the general pattern in the processes of making

sense. That is to say, a group or community was supposed to transfer a doctrine, a meaning system or a way of life in a thoroughly uniform way to newcomers or a new generation. To the extent that we stick to this emphasis on uniformity and 'equalization' of all when speaking about processes of making sense we may well be forced to drop the notion of sense making altogether. Indeed, with growing globalization and urbanization it is not clear at all that uniformity in doctrine or in practices will still be found a generation from now. Then what concept should we use, or how can we think the possibly loosely structured sources of sense or meaning which people will find, use or constitute in this unforeseen new predicament?

d. The final and most encompassing question may be the one that smacks of a late battle with orientalism and colonialism: was the way we thought of sense making and meaning production altogether a 'Western' (maybe a Christian) way of dealing with socialization or enculturation? And do we have to get rid of this *in globo* and focus on particularism and difference, rather than on uniformity and universality?

The theoretical work of concept analysis and problem identification has not yet begun, but at least we are looking into the issue in a detailed way now.

Note

[1] For the past fifteen years the research group Centre for Intercultural Communication and Interaction (CICI) at Ghent University has been exploring a model on identity dynamics. The general metaphor we hold when thinking about cultural identities is a visual one: the chiasm – best known as the butterfly attractor – represents in a graphic way how identities are formed and reshaped in a continuous way, showing temporary structure and ongoing shifts and restructurings at the same time (Pinxten et al., 2004). Members of the research group have been elaborating aspects of the model in processes of gender identity (Longman, 2004), of religious identity (Orye, 2004), of cultural and intercultural identity (Pinxten and De Munter, 2010; Dikomitis, 2005, forthcoming; van Dienderen, 2004). Twice in a row we organized conferences on extremist exclusivist identity as is the case with racism (The Evens Foundation, 2002; Pinxten and Preckler, 2006). The latter symposium posed the question of new forms of exclusion through racism in large cities in the world. That was the first time we explicitly linked our model with the urban issue (the symposium took place in 2002). In becoming more acutely conscious of the importance of the urban context for humanity now and in the future, we decided to explore the link between the urban condition of life and culture more systematically in the following years (see Pinxten and De Munter, 2010, and the international symposium '*Making Sense in the City*', 2006).

Bibliography

Allen, J. and Hamnett, C. (1995), *A Shrinking World? Global Unevenness and Inequality*. Oxford: Oxford University Press.

Appadurai, A. (1996), *Modernity at Large: Cultural Dimensions of Globalization*. Minneapolis, MN: University of Minneapolis Press.

Augustine of Hippo (AD 354–430), *The City of God*. Edition of the Encyclopaedia Britannica. The Great Books.

Bateson, M. C. (2000), *Full Circles, Overlapping Lives. Culture and Generation in Transition*. New York: Ballantine Books.

Castells, M. (1996), *The Information Age*. Oxford: Blackwell.

—. (2002), *Conversations with Manuel Castells*. Oxford: Blackwell.

Dikomitis, L. (2005), 'Three Readings of a Border: Greek Cypriots Crossing the Green Line in Cyprus'. *Anthropology Today*, 21(5), 7–12.

—. (forthcoming), *Cyprus and Its Places of Desire. Cultures of Displacement Among Greek and Turkish Cypriot Refugees*. London: I.B. Tauris.

Denaeghel, I. (1998), 'Het sjamanisme – tussen geheim en post-communisme', in J. Van Alphen (ed.), *Sjamanisme in Tuva*. Antwerp: Ethnographic Museum, pp.123–39.

Dutoit, R. (1989),'De stad in het Antieke Griekenland', *Oudheid*, 23, 34–67.

Evens Foundation (ed.) (2002), *Europe's New Racism? Causes, Manifestations and Solutions*. New York: Berghahn Books.

Friedman, J. (1997), 'Global Crises, the Struggle for Cultural Identity and Intellectual Pork-Barreling, 'Cosmopolitans, Nationals and Locals in an Era of De-Hegemonization', in P. Werbener and T. Modood (eds), *Debating Cultural Hybridity*. London: Zed Books, pp. 70–89.

Geertz, C. (1973), *The Interpretation of Cultures*. New York: Basic Books.

—. (1983), *Local Knowledge*. New York: Basic Books.

Glick Schiller, N., Basch, L. and Blanc-Szanton, C. (1992a), 'Transnationalism: A New Analytical Framework for Understanding Migration', in Glick Schiller, N., et al. (eds), *Towards a Transnational Perspective on Migration*. New York: New York Academy of Sciences, pp. 1–24.

—. (eds) (1992b), *Towards a Transnational Perspective on Migration*. New York: New York Academy of Sciences.

Hannerz, U. (2003), 'Macro-scenarios: Anthropology and the Debate over Contemporary and Future Worlds'. *Social Anthropology*, 11(2), 169–97.

Humphreys, C. (1996), *Shamans and Elders*. Cambridge: Cambridge University Press.

Huntington, S. (1996), *The Clash of Civilizations and the Creation of a New World Order*. New York: Simon and Schuster.

Lasch-Quinn, E. (2003), 'Unschooled: Democratic Life in the Absence of a Moral Culture', in Roberts, A. (ed.), *Constructing Civic Virtue*. Syracuse, NY: Campbell Public Affairs Institute, pp. 25–33.

Long, C. (1964), *Alpha*. New York: Doubleday.

Longman, C. (2004), 'Engendering Identities as Political Processes: Discourses of Gender among Strictly Orthodox Jewish Women', in Pinxten, R., et al. (eds),

Culture and Politics. Identity and Conflict in a Multicultural World. Oxford: Berghahn Books, pp. 49–88.
Martin, D. (2005), *On Secularization*. Hampshire: Ashgate.
Nader, L. (1993), 'Comparative Consciousness', in R. Borofsky (ed.), *Assessing Cultural Anthropology*. New York: McGraw-Hill, pp. 84–96.
Orye, L. (2004), 'Religion, Society and Identity: From Claims to Scientific Categories?', in Pinxten, R. et al. (eds), *Culture and Politics. Identity and Conflict in a Multicultural World*. Oxford: Berghahn Books, pp. 21–48.
Pinxten, R. (1997), *When the Day Breaks. Anthropological and Epistemological Essays*. Frankfurt am Main: P. Lang Verlag.
—. (2010), *The Creation of God*. Frankfurt am Main: P. Lang Verlag.
Pinxten, R. and De Munter, K. (2010), *De Culturele Eeuw*. Meuven/De Haag: Acco.
Pinxten, R. and Preckler, E. (eds) (2006), *Racism in Metropolitan Areas*. New York: Berghahn Books.
Pinxten, R. and Verstraete, G. (2004), 'Introduction', in Pinxten, R., et al. (eds), *Culture and Politics. Identity and Conflict in a Multicultural World*. Oxford: Berghahn Books, pp. 1–19.
Pinxten, R., Verstraete, G. and C. Longman (eds) (2004), *Culture and Politics. Identity and Conflict in a Multicultural World*. Oxford: Berghahn Books.
Smart, A. and Smart, J. (2003), 'Urbanization and the Global Perspective'. *Annual Review in Anthropology*, 32, 263–85.
Taylor, C. (2006), 'Benedict XVI'. *Public Culture*, 18, 7–10.
van Dienderen, A. (2004), 'Flow between Fact and Fiction. Analysis of Identity Dynamics in Visual Representation,' in Pinxten, R., et al. (eds), *Culture and Politics. Identity and Conflict in a Multicultural World*. Oxford: Berghahn Books, pp. 117–33.
Verhelst, T. (2003), *Het recht anders te zijn*. Antwerp: EPO.
Verté, D. and Verhasselt, M. (2006), *Rapport participatie-onderzoek levensbeschouwingen*. Brussels: VUB.
Witherspoon, G. (1977), *Language and Art in the Navajo Universe*. Ann Arbor, MI: University of Michigan Press.

Part Three

Sacred Symbols, Sacred Spaces

Chapter 7

Sacred Symbols of the City: Babel, Barbara and their Towers

Anne-Marie Korte

Introduction

In Western cultural history the image of the Tower of Babel not only refers to an ancient biblical tale that accounts for the divine origins of ethnic and linguistic diversity, its widespread visualizations show that the Tower of Babel has also become both an impressive and complex religious-political symbol of civilization. It is able to represent a grand utopia of urban life as well as its failure to materialize. The image of the Tower of Babel can address a deep human longing for living together and cooperating in spite of great cultural and ethnic differences, while it also stands for a profound distrust of, and resistance to, enforced uniformity. In this chapter, I explore this two-sided impact of the symbol of the Tower of Babel, taking the tension between both sides as a productive means to explore its imaginative power.

As a systematic theologian specialized in gender studies I am particularly interested in textual and visual interpretations of the Tower of Babel story that comment on ethnic, cultural and gender differences and their religious meaning. For this reason I will focus, in this contribution, on an exceptional fifteenth century drawing by the Flemish painter Jan van Eyck,[1] which refers to the Tower of Babel in a very unusual and enigmatic way. I will first present the framework in which my discussion of van Eyck's drawing is situated, followed by an analysis of this drawing, and an exploration of the story of the Tower of Babel in the light of the Christian legends of Saint Barbara and her tower.

The Tower of Babel as an Icon of Cultural Criticism and Political Resistance

The image of the Tower of Babel has an extraordinary significance in Western cultural history. Its representation has become famous as a political symbol of metropolitan ambitions as well as metropolitan megalomania. It has become a well-known icon of criticism of usurpation by hegemonic empires and monolithic civilizations. The most famous example of the latter can be found in the two paintings of the Tower of Babel made by Pieter Bruegel the Elder around 1560, which functioned as a symbol of religious-political criticism during Dutch resistance to the Spanish domination of the Netherlands.[2]

These Bruegel paintings appear to have kept their rebellious expressiveness until today. Digitally reworked versions of these paintings circulate within a number of contemporary movements in Europe protesting against globalization and Americanization, the exhaustion of natural resources and the environment, and the sacrifice of humane and personal dimensions in politics and government. Most recently, the citation and reframing of the Bruegel paintings in the context of cultural criticism and political resistance received new impulses from the attacks on the Twin Towers of the World Trade Centre in 2001. In many comments it was noted that these attacks not only aimed to erase the commercial and economic heart of the Western world, but also meant to destroy the shameless display of Western wealth, power and self-esteem, symbolized by the Twin Towers in New York. As could be expected, conservative Christian opinion leaders and preachers hastened to refer to the biblical story of the Tower of Babel to interpret the attacks as God's wrath for America's major sins. However, it is far more remarkable that political commentators, writers and philosophers also used this image to articulate a self-critical analysis of the meaning of these attacks.[3] Apparently, the biblical story of the Tower of Babel provides images and a normative framework for a self-critical account of these extraordinary events.

The resonance and fame of these visualizations indicate that the Tower of Babel story has a clear moral message and a particular expressiveness: it is widely understood to say that hubris will be punished, and that pride goes before a fall. It is remarkable that this message still sounds so loud and clear, given the fact that in Western culture and media the familiarity with biblical stories has strongly declined during the second half of the twentieth century. Secondly, in this same period longstanding scholarly interpretations of the biblical text of the Tower of Babel have been seriously challenged. Biblical scholars, historians of religion and theologians have developed radically different interpretations of this particular biblical story, which no longer find the warning against hubris and pride to form the essence of the story. I will give a short discussion of these current developments.

The Ambivalent Biblical Text of the Tower of Babel Story

> 1: And the whole earth was of one language, and of one speech.
> 2: And it came to pass, as they journeyed from the east, that they found a plain in the land of Shinar; and they dwelt there.
> 3: And they said one to another, Go to, let us make brick, and burn them thoroughly. And they had brick for stone, and slime had they for mortar.
> 4: And they said, Go to, let us build us a city and a tower, whose top may reach unto heaven; and let us make us a name, lest we be scattered abroad upon the face of the whole earth.
> 5: And the LORD came down to see the city and the tower, which the children of men builded.
> 6: And the LORD said, Behold, the people is one, and they have all one language; and this they begin to do: and now nothing will be restrained from them, which they have imagined to do.
> 7: Go to, let us go down, and there confound their language, that they may not understand one another's speech.
> 8: So the LORD scattered them abroad from thence upon the face of all the earth: and they left off to build the city.
> 9: Therefore is the name of it called Babel; because the LORD did there confound the language of all the earth: and from thence did the LORD scatter them abroad upon the face of all the earth.
> Gen. 11, 1-9 (King James Version)

In the past two decades, postmodern and postcolonial theological reflections in particular have given an important impetus to the reading of the Tower of Babel story (Gen 11, 1-9).[4] These new approaches challenge the long-established theological interpretation of this text in terms of (original) sin, pride and disobedience, focusing on the reproachable human desire to 'be like God'.[5] These new interpretations point to the fact that the biblical text talks about several points of likeness, difference and confrontation between human beings and God, whereas sin, pride and obedience as such are not named or implied in this text. These recent interpretations highlight the story's recognition of difference (between nations, languages and cultures) and focus on the divine predilection for diversity, which confronts the human inclination to remain the same and to resist and suppress what is other and strange (Hiebert, 2007; van Wolde, 1994; Eadem, 2000).

In addition to this alternative reading, these postmodern and postcolonial stances, elaborating on recent exegetical and literary approaches of Gen. 11, 1-9, emphasize that this text is not univocal or coherent at all. They show that the confusion – *Babel* – that lends its name to the outcome of the story is echoed in many ways in this text, as French philosopher Jacques Derrida has shown in his seminal analysis, 'Des Tours de Babel' (Derrida, 1985), literally meaning 'turning round Babel'.[6] In this text, Derrida plays a subtle game with the paradoxes of understanding and confusion that characterize this story. He gives the meaning of the Tower of Babel story his own twist, challenging the dominant Jewish and Christian readings of this story. According to Derrida, this story shows the powers as well as the delusions of language, the weak borderline between understanding and misunderstanding, and the necessity as well as the fundamental impossibility of translation. Drawing from different and partly opposite translations and interpretations, and using some speculative Jewish and Muslim comments to this story, Derrida argues that the meaning of 'Babel' on the one hand is evident, given that Babel as a symbol of confusion is universally known and comprehensible across the borders of languages and cultures. But on the other hand the exact meaning of the name of Babel eludes and confuses us: is Babel a proper name, the name of a city named after God, the city of the Father-God (Bab-El), or is it the gate to the gods (the Akkadic Bab-illi), as translations throughout the times have suggested? Who has given Babel its proper name, is this a personal gesture of God? And who is this God who bestows language as well as confusion on humankind, and who creates unity as well as difference and diversity? Would we be able to 'reach' this God if we all spoke the same original language, or does the story of the Tower of Babel definitely reveal that this longing will never be fulfilled? With questions like these Derrida situates the interpretation of the story of the Tower of Babel in contemporary debates about language, culture, difference and desire.[7]

Most interestingly, the postmodern and postcolonial readings of Gen. 11, 1-9 result in the open question of whether ethnic and cultural diversity should be seen as either divine punishment or divine gift. We can consider this question to be the theological articulation of a fundamental ambivalence towards the reality of ethnic and cultural diversity. The text of Gen. 11, 1-9 does not provide unambiguous answers here; rather, it seems to harbour this question as an *aporia*, thereby urging the listeners and readers to respond and to step into this debate.

Visual Responses to the Textual Ambiguities of Gen. 11, 1-9: Looking Upward versus Looking Downward

Given these textual ambiguities, it becomes hermeneutically very interesting to look at the visual history of this story.[8] Do the imaginative interpretations of the Tower of Babel reflect the different views on ethnic and cultural diversity in the text of Gen. 11, 1-9, and what do artists make of these differences? Art historian Helmut Minkowski's lifelong comprehensive work on the iconography of the Tower of Babel contains huge collections and overviews that make it possible to draw some lines and conclusions regarding this question (Minkowski, 1991).

Until the fifteenth century, in Western visual culture the image of the Tower of Babel regularly appeared as an illustration in the biblical text, mainly in miniatures, but also in floor mosaics and in stone ornaments of churches. These pictures in most cases show, in a very compact form, both the actual building process of the tower and God's impending verdict, visualized by God's head, hand and words, or by God's angelic messengers above the tower. From the middle of the fourteenth century new and more autonomous genres of visualization of the Tower of Babel emerged, in particular in northern Europe. The image of the Tower of Babel became used to express, first, the rise of a new self-conscious urban culture, and second, to articulate criticism of the usurpation exercised by hegemonic sovereigns and empires.

This first tendency, the depiction of new urban self-awareness, can be found in late medieval representations of the Tower of Babel in books, panels and windows, which show an increasing fascination for the building process in all its aspects. In these pictures there are no references to God's judgement or to the doomed ending of the building project. The depicted tower becomes higher and gets rather varied forms, while the scene around the tower becomes quite spacious and more elaborate, showing all the wealth, preparations and work that is required to build a metropolitan edifice like this.

The second tendency, the depiction of the Tower of Babel scene to formulate a critical stance towards foreign powers, starts at the beginning of the sixteenth century, and can be found in the many huge paintings from the Low Countries in particular. Here the tower dominates the whole landscape, it touches the sky, and is on the brink of collapse or abandonment. These images no longer focus attention on the building process or the joint efforts to finish the building, but on the fate of the tower itself: we see how it remains uncompleted, gets abandoned and destroyed, and finally falls into ruins. The fascination with destruction and punishment, in other words, becomes stronger than with the awe-inspiring capacity of constructing such a tower.

So with respect to the ambiguities in the textual version of the story of the Tower of Babel, we find in the fifteenth century visual interpretations an increasing divide between looking upward and downward, based on the recognition of different points of view: an identification with either the citizens as builders or with God's judgmental point of view.

The Tower of Saint Barbara

Studying the period of these new contextualizing and moralizing visual interpretations of the Tower of Babel, I came across the enigmatic drawing by the Flemish painter Jan van Eyck picturing the Christian virgin and martyr Saint Barbara. It was made in 1437, and is part of the collection of the Royal Museum of Fine Arts in Antwerp, Belgium. It concerns a small panel of 20 × 30 centimetres, and at first sight this drawing seems to be a sketch for a painting; the drawing, however, is completely elaborated, framed and signed. On the other hand the sketch is only partly coloured, so the question remains of whether or not this drawing was finished.[9] At first I was struck by the fact that I had found a single female character portrayed at the foot of the Tower of Babel, which seemed to me completely unique in Christian visual culture. But immediately afterwards it became clear to me that this drawing does *not* represent the Tower of Babel.[10] It is this initial confusion that made me study this drawing, its subject and its interpretations in more detail (Korte, 2009).

In Christian iconography, Saint Barbara's characteristic attribute is a tower. Mostly, it is portrayed as a small tower that she holds in her hands, or is standing at her feet. van Eyck chose a very different and spectacular visualization: he depicted Saint Barbara sitting in front of a huge tower that is still under construction, and the depiction of this tower shows similarities to the type of representation of the Tower of Babel that was incipient in the fifteenth century in the Low Countries.[11]

The composition of the drawing poses the question of why Saint Barbara and the enormous tower are both pictured in great detail and why both objects are equally impressive. Looking upward, starting at the bottom of the drawing, we see that the lower half of the picture is dominated by the beautiful Barbara, seated with her book and feather, with her long skirts draped widely around her, the fabric of her dress almost streaming over the borders of the drawing. Looking downward we see that the upper half of the drawing is dominated by a big tower in the style of medieval cathedrals. It is still under construction and its unfinished steeple reaches the sky above the upper borderline of the drawing, an element that links this tower to the Tower of Babel visualizations. The face of the reading Barbara is placed right in the middle of the drawing. Behind Barbara, at the level of her face, a workplace for building materials at the foot of the tower is visible. Around the tower and at its top we see engineers and construction workers. In the background of the tower we see a big city, which nevertheless appears diminutive compared to the enormous tower.

The tower has become Saint Barbara's characteristic symbol because it represents the most famous and intriguing element of her hagiography.[12] According to Christian legends, Saint Barbara became locked up in a tower by her father, who wanted to keep her away from men eager to marry her. Because of this element, as well as the lack of evidence for her historical existence, it seems likely that Barbara's story has been conceptualized from older, non-Christian mythic tales. Christian legends date her life between the third and seventh century C.A. and her story knows many versions. The main features tell us that Barbara was the daughter of a pagan Roman merchant and lived alone with her father in the city of Nicomedia – or sometimes Heliopolis – in Asia Minor. By putting her in a tower her father wanted to protect her against obtrusive men as well as foreign influences, in particular that of Christianity. However, while her father was out on a journey, Barbara, locked up in her tower, took on the Christian faith, destroyed her father's idols that were kept in the tower, and ordered an extra window to be made in her tower. With three windows, the tower now referred to the Holy Trinity. When her father returned and noticed the extra window, Barbara told him she had turned Christian. Her father was so enraged that he hit her and handed her over to the local authorities to be sentenced to death for the crime of blasphemy. Barbara escaped from her tower, but was found and killed by her father, who immediately after the murder was struck by thunder and wasted away to ashes. In some versions Barbara did not die by her father's hand, but was directly taken up to heaven with body and soul.

In Christian iconography Saint Barbara was not only depicted with her tower; she was also portrayed with the martyr's palm, a chalice and a book. Van Eyck has played with all these attributes in his drawing. The long palm in Barbara's hand can also be a huge writing quill, while the tower is not only Barbara's tower with its three main windows at the front, but at the same time the enormous tower of a city cathedral. There is no chalice in Barbara's hands, but the shape of the chalice can be found in Barbara's full skirts that fan out into a large bowl at the bottom of the drawing. The book that lies in Barbara's lap could actually be a Bible, but the fact that the open page of the book contains drawings could be a hint that the book refers to alchemy and freemasonry. Saint Barbara was the patron saint of the alchemists, and in the fifteenth and sixteenth century sources van Eyck himself was named an alchemist.

Another playful game concerns van Eyck's own presence in the drawing; he clearly wanted to be known as Barbara's painter. He gave his drawing a 'speaking autograph': *Iohannes van Eyck me fecit* (made me), is painted in golden letters on the wooden frame of the drawing.

Barbara's Tower and the Tower of Babel

Whether van Eyck has connected Barbara's tower to the Tower of Babel intentionally we do not know, but his unique drawing implicates and evokes this connection, stimulating the comparison and confrontation between these two symbols of power, identity and holiness in an urban setting of ethnic and cultural diversity.

In the first place, by the image of a beautiful woman in front of a Babel-like city, van Eyck's drawing points to those internal biblical associations in which Babel is equated with the city of Babylon and associated with the abhorrent figure of the Whore of Babylon. Sitting on her throne high above civilization and portrayed as a holy virgin and martyr, Barbara seems the complete counterpart of the Whore of Babylon, the woman who in the Christian imagination symbolizes the excesses of urban life in the most horrible way (Rev. 17,3 – 18,24).[13] The Whore of Babylon epitomizes centralistic power and ruthless domination, resulting in oppression and gross injustice. Arrogance, extravagance, blasphemy, fornication and cruelty are typical of her, all expressed in the 'golden cup in her hand full of abominations and filthiness of her fornication' and her being 'drunken with the blood of the saints'. There can be no greater contrast than between this legendary evil woman and the Holy Barbara. Yet the wealth and complexity of detail Christian legend has given to Saint Barbara make it impossible to reduce her to this innocent counterpart of the Whore of Babylon. For Barbara is also rich, beautiful, attractive and exquisitely dressed, she takes to sitting 'enthroned as a queen', and arouses aversion and rage because of her stubbornness. Her performance is highly ambivalent: is the Holy

Barbara a loyal daughter who waits in her tower for her father to return, or is she a rebellious and provocative young woman who rejects her father's national and religious identity? To which extent can Barbara be seen as honest, pure and innocent?

At this point van Eyck's drawing offers an important second association: the relation between the names of Barbara and Babel, which both mean 'incomprehensible' and both are mimicries of strange utterances. Considering her name Barbara is literally a barbarian, a stranger and outsider, someone whose integrity and innocence are not given from the outset. Barbara and Babel refer to each other, and both confront us with the question of how to react to what and who is other and strange. But Barbara not only stands for the unfamiliar other and the reality of diversity, as Babel does. The stories contributed to her in Christian legend also turn her into an example of how to act in confrontation with the unfamiliar other and the reality of diversity. The Barbara stories answer questions that the biblical story of the Tower of Babel leaves open, in particular with respect to the *aporia* of the divine predilection for diversity and the human inclination to stay the same and to resist and suppress what is other and strange.

The Christian stories about Barbara, who is a stranger in her city, a motherless daughter, and a young woman who resists her father without turning away from him, illuminate how to face and handle difference in language, culture, origin and religion in a very concrete way. Motherless and left behind by her father Barbara has no option but to define her own affiliations. She chooses to become part of the Christian community as a kind of new family, but she does so without denying her actual origins. That is, she confronts her father with her choice by staying in her tower and changing this building into a public symbol of her oppositional stance. She destroys, like the biblical Abraham, the idols her father kept in the tower, which could be seen as a symbolic patricide, and she opens her tower to the light of the triune God.

To affirm her own beginnings Barbara does not need a total erasure or a creation ex nihilo. She does not have to murder her own father or mother, as happens in the famous myths of origins – featuring Marduk, Zeus and Oedipus – of the old Middle Eastern and Western culture. Being called a stranger, abiding in a strange city and left alone by her parents, Barbara has to choose herself to whom she belongs. This choice results in her martyr's death, the erasure of her father and her elevation into the community of saints – her new kinship. The attributes that recall and symbolize Barbara's earthly existence, the tower (in which she was locked up by her father) and the chalice (given to her, according to legend, from heaven by her deceased mother), are both ancient symbols of masculinity and femininity, and represent the bonds with both her parents. Barbara's multiple roots and various loyalties continue to be remembered and confirmed. They do not have to be cut off or denied, because they have become part of her new religious identity.

The Tower of Babel and the Recognition of Multiple Origins and Affiliations

Van Eyck's drawing encourages the reconsideration of the interpretation of the symbol and the story of the Tower of Babel. His painting does not confirm the dominant theological and moralizing interpretative frameworks: it neither connects the pride and *hubris* interpretation to the image of the Tower of Babel nor does it join the split between looking downward and looking upward that marks the fifteenth century visual interpretations of the Tower of Babel.

Instead of affirming the *aporia* of unity versus diversity characterizing the biblical story, van Eyck's drawing suggests a relocation of the central problem: the confrontation with the reality of ethnic and cultural diversity should not be formulated in terms of unity versus diversity but as the recognition of multiple origins and affiliations.

By means of the Barbara story the drawing takes us to a fundamental and topical question in these biblical stories, that is, the tension between the longing for unity and the challenge posed by diversity in multicultural and multi-religious urban culture. It is through the eyes of a female protagonist that it shows us how to deal with this: Barbara neither denies nor destroys diversity but faces up to it even if a fortunate outcome is not assured.

Van Eyck's drawing contains another indication of how to read the Babel story. His drawing still raises the issue of whether or not it was finished, of whether it was only a preliminary study or a completed work. This question is reiterated in the unfinished tower and in the question of which moment of Barbara's life van Eyck depicted here: is she in anticipation of the confrontation with her father, or already transcending her earthly life? The drawing, the tower and Barbara are all uncompleted, demonstrating that this is the only way to tell a convincing story about descent and origins, both acknowledging diversity and resisting stories of faith that are used as rights to power.

Notes

[1] Jan van Eyck, 'Heilige Barbara', (Brush point on plastered panel 31 × 18 cm, with original frame 41.2 × 27.6 cm), 1437. Koninklijk Museum voor Schone Kunsten, Antwerpen, Belgium. See for example: http://www.go2cit.nl/epubVKB/uploads/images/Collectie/Meesterwerken/MW-Van-Eyck_Heilige-Barbara.jpg.

[2] For art historical backgrounds of these paintings see Mansbach (1982), Weiner (1985), Wegener (1995) and Morra (2007).

[3] See, for example, Hankiss (2002), Wallerstein (2002) and Davison (2005).

[4] See, for example, Miguez-Bonino (1999), Song (1999) and Wagenaar (2003).

[5] For classical 'pride and punishment' interpretations see for example Cassuto (1964, p. 248), von Rad (1972, p. 151), Sarna (1989, p. 84), Van Seters (1992, pp. 182–5) and Blenkinsopp (1992, p. 91).

[6] With these accents Derrida also incorporates the Jewish and Islamic interpretative traditions of the story of the Tower of Babel into his 'turnings around Babel', in which the theme of the giving and receiving of names has predominantly been developed.

[7] See, for example, Druart (2007).

[8] I have expounded the hermeneutical interest that underlies this approach in Korte (1998). See also Eadem (2004, 2010), O'Kane (2005) and Bergmann (2009).

[9] Strictly speaking, this work is not a drawing but a work on a panel containing a drawing on the chalk layer. It is considered to be one of the first drawings that are an autonomous art form in Western painting. There are long and ongoing debates on its status as either a drawing or a painting as well as on the question of whether or not it was finished (see Koldeweij, 2002, pp. 12–14; 2006, p. 92).

[10] Ever since the 1940s there have been debates about the issue of whether or not the drawing refers to the Tower of Babel (see Bol, 1965, pp. 84–5).

[11] For art historical background information see Pächt (1989), Harbison (1991), Rothstein (2005), Graham (2007) and Augath (2007).

[12] Information about Saint Barbara was derived from Farmer (1978), van der Linden (1999, pp. 111–12). For gender critical views on Saint Barbara see Caprio (1982), Roberts (1998), van Dijk (2000) and O'Grady (2002).

[13] For an analysis see of the lemma 'Great Whore' in Meyers et al. (2000), pp. 528–9.

Bibliography

Augath, S. (2007), *Jan van Eycks 'Ars Mystica'*. Munich: Wilhelm Fink.

Bergmann, S. (2009), *In the Beginning is the Icon: A Liberative Theology of Images, Visual Art and Culture*. London: Equinox.

Blenkinsopp, J. (1992), *The Pentateuch: An Introduction to the First Five Books of the Bible*, ABRL. New York: Doubleday.

Bol, L. J. (1965), *Jan van Eyck*. Berlin: Gebr. Weiss/Verlag Lebendiges Wissen.

Brown, W. P. and Carroll, J. T. (2000), 'The Garden and the Plaza'. *Interpretation: A Journal of Bible & Theology*, 54(1), 3–12.

Caprio, B. (1982), *The Woman Sealed in the Tower: A Psychological Approach to Feminine Spirituality*. New York: Paulist Press.

Cassuto, U (1964), *A Commentary on the Book of Genesis, Part 2, From Noah to Abraham, Genesis VI 9–XI 32*. Jerusalem: Magnes.

Collins, A. Y (1993), 'Feminine Symbolism in the Book of Revelation'. *Biblical Interpretation*, 1, 20–33.

Davison, G. (2005), 'The Fallen Towers: Pride, Envy and Judgement in the Modern City'. *The Bible and Critical Theory*, 1(3), 141–9.

Derrida, J. (1985), 'Des Tours de Babel', in Anidjar, G. (ed.), *Acts of Religion*. New York: Routledge, pp. 102–33.

Druart, T.-A. (2007), 'Islam and Christianity: One Divine and Human Language or Many Human Languages'. *Journal of Religion & Society*, 9, 1–13.

Eadem (1994), 'The Tower of Babel as Lookout of Genesis 1–11', in Eadem, *Words Become Worlds: Semantic Studies of Genesis 1–11*. Leiden: Brill, pp. 84–109.

— (2000), 'The Earth Story as Presented by the Tower of Babel Narrative', in Habel, N. C. and Wurst, S. (eds), *The Earth Story in Genesis*. Sheffield: Sheffield Academic Press, pp. 147–57.

— (2004), 'Recapturing the Sacred: Feminist-Theological Hermeneutics and the Authority of Holy Texts'. *Yearbook of the European Society of Women in Theological Research*, 12, 12–32.

— (2010), 'Paradise Lost, Growth Gained: Eve's Story Revisited. Genesis 2–4 in a Feminist Theological Perspective', in Becking, B. and Hennecke, S. (eds), *Out of Paradise: Eve and Adam and Their Interpreters*. Sheffield: Sheffield Phoenix Press, pp. 140–56.

Farmer, D. H. (1978), *The Oxford Dictionary of Saints*. Oxford: Clarendon Press.

Graham, J. (2007), *Inventing Van Eyck: The Remaking of An Artist for the Modern Age*. Oxford: Berg.

Hankiss, E. (2002), 'Symbols of Destruction'. *After September 11 Archive*. New York: Social Science Research Council (www.ssrc.org/sept11/essays/hankiss.htm) (consulted 24-04-2010).

Harbison, C. S. (1991), *Jan van Eyck: The Play of Realism*. London: Reaktion Books.

Hiebert, T. (2007), 'The Tower of Babel and the Origin of the World's Cultures'. *Journal of Biblical Literature*, 126(1), 29–58.

Hyung Kyung, C. (1991), *The Struggle to Be the Sun Again: Introducing Asian Women's Theology*. Maryknoll, NY: Orbis Books.

Keller, C. (1990), 'Die Frau in der Wüste: Ein Feministisch-theologischer Midrasch zu Offb. 12. *Evangelische Theologie*, 50, 414–32.

Koldeweij, J. (2002), 'Een onvoltooid heiligenleven of een onvoltooid schilderij? Vorm en inhoud bij de Heilige Barbara van Jan van Eyck te Antwerpen'. *Desipientia*, 9(1), 12–14.

Koldeweij, J. and Hermesdorf, A. And Huvenne P. (eds) (2006), *De schilderkunst der Lage Landen, Volume 1, De middeleeuwen tot en met de zestiende eeuw*. Amsterdam: Amsterdam University Press.

Korte, A.-M. (1998), 'Significance Obscured: Rachel's Theft of the Therafim', in Bekkenkamp, J. and de Haardt, M. (eds), *Begin with the Body: Corporeality, Religion and Gender*. Leuven: Peeters, pp. 157–82.

—. (2009), 'Babel, Barbara en hun torens: Gen 11,1-9 genderkritisch belicht', in van Grol, H. and van Midden, P. (eds), *Een roos in de lente: Theologisch palet van de FKT*. Utrecht: FKT, pp. 145–58.

Mansbach, S. A. (1982), 'Pieter Bruegel's Towers of Babel'. *Zeitschrift für Kunstgeschichte*, 45(1), 43–56.

Meyers, C., Craven T. and Kraemer R. S. (eds) (2000), *Women in Scripture: A Dictionary of Named and Unnamed Women in the Hebrew Bible, the Apocryphal/Deuterocanonical Books, and the New Testament*. Boston: Houghton Mifflin Company.

Miguez-Bonino, J. (1999), 'Genesis 11: 1–9: A Latin American Perspective', in Levison, J. R. and Pope-Levison, P. (eds), *Return to Babel: Global Perspectives on the Bible*. Louisville Kt: Westminster John Knox Press, pp. 13–16.

Minkowski, H. (1991), *Vermutungen über den Turm zu Babel*. Freren: Luca Verlag

Morra, J. (2007), 'Utopia Lost: Allegory, Ruins and Pieter Bruegel's Towers of Babel'. *Art History*, 30(2), 198–216.

Niditch, S. (1995), 'Genesis', in Newsom, C. A. and Ringe, S. H. (eds), *Met eigen ogen: Commentaar op de bijbel vanuit het perspectief van vrouwen*. Zoetermeer: Meinema, pp. 37–56.

O'Grady, K. (2002), 'The Tower and the Chalice: Julia Kristeva and the Story of Santa Barbara'. *Feminist Theology*, 10(29), 40–60.

O'Kane, M. (2005), 'The Artist as Reader of the Bible: Visual Exegesis and the Adoration of the Magi'. *Biblical Interpretation: A Journal of Contemporary Approaches*, 13(4), 337–73.

Pächt, O. (1989), *Van Eyck: Die Begründer der altniederländischen Malerei*, (ed.Maria Schmidt-Dengler). Munich: Prestel.

Pippin, T. (1992a), *Death and Desire: The Rhetoric of Gender in the Apocalypse of John*. Louisville: Westminster John Knox.

—. (1992b), 'The Heroine and the Whore: Fantasy and the Female in the Apocalypse of John'. *Semeia*, 60, 67–82.

Roberts, M. (1998), *Impossible Saints*. London: Virago Press.

Rothstein, B. L. (2005), *Sight and Spirituality in Early Netherlandish Painting*. Cambridge: Cambridge University Press.

Sarna, N. M. (1989), *Genesis*. Philadelphia: Jewish Publication Society of America.

Schüssler Fiorenza, E. (1984), *The Book of Revelation: Justice and Judgement*. Philadelphia: Fortress Press.

Selvidge, M. J. (1992), 'Powerful and Powerless Women in the Apocalypse'. *Nectestamentica*, 26, 157–67.

Song, C.-S. (1999), 'Genesis 11, 1–9: An Asian Perspective', in Levison, J. R. and Pope-Levison, P. (eds), *Return to Babel: Global Perspectives on the Bible*. Louisville Kt: Westminster John Knox Press, pp. 27–33.

van der Linden, S. (1999), *De heiligen*. Amsterdam/Antwerpen: Contact.

Van Dijk, M. (2000), *Een rij van spiegels: De Heilige Barbara van Nicomedia als voorbeeld voor vrouwelijke religieuzen*. Hilversum: Verloren.

van Seters, J. (1992), *Prologue to History: The Yahwist as Historian in Genesis*. Louisville: Westminster John Knox.

van Wolde, E. (ed.) (2004), *De toren van Babel*. Zoetermeer: Meinema.

von Rad, G. (1972), *Genesis: A Commentary*. Philadelphia: The Westminster Press.

Wagenaar, H. (2003), 'Babel, Jerusalem and Kumba: Missiological Reflections on Genesis 11:1–9 and Acts 2:1–13'. *International Review of Mission*, 92(366), 406–22.

Wallerstein, I. (2002), 'America and the World: The Twin Towers As Metaphor'. *After September 11 Archive*. New York: Social Science Research Council (www.ssrc.org/sept11/essays/wallerstein.htm) (consulted 24-04-2010).

Wegener, U. B. (1995), *Die Faszination des Maßlosen: der Turmbau zu Babel von Pieter Bruegel bis Athanasius Kircher*. Hildesheim: Olms.

Weiner, S. E. (1985), *The Tower of Babel in Netherlandish Painting* [Dissertation Columbia University]. Ann Arbor, MI: UMI.

Wilson Carpenter, M. (1995), 'Representing Apocalypse: Sexual Politics and the Violence of Revelation', in Dellamora, R. (ed.), *Postmodern Apocalypse: Theory and Cultural Practice at the End*. Philadelphia: University of Pennsylvania Press, pp. 107–35.

Chapter 8

Communicating the Elemental Cosmos: The Hereford *Mappa Mundi*, Sacred Space and the City

Renée Köhler-Ryan

A religiously defined sacred space can quite often evoke a sense of eerie familiarity. Such is its elemental nature. Everything there is of and from the world as we know it, and yet, it is changed, by being explicitly placed in relation to divine transcendence. The everyday city-dweller may well be astounded to find that, in such a space, the earth on which one moves, the air that one breathes, the light that enables vision and warmth and the water that nourishes and cleanses, are more manifestly charged with meaning. The elemental is emphasized in a sacred space, for there the world is offered and at the same time transformed: an elemental microcosm that enables integration into wider senses of reality. Amazement can become a deepened form of awareness when one sees that the elemental is also at the foundation of the city. Without the elemental, the space and human interactions of the metropolis would be impossible.

While the contemporary city in its secular and heterogeneous forms can seem anything but receptive to a sense of divine transcendence, this contribution discusses how comparisons between sacred spaces and the city can both instantiate and reawaken awareness of what it is to be of the elemental order, which constantly transcends itself while being at the same time as much of the living cosmos as it is of humans. Discussion begins with some preliminary definitions of the nature of the elemental, before contrasting two ways of thinking the human relationship to everyday spaces. The space of rationality, particularly influenced by Descartes, is so abstract that it tends to separate us from imaginative ways of understanding our place in the cosmos. On the other hand, place theory, as I will discuss it, credits so much value to personal experience and the individual body in Nature that possibilities of communication and community break down. There can be neither a city nor a robust understanding of the sacred if place theory's presuppositions and consequences are taken to their extreme.

The median way between these two positions is explored in this chapter by bringing together the most important aspects of rational thought and lived bodily experience. Thus, I proceed to think through ways of mapping the world, in particular the medieval *mappaemundi*, that allow for elemental ways of knowing space. I then outline some key features of the elemental thinking of Gaston Bachelard and Saint Augustine. These two very different theorists enable us to think of the sacred and the city together, through the elemental cosmos.

The Main Attributes of the Elemental

The elemental can be defined first as comprising what is most basic to the human experience of living in the world. As such, the elemental is what is absolutely essential to life. It is most often taken for granted. I will consider the elemental primarily in terms of the categories of earth, air, fire and water. Each of these individual elements enables life, makes up the cosmos, and simultaneously provides ways in which we know and communicate meaning to ourselves and to others. Tied to these capacities of communication are the historical facets of the elemental. That is, in a secondary way, one can distinguish the elemental in the details that comprise our everyday lives and which communicate themselves through the cultural artefacts of history. If we had nothing in common with those of other eras, if we did not still share their cosmos, then nothing of the past could make sense to us. Since all humans share the qualities of the given world, cultural meaning can at its most significant points transcend the limitations of chronological time.

Another way to consider the two main attributes of the elemental – as the basic stuff of the cosmos and as enabling communication throughout history – is through a sense of sacred transcendence, particularly as found in the human-made sacred space. Expressions of the elemental have transcendent value. This link between sacred transcendence and the elemental will be particularly explored in what follows through considering the medieval Hereford *mappa mundi*. The same connection is evident in sacred spaces, which are of the world while at the same time constantly referring to divine transcendence.

Integral to the discussions that follow here is William Desmond's idea that the elemental is 'strangely intimate'.[1] That is to say, each of the elements affects quotidian experience and concerns, while simultaneously communicating to us the senses of integral value and transcendent worth of the world that we share with others. Such communications carry with them the immediacy – or, intimacy – that is the fundamental attribute of being elemental. We live the elements, even as they compose our world. Desmond describes, 'the elemental is such that its expression is just its simple being. There is no disjunction between expression and being' (Desmond, 1990, p. 272). The elemental life, shared with others, comes to fruition in sacred spaces as well as in metropolises that are manifestly elemental.

(Cartesian) Modern Space and the Elemental

The modern Cartesian sense of space, which is in many ways still with us today, has several aspects that prove inimical to elemental expressions of being human and open to divine transcendence. Such space is *abstract* in that it emphasizes but a part of the whole of reality. It abstracts rationality from the particularities that make up our everyday lives and claims extraordinary significance for the solitary working mind. Abstract space thereafter tends to take on a life of its own. Senses, imagination, anything in fact which cannot at face value be quantified and set out in a visually clear form, are either renounced or else forced to submit to a fabricated order of reality. Abstract space is, then, particularly inappropriate to sacred space, which, qua elemental, is innately open to transcendence. The elemental, as will be discussed more fully later when considering Augustine and Bachelard, always directs us beyond the mere immediate, integrating us into a greater sense of reality. In contrast, abstract space can prove alien to the formation of cities that nurture human life.

Instances of abstractly delineated cities are numerous – they replace central spaces for community and commerce with gridded zones where meetings between people lack spontaneity. The paradigm for these cities was already set in place by René Descartes who, in his *Discourse on Method* proposes to knock down the entire realm of learning as he finds it, so as to rebuild according to the plumb-line of reason. Descartes argues that the learning of his time is like an old and irregular city, whose buildings and streets need to be cleared away so as to make way for straight, orderly, rational delineations (Descartes, 1985a, p. 116).[2] In each instance of such a city, discord is instantiated between the given cosmos and the human-made space. The elemental world is not composed of straight lines; living the elements, we know this to our deepest core.

So as to imaginatively comprehend the implications of abstract space, it is helpful to remember that the representation of space most fitting for the rationalist is given on a graph, according to the coordinate system developed by, among others, Descartes.[3] Unsurprisingly, the perspective that such graphing offers, if not situated within a larger whole, can actually distort lived reality. To illustrate this point, one can consider the problems inherent in mapping the lived world. A modern map takes the imperfect sphere of earth and makes it flat. This is evident from the mere fact that almost every such map will give in fine print, in a corner off to the side, the calculations according to which such inevitable distortion in its instance occurs. For example, when maps composed according to the Mercator scale bend what is not flat, so that it can be depicted on the surface of a plane, they bring about at least two significant consequences (Fig. 8.1).[4] First, geographical land masses change in appearance of size as well as in nature of proximity when they are drawn up to fit on a rectangular grid. Secondly, some parts of the world simply cannot fit onto the grid pattern that the map uses, and so they do not appear at all.

These necessary deviations from lived space influence those who plan their lives according to such maps. Maps can, then, actually affect one's intentions. If I rarely see the antipodes depicted on a map, I will think even less about what they might be like, or what they might mean for the planet, for me, and for those with whom I share the space of the world. Also, the distance between two points can be easily mistaken when using a flat grid map. Lynn S. Liben relates the story of how American President Ford was

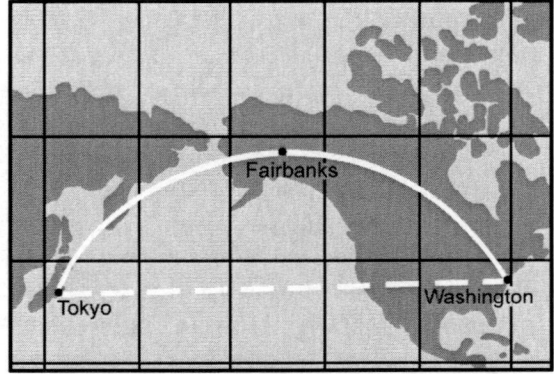

FIGURE 8.1 President Gerald Ford's route from Washington, DC, to Tokyo, Japan, via Fairbanks Alaska. Gattis, Merideth, ed., Spatial Schemas and Abstract Thought, Figure 3.4, p. 71, © 2001 Massachusetts Institute of Technology, by permission of The MIT Press.

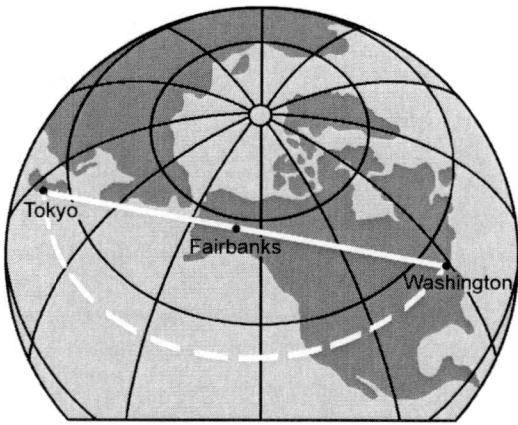

FIGURE 8.2 President Gerald Ford's route from Washington, DC, to Tokyo, Japan, via Fairbanks Alaska. Gattis, Merideth, ed., Spatial Schemas and Abstract Thought, Figure 3.4, p. 71, © 2001 Massachusetts Institute of Technology, by permission of The MIT Press.

once reproached for taking what his critics claimed was a detour to Alaska on a tax-paid trip to Tokyo, in order to make a re-election campaign stop (Liben, 2001, p. 71). That this was not a detour at all can only be pictured by viewing a map (or globe) of the surface of the earth that is not drawn up according to the Mercator scale (Fig. 8.2). The ways that we corporeally experience and move through space are at least overlooked and at worst undermined by abstract space, which is prone to deny the physicality of human bodies in space.

One should caution that it certainly should not be forgotten that abstract thought has its own range of advantages. Without the gridded map and clear timetable, contemporary life as we know it would not exist. Only when abstract, but beneficial, qualities are removed from the broader context of the cosmos do they become detrimental. The major difference between abstract space and the elemental spaces being proffered here is as follows: whereas abstract space takes a part of human existence in the world and proclaims it to be all-important, the elemental emphasizes each aspect of being human in the world. A truly elemental space constantly refers beyond itself, by representing the elements such that they cannot be simply explained and thus exhausted in meaning. Such space involves the whole person, physically, but also rationally and imaginatively, in an integrated whole space of significance. As such, one might think that theorizing about specific places would be a fitting counter to abstract, rational space.

However, some of the problems of contemporary place theory, to which we now turn, give pause in this respect.

Places and False or True Transcendence

In the elemental space, then, meaning is present and it is communicable. Anyone who enters into an elementally defined space is in a very basic way already familiar with his or her surroundings. Incorporating the modes through which we already experience daily life, the person entering such a space need not puzzle it out, but is instead more likely to feel at home. This ready communicability, albeit inexhaustible, is very often missing from the places described by 'place theory', which seeks to differentiate itself from rationalized Space.

By 'place theory' I refer to a range of thinkers who see immense philosophical significance in the idea of 'place'. Places, such thinkers maintain, provide a concept through which to understand what has been undervalued by the modern sense of Space. At the same time, places in their heterogeneous nature appeal to the many different and highly individual experiences that humans have of being in the world.[5] It is impossible here to go into all the pros and cons of place theory. I will, instead, outline two points most appropriate to the elemental nature of sacred space and the city. First, in dwelling so much on what is incommunicable, theorists of place are not entirely true to the deeper senses of community and belonging essential to elemental metropolitan and sacred spaces. Secondly, when place theory turns to something that only looks like elemental appreciation, it can very easily end in pantheism. Namely, when it bows down to raw Nature, it runs the risk of generalizing the very specific ways in which the elemental affects our daily lives with others in the world. Therewith, that same world, rather than indicating what is present beyond, becomes an object of worship. Moreover, such pantheism runs counter to one of the main arguments of place theory, which is that highly specific aspects of a place should be upheld – rather, one would think, than something as general and impersonal as Nature.

Place theory brings with it a range of advantages when considering antidotes to the totalizing nature of rationalized space. It concentrates on the particular values of concrete places, claiming that place, rather than a modern sense of Space, is of great importance. Thus, place theory strives to protect the places in which we live from becoming consumed by Space that gives pre-eminence to universalized utility. Place theory tends most often to be concerned with the history of specific places, with all their contingencies and sociological aspects. This, though, brings with it a significant problem, indicated by Jonathan M. Smith, Andrew Light and David Roberts, who identify what they call the 'exclusive' nature of place (Light and Smith, 1998, p. 8). That is, the places of place theory denote aspects that are ultimately incommunicable to any who do not belong to the place under consideration. The authors state: 'The placeness of a place is a subjective or intersubjective creation, and therefore apparent only to the individual or group members who create it.' (Light and Smith, 1998, p. 6) The modern person, under the sway of a desire to find values common to all – and thus effectively to trace the roots of a cosmopolitan order – shies away from such accentuated exclusivity. It is important to the present exploration that he does so. For, the significance of the kinds of place we are considering here – sacred space and the city – extends beyond any specific collection of experiences or data proper only to a certain religious site or metropolis.

The challenge here is to find those qualities of meaningful locations that speak in ways communicable to more than a sharply defined set of individuals, and which still allow for real experience of what is common to all humans. Thereby the best of what is aimed for by abstract space and by place theory are retained. Alertness to the elemental in a particular space makes this possible, by opening us to something more – to what is granted in the cosmos, which is beyond anything we could have given to ourselves. Place theory shies away from this point when it insists on exclusivity, paradoxically becoming like those who hold to abstract space by insisting on the overriding significance of the human-made rational qualities of spaces.

Place theory can become problematic, too, when it speaks of the importance of Nature, instead of an elemental cosmos. Place theory is such a variegated field of research that it would be remiss to imply that each of its proponents is prey to the same fallacy. However, it is noteworthy that one of the more well-known theorists, Edward Casey, moves toward a kind of pantheism when considering the wilderness places of Nature. For Casey, the best place of all is in the wilderness (Casey, 1993, pp. 183–270). Away from city life, the subject is disclosed for Casey as first and foremost situated within a field of experience separated from community. Additionally, the person in wilderness places is apart from transcendence that can point both through the world and beyond it. Casey describes his wilderness places in terms of the Kantian sublime (Casey, 1993, pp. 199–202), but they lack the sense of leading beyond – of signifying something more. Further, Casey's wilderness places do not venture into those personal elemental dimensions that are essentially interconnected with divine transcendence.

It is in this respect both perplexing and telling that place for Casey performs a pseudo-religious role. He states that he wishes to 'accord to place a position of renewed respect by specifying its power to direct and stabilize us, to memorialize and identify us, to tell us who and what we are in terms of *where we are* (as well as where we are *not*).' (Casey, 1993, p. xv) Casey's paradigmatic example of being in place makes clear that the best place to be is not with others in the city, but instead alone in the wilderness. Given that the ultimate place is more amenable to isolation than to community, Casey's theory in the end misses those dimensions essential to understand the importance and possibilities for transcendence in the city. If Casey's places really do save, they claim to do so more by calling us away from the metropolis than by finding those patterns and capacities within the city that hold promise for personal and communal communications of divine transcendence in everyday life.[6] Casey's theory reminds us of the compelling aspects of particular places, as well as significant qualities of embodiment. However, these points need to be incorporated into a greater understanding of the meaning of space if they are to speak to the meaning of the sacred in the life of the city.

Such a vision is possible when sacred spaces are considered to be elemental microcosms that emphasize the world as a communal realm that is by nature open to transcendence. As such, these spaces shed light on the same qualities possible in the metropolis. To achieve such a perspective, several tools for the imagination can be employed. To these I will now turn, by first approaching some ways of mapping that have been mostly lost to us, but which offer significant insights into how we imagine and navigate our everyday lives in light of ultimate meaning. I will then consider how such considerations are at work in the elemental through two key figures, Gaston Bachelard and Saint Augustine.

The *Mappaemundi* and Spaces of the Elemental Cosmos

In order to appreciate the modes of cartography most amenable to thinking elementally about the city and sacred spaces, it is worthwhile to recall what one expects from a map and what that tells us about how we see the world.[7] Today, a map is more often than not a tool, enabling us to move in the most efficient way possible from one point to another. Or, a map is a way to see very quickly a range of information – of geographical features, tourist attractions, demographic information, and so forth.[8] In each instance, a map allows the viewer to find the answer to a question or grasp the solution to a problem. Contemporary maps are for the most part closely related to those of modernity, and they tend to eclipse the existence of maps that were in an earlier era concerned to give information that continually made reference to the world as cosmos with transcendent significance.

Perhaps no maps better represent the sense of elemental orientation that is our subject than the medieval *mappaemundi*. These depict the world by underscoring the detailed ways that the medieval person imagined lived spaces in relation to divine transcendence. Scott D. Westrem notes, when speaking of the Hereford map, that '*mappaemundi* were not assumed to be precise representations of geographical reality. They were thought to be *true*, however.' (Westrem, 2001, p. xvii). That is, they were held to correspond to a wholeness of vision that was quintessentially human by being cosmically oriented, striving to leave no essential attribute of existence in the elemental order unrecognized. Medieval *mappaemundi* offer very human representations of space. That is, they speak to both sides of the basic human tendencies in drawing up any kind of map. To borrow Erwin Straus's terms, they neglect neither the urge to think in terms of abstract geography nor to move along the horizon of a landscape.[9] Instead, these maps are both abstract enough to offer a vision of the whole world, and so concerned with the lived world of experience that they are punctuated with what can appear to the (post-)modern viewer even quaint details and peculiarities of custom and history. The point of these minutiae seems in part at least to give the reader of the map pause, so as to consider how variegated and wondrous the world is, as natural and historical living artefact.

Let us consider for a moment some of the aspects of the Hereford map,[10] which is one of the few and the largest of its peers known to exist. Cast in the shape of a circle, the world of this map is represented as a sphere – 'as medieval people knew it to be' (Westrem, 2001, p. xxxviii). Medieval mapmakers believed that the great seas took up the space of the world remaining beyond the land masses on which people lived. Since the existence of these waters was not of the greatest concern in their everyday lives, medieval cartographers excluded the waters when they depicted the world, concentrating instead on how peoples relate to each other, historically, but, more importantly, soteriologically.

On the Hereford map, the elemental is constantly referenced, both in word and in image. In concert, the eternal presence of Christ, in every detail of past, present and end time, is evident throughout. The map is oriented to the East, where the onlooker finds Christ in the direction where the sun rises. The redeemer of the cosmos, through whom that world was also made, sits regally at the uppermost point of the map and outside the perimeters of the land mass. Then, at the exact centre of the map are the circular walls of Jerusalem, with the crucifixion depicted above. Christ is the reference point both at the centre and along the perimeters of this given world. From these marks of orientation the rest of the cosmos falls into place. It is a well-ordered whole in which associations are constantly made between places vis-à-vis their particular significance along a seemingly immanent horizon of human experience as well as their importance within the salvation history to which everything ultimately refers. Christ the redeemer sits also as the judge in this worldview. To his left are cast away those who have rejected him, while to his right are those faithful who are to be guided by angels into eternal life. The presence of the heavenly Jerusalem on the outer edge of what can be concretely imagined illuminates the intrinsic value of everything within.

The maker of the medieval map can render such associations because he takes things, people, places and events, and draws them together into a world held together by the links between centre and perimeter. Within the circumference of the mapped world, all pivots around the earthly Jerusalem that leads toward its transcendent urban counterpart. The city on both levels of meaning draws together the significance of every person within the cosmos. That is, all persons are called toward a city, which they can find by exploring what is within the perimeters of the world, as these same boundaries also touch on what is unknown and beyond. Every particular and concrete thing on the map holds universal value because it is held in constant tension between all that centre and perimeter signify. That is, everything represented is given universal meaning by manifesting what is ultimately at stake for all humans: the quest for meaning, which in religious terms is the search for divine transcendence.

This is all possible because the map-maker shares the world with those who view his map; theirs is the same elemental microcosm, with common end: the transcendent city of Jerusalem constantly interconnected with the immanent city of Jerusalem. Every other point in the depicted elemental cosmos is valuable because it shares the world of the historical city of redemption, and thereby already partakes of the life of the ultimate city beyond. This is effectively a very Augustinian understanding of how individuals and communities here are already in the City of God. Before considering this point, we will first turn to Bachelard's appreciation of how a city is elemental, and to Augustine's affirmation that God himself is to be found by hearkening to the elements that compose our world.

Bachelard's Elemental City and the Role of Imagination

This moment of considering Bachelard before Augustine is indulged in order to underline that the elements have both cosmic and sacred significance within the city. Bachelard's work is not overtly concerned with anything religious. However, it is important to note that Gaston Bachelard speaks of a poetics of space in terms that connote the religious and therewith the sacred. While he does not draw attention to the religiously weighty nature of these terms, his ready employment of 'soul' to refer to where the poem relates to the human, and 'Logos' for everything that is 'specifically human' (Westrem, 2001, p. xxiii) takes him into a domain that can at the very least be called transcendence. When known through the elemental, the specifically human has religious overtones that are ignored at our peril. For Bachelard, a poem is true if it speaks to the soul, and its work is possible because of our shared human Nature. We are elemental; we experience and communicate through Logos. We dwell in spaces together by virtue of a shared world of meaning.

An example of the work of poetic elemental imagination very pertinent here can be found in the *Poetics of Space*. At first, Bachelard speaks of the city as potentially alienating. Then, however, he provides an example of imagination at work that renders a link between city and elemental cosmos. Bachelard's city becomes the city of every human. It is available to every human subject; it is universal because, as made by humans, it derives first from the elemental. The elemental can even override features of the abstractly construed modern city that might otherwise alienate us. Bachelard begins by saying that in Paris, the city with which he is most familiar, humans live mainly in rooms. He describes such an abode as 'a sort of geometrical site, a conventional hole' (Bachelard, 1964a, p. 27).[11] City houses, furthermore, have no roots and the city in its entirety lacks a horizon that intersects with verticality. Consequently:

> *Home* has become mere horizontality . . . in addition to the intimate value of verticality, a house in a big city lacks cosmicity. For here, where houses are no longer set in natural surroundings, the relationship between house and space becomes an artificial one. Everything about it is mechanical and, on every side, intimate living flees. (Bachelard, 1964a, p. 27)

For Bachelard, the intimacy of verticality is most present in a complete house, which is rooted in the earth and reaches up to the heavens. Like a whole human being, such a house has heights and depths that allow for multi-faceted imagination and for a sense that when humans share such a cosmic appreciation of life, their commonly held possibilities have greater reach. To be merely horizontal is, then, to lack the capacity to reach beyond, into the furthest reaches of what it means to be human.

Or so it would only seem, for Bachelard nonetheless refuses to despair at the spaces of the city, which he argues can be humanized by drawing precisely upon affiliations between metropolis and the cosmos elementally construed. He demonstrates this by showing how thinking of the city as an ocean can incorporate one into its life and its movement, so that the metropolis is no longer alienating and disruptive. For Bachelard, the interrelations between city and ocean indicate that the city is not intrinsically non-elemental. Deeply human, it can be known as profoundly cosmic. Namely, Bachelard muses:

> When insomnia . . . is increased through irritation caused by city noises; or when, late at night, the hum of automobiles and trucks rumbling through the Place Maubert causes me to curse my city-dweller's fate, I can recover my calm by living the metaphors of the ocean. We all know that the big city is a clamorous sea, and that it has been said countless times that, in the heart of night in Paris, one hears the ceaseless murmur of flood and tide. So I make a sincere image out of these hackneyed ones, an image that is as much my own as though I myself had invented it. If the hum of cars becomes more painful, I do my best to discover in it the roll of thunder, of a thunder that speaks to me and scolds me . . . I dream an abstract-concrete daydream . . . I talk to myself to give myself cheer: there now, your skiff is holding its own, you are safe in your stone boat. Sleep, in spite of the storm. Sleep in the storm. Sleep in your own courage, happy to be a man who is assailed by wind and wave. And I fall asleep, lulled by the noise of Paris. In fact, everything corroborates my view that the image of the city's ocean roar is in the very "nature of things," and that it is a true image. (Bachelard, 1964a, p. 28)

To Bachelard, this reverie is not the result merely of free association. It is only because the city really is like the ocean that his musings are so effective. There is a fundamentally true relationship between ocean and city. Such imaginative associations have their foundation in the nature of the cosmos itself, just as elemental – historically and communally defined and developed – details did for the medieval map-maker. This means too that they can be conveyed from person to person. For Bachelard, the elemental image, especially in the form of a poem, is peculiar and readily communicable. Namely, when a poet speaks in elemental terms, the reader of the poem feels as though she could have spoken – or written – these same words herself (Bachelard, 1964a, p. xxiii). They echo in the depths of the soul.

Bachelard's claims would be superfluous to this discussion were it not that they counter some of the main presuppositions about the spaces in which we live, which we have inherited from modernity. Bachelard is, in exploring the poetic imagination, deliberately grappling with what cannot be fathomed by rationality alone. This, he admits quite frankly, constitutes for him a 'daily crisis' (Bachelard, 1964a, p. xviii). To listen to what the poetic, elemental imagination has to say is to set aside modern assumptions about what is important in everyday life. That is, it is to reject the notion that to live in space is simply to move between points in geometrical, flat space. The presuppositions of a scientific worldview are eschewed. Movement is not simple relocation; it can instead forge new affiliations between self and elemental space. Some spaces, and certain representations of space, facilitate this better than others. The most appealing and beneficial spaces are deeply in tune with the elements that make our world.

To be more precise, for Bachelard it can be ascertained that the elements are significant to human nature because they form a cosmos that humans share in common. The elemental image, poetic or otherwise, has the capacity to engage us with places and elements that we share with others. For Bachelard, to be human is to have the capacity constantly to change the inner recesses of the shared psyche, by entering into various elementally defined spaces. Moreover, it is to possess the capacity, through poetry, to convey such an experience of immersion into cosmic dimensions. Bachelard speaks mainly of the poet who does this through the poetic image that is the product of the poetic imagination. One might argue in the same vein that the architect designing a space that communicates universal values is also a poet, who is similarly attuned to the media given by the cosmos: the elements. Further too, those involved in the formation of cities have the opportunity to draw citizens together, by appealing to recognizable and valuable elemental spaces of the inner psyche. By calling upon the types of space that humans can share as elemental, urban planners can open up greater possibilities of community, which are at the same time nurtured by their communications of transcendence.

Elemental Ways to God and the City: Augustine and the Cosmos

When exploring the ways in which sacred meaning is already present in the elemental, as well as how the elemental can convey that same significance, Bachelard can only take us so far. Bachelard demonstrates how the elemental is a rich source and medium of meaning. However, to find the link between elemental cosmos and divine transcendence, one can turn to a much earlier thinker of the sacred and the city: Saint Augustine. Augustine develops a philosophy of relationship to divine transcendence whereby both the elemental order *and* the city are extremely important. Without either of these, there is something lacking in a human relationship to the sacred. Taken together, Augustine's and Bachelard's thoughts about the elemental yield that the sacred finds its place in the city when represented by that which first brings persons together: their shared lived world.

For Augustine, as for Bachelard, the elemental world draws people into community by providing a common context through which to connect to the creation in which we always participate.[12] As he discovers, each element reveals particular possibilities of how to relate and at the same time bear witness to elementally lived transcendence. He experiences also that one cannot remain aloof when considering and questioning the elements. One needs to acknowledge that the cosmos constantly challenges by presenting its elemental possibilities of relationship to transcendence. Like the elements, we are created. Unlike them, we can turn away from our source, acting against our nature. Reflection on the elements can be transformed into self-reflection when this is realized. Seeing the beauty of an element responding spontaneously to divine transcendence can strike a chord that resonates throughout one's whole existence. Thus, the elements can transform our inner nature, by demonstrating and evoking what is for Augustine the proper orientation of desire toward God.

One can see the attitude that Augustine adopts to do this when he contemplates the elements in his telling and re-telling of *Genesis*,[13] but also in a particular passage in Book X of the *Confessions*, where he calls upon each element in turn: the earth, 'the sea and the great deep and the teeming live creatures that crawl', 'the gusty winds, and every breeze with all its flying creatures' and 'the sky...sun, moon, stars'. They are so compelling in their majesty that he 'puts [his] question' to them, begging 'Tell me of my God . . . You are not he, but tell me something of him'. Each in its own way points him beyond. These elements, which stand 'around the portals of [his] flesh', '[lift] up their mighty voices and [cry] "He made us"'. Each tells them this in its own way, in consonance with the other elements. He remarks that: 'My question was my contemplation and attentive spirit, and their reply, their beauty' (Augustine, 1997, pp. 185–6). This beauty takes on very concrete forms for Augustine, each of which points beyond itself, while retaining its specific nature. Furthermore, in making up the cosmos, each element conveys a relationship between human subjects, who are also made, and the world in which we live. As on the Hereford map, God proves to be the point of common reference – of shared understanding, as it were – between us and all that is of the world. The elements can speak to us because they are like us. We too, are like them.

This elemental awareness is essential to the Augustinian City of God, which has its foundations in appreciation of the fullness of being religious that is available to every human subject. To be religious is, for Augustine, to participate in one's own creation, tracing the line from Creator to creature that was and is there at the constant beginning of all that exists in the world. To convert is to be religious; to be re-aligned, as one was meant to be, from the beginning of creation.[14] Here, then, is the foundation for a community of members of the City of God, which, ideally, is mirrored in a community of people who come together and may even together form a sacred space. All religious architecture meets with the challenge to mirror that religious society – a city that for Augustine stretches throughout the ages and into eternity. In Augustine's vision, city and sacred space merge. Each is grounded in an elemental appreciation of the meaning of living in the cosmos, in that each is religiously oriented.

The Sacred in the City: Elemental Community in the Cosmos

Augustine develops the notion that the person in relationship to God is never without company. Instead, those who strive to live in accord with sacred values form a city that includes but also transcends the physical boundaries of space and time. Without earth, air, fire and water, we could not exist. In company, we can raise our appreciation of the elements to a shared higher level. Each time a person discovers a new possibility of finding God through creation, an opportunity of interpersonal communication is awakened. Knowing how an element expresses itself, we can use its language to speak to another person about elementally conveyed meaning, and ultimately something of divine transcendence. When the city is capable of incorporating this elemental vision, it can be raised toward its greatest heights of communal awareness of divine transcendence. Specifically religious sacred spaces within the city can remind us of this possibility, by presenting an integrated vision of the world in relationship to transcendence. By striving to overcome tendencies to reduce the meaning of our shared world to abstraction, exclusivity or pantheism, the makers and dwellers of cities can become more attuned to sacred realities. Sacred spaces can express such truths in their modes of being elemental.

That is, features within such religious spaces accentuate the possibilities inherent in living in an elemental cosmos. The sacred space's expressions of elemental existence manifest possibilities for making the metropolis more elemental, and thus more apt for communal life. In the past, it was perhaps simpler to find such manifestations of the human appreciation of the elemental. Gothic cathedrals[15] continue to transform interior light and air through the use of different kinds of glass, incense and candles. Traditional churches still use water in fonts, to remind us of the different ways that this element cleanses and nourishes, which are extended into notions of ritual purification with water. The baroque is lavish in many ways, including its decoration of the earth with marble and intricate mosaics. And in the Byzantine Christian style, mosaics too can have a fiery light within, which refers both to this element as we know it here, but also beyond, in the heavens that we imagine to be like the world as we know it, and yet transcendent and refined. In each instance, the element is both of and beyond us, revealing the 'strange intimacy' of William Desmond's elemental referred to above. Each can reach us now, from the distance of the past, speaking to us of what it is to be human and live in the world with others.

In the elemental, 'expression and being' are inseparable. This means that in its purest forms, the elemental allows no disjunction between experience and expression. The Hereford map may again provide a means to understand such strange confluence, by depicting how the elemental and the city are intertwined through the workings of sacred transcendence. In that portrait of the elemental and historically oriented cosmos, the city of Jerusalem is both centre and ultimate goal. In the imagination of the medieval map-maker, a metropolis represents the core of what we are as well as what we are called to become. All orientations to Jerusalem in the cosmos and at its periphery are elemental, because the sacred is present at the heart of the known, lived world, but it is simultaneously elsewhere. This view of the sacred is the natural outgrowth of imagination that knows what it is to be elemental. Humans are of the elements. They also build and live in cities. By portraying how we imagine ourselves in a realm seemingly completely beyond, both sacred space and the medieval map enable the elemental metropolis to emerge in its vibrant potentiality.

Notes

[1] 'Strange intimacy' is a phrase borrowed from Christopher Ben Simpson when describing the elemental in Desmond's thought. (Simpson, 2009, p. 35) The phrase is particularly apt in that it captures the richness of the idea of the elemental at stake. To live the elemental requires immediacy on the part of the subject, such that experience seems even to be unmediated by rationality. This is mindfulness untrammelled by abstraction from human ways of living in the richness of the given world. One is opened up to the strangeness of being (see for instance Desmond, 1990, pp. 271–5; 1995, p. 188; 2001, pp. 170–7; 2008, pp. 35–7). This list is by no means exhaustive as ideas pertaining to the elemental run throughout Desmond's writings.

[2] See Kunstler's (2001) study for the consequences of such modern thought for the contemporary city-dweller.

[3] Discussions and critiques of the abstract nature of Cartesian space abound. Those which have very much informed the views given in this paper include: Bachelard, 1984, pp. 135–77; Dijksterhuis, 1986; Dupré, 1993; Lachterman, 1989; Ong, 1983; Pickstock, 1998; and Straus, 1963 (especially pp. 9–12). While I tend not to agree wholeheartedly with Edward Casey's conclusions as to the nature and significance of place, his discussion of Cartesian space is quite interesting and sometimes helpful (see in particular Casey, 1997, pp. 151–61; 1993).

[4] For a fuller discussion of the points mentioned here see Liben (2001).

[5] For examples of place theory (see Casey, 1993, 1997; Chidester and Linenthal, 1995; Feld and Basso, 1996; Light and Smith, 1998; Tilley, 1994). Sheldrake (2001) and Brown (2004) each take place theory into account but build upon it to provide theological and aesthetic perspectives.

[6] On this point, cf. Sheldrake. Sheldrake points out the necessity that ultimate space not be only naturalistically understood. He states: 'To put matters theologically, God is not revealed to us in the immediacy of raw nature. The only spirituality that is accessible is incarnational – that is mediated through the cultural and contextual overlays we inevitably bring to nature and to our understandings of the sacred. "Every habitat is approached by means of a particular, a way of reading the natural world that has accumulated over time." [quoting Simon Schaua]' (Sheldrake, 2001, p. 16).

[7] See Harvey (2000) for an imaginative appreciation of the potencies of different kinds of maps for seeing the world.

[8] For a very simple overview see Wilford (2002).

[9] Roughly speaking, space is that of the map and the timetable. It is derived and planned. The space of, on the other hand, is the perceptual space of the body, together with all that goes along with it. These, Straus argues, are the two ways in which we know the world spatially. Whereas often one or the other is more pre-eminent in a certain situation or age, to be human is to strive to keep the two in balance. Each must be present, or aspects of being human are lost. The precarious nature of this balance can be addressed by comparing rational abstract space with the space given to us by contemporary place theory (see Straus, 1963, p. 318ff).

10 See http://www.herefordcathedral.org/visit-us/mappa-mundi-1/mappa1.jpg/ view?searchterm=Hereford%20mappa%20mundi. The Hereford *mappa mundi* is copyright of The Dean and Chapter of Hereford and the Hereford Mappa Mundi Trust.

11 He is quoting Paul Claudel.

12 Augustine's idea of creation cannot be given the attention it deserves in this discussion. Creation is for him a philosophical and theological notion, tied to his understanding of conversion and ultimate salvation. For him, to be religious is to participate in one's own creation, by tracing the line marked out from the beginning between Creator and creature. For a brief discussion of this point and Augustine's repeated effort to write a commentary on the biblical book of (see Fiedrowicz, 2002).

13 'The effort to think through the mystery of creation runs like a leitmotif through Augustine's work. Over a period of almost thirty years Augustine composed five commentaries on the biblical creation stories' (Fiedrowicz, 2002, p. 13)

14 See Fiedrowicz: 'For Augustine, religion is simply the free and deliberate acknowledgement of human beings that as creatures they are ontologically dependent on God. It is not without good reason that his ends with an interpretation of the creation story, for it is here that, the human being's praise of God, finds its real meaning: becomes the acknowledgement , accompanied by praise, of the creative bond that constitutes the nature of the human person at its deepest level. It is in praise of God that the ontological bond () is acknowledged and thereby becomes religion ()' (Fiedrowicz, 2002, p. 15).

15 See Sauvanon (2004) for discussion of the presence of the elements in Chartres Cathedral.

Bibliography

Augustine, A. (1984), *City of God*, (trans. H. Bettenson). London; New York: Penguin Books.

—. (1997), *The Confessions*, (trans. Boulding, M. O.S.B.). Vol. I/1 of *The Works of Saint Augustine: A Translation for the 21st Century*. New York: New City Press.

Bachelard, G. (1964a), *The Poetics of Space*, (trans. M. Jolas). Boston: Beacon Press.

—. (1964b), *The Psychoanalysis of Fire*, (trans. A.C.M. Ross). London; New York: Quartet Books.

—. (1984), 'Non-Cartesian Epistemology', in *The New Scientific Method*. Boston: Beacon Press, pp. 135–77.

—. (1987), *On Poetic Imagination and Reverie*, (trans. C. Gaudin). Dallas: Spring Publications.

Brown, D. (2004), *God and Enchantment of Place: Reclaiming Human Experience*. Oxford: Oxford University Press.

Casey, E. S. (1993), *Getting Back Into Place: Toward a Renewed Understanding of the Place-World*. Bloomington; Indianapolis: Indiana University Press.

—. (1997a), *The Fate of Place: A Philosophical History*. Berkeley; Los Angeles; London: University of California Press.

—. (1997b), 'Smooth Spaces and Rough-Edged Places: The Hidden History of Place', *The Review of Metaphysics*, 51, 267–96.
Chidester, D. and Linenthal, E. T. (1995), *American Sacred Space*. Bloomington; Indianapolis: Indiana University Press.
Descartes, R. (1985a), 'Discourse on the Method', in J. Cottingham, R. Stoothoff and D. Murdoch (trans.). *The Philosophical Writings of Descartes (Vol. I)*. Cambridge: Cambridge University Press, pp. 111–51.
—. (1985b), 'Rules for the Direction of the Mind', in J. Cottingham, R. Stoothoff and D. Murdoch (trans). *The Philosophical Writings of Descartes (Vol. I)*. Cambridge: Cambridge University Press, pp. 7–78.
—. (1985c), 'The World or Treatise on Light', in J. Cottingham, R. Stoothoff and D. Murdoch (trans). *The Philosophical Writings of Descartes (Vol. I)*. Cambridge: Cambridge University Press, pp. 79–98.
Desmond, W. (1990), *Philosophy and Its Others: Ways of Being and Mind*. Albany: SUNY Press.
—. (1995a), *Being and the Between*. Albany: SUNY Press.
—. (1995b), *Perplexity and Ultimacy: Metaphysical Thoughts From the Middle*. Albany: SUNY Press.
—. (2001), *Ethics and the Between*. Albany: SUNY Press.
—. (2005), *Is There a Sabbath for Thought? Between Religion and Philosophy*. New York: Fordham University Press.
—. (2008), *God and the Between*. Oxford: Blackwell.
Dijksterhuis, E. J. (1986), *The Mechanization of the World-Picture: Pythagoras to Newton*, (trans. C. Dikshoorn). Princeton: Princeton University Press.
Dougherty, J. (2001), 'The Sacred City and the City of God', *Augustinian Studies*, 32(1), 81–90.
Dupré, L. (1993), *Passage to Modernity: An Essay in the Hermeneutics of Nature and Culture*. New Haven: Yale University Press.
Ellul, J. (1989), *What I Believe*. Grand Rapids: Eerdmans.
Feld, S. and Basso, K. H. (eds) (1996), *Senses of Place*. Santa Fe: School of American Research Press.
Fiedrowicz, M. (2002), 'General Introduction', in *On Genesis, The Works of Saint Augustine: A Translation for the 21st Century* (Vol. I/13). New York: New City Press, pp. 13–22.
Harvey, M. (2000), *The Island of Lost Maps: A True Story of Cartographic Crime*. New York: Random House.
Jones, M. M. (1991), *Gaston Bachelard, Subversive Humanist: Texts and Readings*. Madison: The University of Wisconsin Press.
Kunstler, J. H. (2001), *The City in Mind: Notes on the Urban Condition*. New York: The Free Press.
Lachterman, D. R. (1989), *The Ethics of Geometry: A Genealogy of Modernity*. New York: Routledge.
Lancian, R. (1967), *Pagan and Christian Rome*. New York: Benjamin Bloom, Inc.
Liben, L. S. (2001), 'Thinking Through Maps', in Gattis, M. (ed.), *Spatial Schemas and Abstract Thought*. Cambridge: A Bradford Book, pp. 45–77.
Light, A. and Smith, J. M. (eds) (1998), *Philosophy and Geography III: Philosophies of Place*. Lanham: Rowman & Littlefield.

Livermore, A. (1964a), 'The Augustinian Origins of Gothic: Part I – Abbot Suger'. *Downside Review*, April 1964, 141–55.

—. (1964b), 'The Augustinian Origins of Gothic: Part II – The Art-Historians'. *Downside Review*, July 1964, 222–32.

MacDonald, W. L. (1967), *Early Christian & Byzantine Architecture*. New York: George Braziller Inc.

O'Connell, R. J. (1978), *Art and the Christian Intelligence in Saint Augustine*. Oxford: Blackwell.

—. (1986), *Imagination and Metaphysics in St. Augustine*. Milwaukee: Marquette University Press.

Ong, W. J. (1983), *Ramus, Method and the Decay of Dialogue: From the Art of Discourse to the Art of Reason*. Cambridge: Harvard University Press.

Pickstock, C. (1998), *After Writing: On the Liturgical Consummation of Philosophy*. Oxford, Malden: Blackwell Publishers.

Robertson, D. S. (1977), 'Basilicas, Theatres, Amphitheatres, and other Roman Monuments', in *Greek and Roman Architecture*, 2nd edn. Cambridge: Cambridge University Press, pp. 267–96.

Sauvanon, J. (2004), *La Cathédrale de Chartres: Miroir de la nature: l'air, l'eau, le feu, la terre*. Éditions Legué-Houvet. Le Coudray: L'imprimerie Chauveau.

Sheldrake, P. (2001), *Spaces for the Sacred: Place, Memory and Identity*. London: SCM.

Simpson, C. B. (2009), *Religion, Metaphysics and the Postmodern: William Desmond and John D. Caputo*. Bloomington: Indiana University Press.

Smith, M. A. (1982), *Gaston Bachelard*. Boston: Twayne Publishers.

Strachan, G. (2003), *Chartres: Sacred Geometry, Sacred Space*. Edinburgh: Floris Books.

Straus, E. (1963), *The Primary World of Senses: An Indication of Sensory Experience*, (trans. J. Needleman). London: Free Press of Glencoe.

Tilley, C. (1994), *A Phenomenology of Landscape: Places, Paths and Monuments*. Oxford: Berg Publishers.

Van Herck, W. and De Dijn, H. (2002), *Heilige Plaatsen: Jeruzalem, Lourdes en shopping malls*. Kapellen: Uitgeverij Pelckmans.

Van Oort, J. (1991), *Jerusalem and Babylon: A Study into Augustine's City of God and the Sources of His Doctrine of the Two Cities*. Leiden: E.J. Brill.

Westrem, S. D. (2001), *The Hereford Map: A Transcription and Translation of the Legends with Commentary*. Turnhout: Brepols.

Wilford, J. N. (2002). *The Mapmakers: The Story of Great Pioneers in Cartography – From Antiquity to the Space Age*. London: Pimlico.

Chapter 9

Relocating and Negotiating the Sacred: The Reception of a Chapel in a Shopping Mall

Peter Nynäs & Anne Birgitta Pessi

Introduction

Late-modernity and secularization have shaped the urban religious landscape. We might also acknowledge the impact of resacralization and a post-secular urban culture. Among individuals certain elements of spirituality (e.g., praying) are rising, for example, in the Nordic countries, there seems to be new interest in spiritual matters. Also, there are novel public roles of religion and religious institutions all over the world. The processes of secularization and resacralization are intertwined and complex. Still, taken together they seem to indicate a shift away from religion in its traditional form and tend to foster a spirituality that corresponds to personal needs fulfilled through consumption or cultural practices. Religion is not only declining or rising but indeed transforming.

In this context of religious transformation we can also observe how religious architecture has been both marginalized and made more invisible in contemporary society and in public space. Further, we also witness a relocation of facilities for worship, prayer and contemplation. They are, for instance, found in airports and shopping malls. Additionally, the character of new prayer rooms is changing as well as the location. They are often intended to be used by people of all faiths or by people of no faith at all; they are designed in a more inclusive, more communal sense. The sacred and the profane are in a complex, interrelated relation to each other.

These developments have contributed to a need to re-evaluate the assumed distinction between the sacred and the profane. For instance, researchers have recently more explicitly emphasized the need to acknowledge the question of how sacred places are negotiated or reinvented due to these contextual changes. Modernity and late-modernity do not simply lead to the downfall of religious beliefs and practices but also allow for the continuation of religion: traditional rituals are being modified, reinterpreted and invented. Modernity, late-modernity, and secularization also develop new and novel 'sacred' conditions that have less to do with religion in the conventional understanding of the word. When late-modern individual and choice oriented ways of life make new demands on society and individuals, this affects, and is embedded in, the relationship between social processes and spatial conceptions, forms and structures. Hence, resacralization also generates semi-religious practices and symbolic spaces that blur – or even invert – the traditional boundaries between the sacred and the profane. For instance, shopping malls – the cathedrals of commerce in a religion of the market – are acknowledged to use a similar formula to other sacred places to produce identity, meaning and enchanting effects among their visitors.

In this chapter we will address this changing, transforming religious landscape and examine the blurred boundaries between the sacred and the profane. The chapter is based on a study of The Chapel of Silence, a particular chapel situated in a suburb of Helsinki, the fastest growing area of Finland. This particular chapel is situated in a shopping mall called the Big Apple, and our focus is on the reception of this chapel. How is the chapel appreciated and experienced by the presumed users within the specific context of a shopping mall? With the help of several empirical methods and data, both qualitative and quantitative, the article will propose both more general, as well as deeper understanding, of the complex processes addressed above. From this mixed-methods based analytical approach we will shed light on how the sacred dimension is negotiated in post-secular urban settings.

Transforming Religious Landscape

The erosion of religion – secularization – was long held to be an inevitable feature of modernity, and a condition of modernization. However, today most scholars argue that religion has not, after all, lost influence and relevance as predicted – quite the contrary. For instance, immigrant religions, charismatic movements, new religious movements and alternative spiritualities exemplify this trend. Also, traditional religions and religious institutions have gained novel public roles. As José Casanova (Casanova, 1994) writes, the present development does not necessarily imply that religion loses influence and relevance either in the political arena and the culture of a society, or in the personal conduct of life. Therefore, the validity of the secularization thesis has been subject to questioning and debate; empirical findings do not support it (see e.g., Stark and Bainbridge, 1985; Hadden, 1987;

Berger, 1999). Besides the novel public roles of religion, we can also detect examples of resacralization, or de-secularization, and post-secular urban culture on an individual level. For instance, certain elements of spirituality (e.g., praying) are rising, for example, in the Nordic countries there seems to be new interest in spiritual matters. All in all, religion is not (only) declining or rising but indeed transforming.

In contrast to the idea of secularization, and in order to conceptualize the new situation, Western societies of today are often referred to in terms of a post-secular culture (see e.g., Barbato and Kratochwil, 2008). The term post-secular is ambiguous but generally used to depict complex and diverse changes that in different ways involve, among others, resacralization or revitalization of religion, as well as the profound transformation of the religious landscape. In his recent book Charles Taylor reflects on the process of secularization and the term 'post-secular' (Taylor, 2007). He refers to 'a time in which the hegemony of the mainstream master narrative of secularization will be more and more challenged' (Taylor, 2007, p. 534). This master narrative is the idea that secularization is a linear regression in belief and practice caused by an 'incompatibility between some features of "modernity" and religious belief' (ibid., p. 530).

It is central to note that in the post-secular religious landscape, processes of secularization on the one hand and resacralization on the other are not mutually exclusive. The sacred and the profane, as well as secularization and de-secularization, are complexly interrelated to each other. Co-existence theories propose that secularization and revitalization of religion appear simultaneously but (often) in separate locations or areas of life (e.g., Woodhead and Heelas, 2000). This entails the fact, however, that religion has taken on new forms in a way that poses theoretical and methodological challenges. Sophie Gilliat-Ray depicts the ongoing transformation of the religious landscape in terms of a shift away from religion in its traditional forms, constituted by a normative and unifying role, towards more holistic and eclectic spirituality that corresponds to personal needs often fulfilled through consumption (Gilliat-Ray, 2005). Looking at the changes on a more general level, we can add that the religiosity of today is affected by individualism (see Motak, 2009), as well as by its novel public roles, for instance in the public sphere of welfare (e.g., Casanova, 1994; Yeung et al., 2006a; 2006b; Pessi, 2008).

We have found it to be of relevance to investigate a place that embodies both these transformation processes of religion and the late-modern transformation space – of which more will follow in the next section. Our focus is on the blurred boundaries between the sacred and the profane and the role of relocated facilities for worship among people. The article concerns one particular chapel, The Chapel of Silence,[1] situated in a shopping mall, the Big Apple, located in a suburb in Helsinki, the fastest growing area of Finland. Our focus is on the reception of this chapel: How is the chapel appreciated and experienced by the presumed users within the specific context of a shopping mall?

Spatial Turn – Place and its Reception

A concern with place has been a part of religious studies from the beginning, and the effort to study and understand ongoing changes in society should also be approached from a perspective of geography and spatial analyses. However, the interest in religious studies with place has mainly been related to a basic distinction between the holy and the profane. Within this paradigm there have been different theoretical and conceptual emphases of a psychological, phenomenological or sociological nature. Such clear distinction is no longer sufficient to describe the late-modern religious transformation.

At the beginning of the twentieth century, the concern with place involved an interest in people's experience of sacred places (James, 1902; Otto, 1950), with an emphasis on experiences of the wholly other (*ganz andere*) and the numinous. However, it was with Mircea Eliade that the sacred place became the subject of theoretical inquiry (Eliade, 1957). Eliade brought to the discussion a process of sanctification, that is, how the sacred arises in the world in 'hierophanies' as sacred places, imbued with religious meanings. Thus, the emphasis was on the sacred place as a centre (*axis mundi*), set apart from ordinary and profane space, enabling communication between different domains. Also Émile Durkheim, in his classical analysis of the role of religion in building a community, underscored that sacred reality is a projection of a social reality; the intensification of feelings that goes with experiences of sacredness is related to social reality, whether or not it is symbolized by a building, an image or a totem (Durkheim, 1912).

With modernity, secularization, and a growing awareness of diversity followed a need to re-evaluate the assumed distinction between the sacred and the profane. According to Kim Knott (Knott, 2005a, p. 110), Jonathan Z. Smith (Smith, 1987) has 'dislodged theory on sacred space from its previous base in a phenomenological conception of the sacred and re-engaged it with social and cultural constructionist approaches'. A recent article by

Lily Kong and Tong Chee Kiong (Kong and Kiong, 2000) exemplifies this shift. They emphasize the need to acknowledge how sacred places are negotiated or reinvented because of the contextual and contentual changes related to the transformation of religion. Modernity, and late-modernity, do not simply lead to the downfall of religious beliefs and practices but also allows for a continuation of religion in its novel forms. For instance, traditional rituals are being modified, reinterpreted and invented to fit with late-modernity. In this article we do not apply a particular understanding of late-modernity. Instead we rely on how various scholars have acknowledged how religion is not fading away but is rather transformed in several ways (cf. Frisk, 2009). Our focus places further emphasis on how this is embedded in spatial processes. In their study of how religion is modified and negotiated as late-modern living makes new demands on society and individuals, Kong and Kiong (2000) point out that these processes are part of both the relationship between social processes and spatial conceptions, forms and structures. Further, the neo-liberal form of the market economy characteristic of late-modernity can also be expected to develop its own sacred conditions that have little or nothing to do with religion or the sacred in the conventional understanding of the words.

The theoretical perspective represented by Kong and Kiong is situated within a theoretical development that has recently taken place in the understanding of place and space, particularly within human and cultural geography; this so-called spatial turn focuses on how socially constructed and negotiated cultures, identities and meanings both produce and are produced by place and space. Spatial turn implies a rejection of the idea that space would be a box without content; it fosters a re-conceptualization of space. Spatial turn emphasizes space as a tripartite synthesis of physical, mental and social spaces operating simultaneously (Lefebvre, 1991). An observance of this complexity is also important for the study of religion (see Knott, 2005b; Knott, 2005c; McAlister, 2005). Spatial turn brings about an understanding of place and space as, for instance, symbolically condensed – which resembles earlier studies of symbolism and religious space (see, e.g., Tillich, 1966; Dillistone, 1966).

A very common and visible part of the present spatial change in the religious landscape is the relocation of facilities for worship, prayer and contemplation. They are, for instance, found in airports and shopping malls, embedded in the specific symbolic world and design of these specific environments. Not only is the location altering, but also the character of new prayer rooms. They are often intended to be used by people of all faiths or by people of no faith at all; that is, they are designed in a more inclusive direction. These processes are affected by resacralization tendencies and late-modern individualism and they contribute to a need to re-evaluate the assumed distinction, and the complex relation, between the sacred and the profane.

Further, in addition to a change in the location and character of institutionalized sacred places '[t]he geographer of religion is therefore required to go beyond a focus on religious landscapes of churches, temples, mosques, synagogues and so forth, as has hitherto been the primary focus' (Kong, 2005, pp. 246–7). Graham Ward exemplifies the concrete nature of this:

> The staging of public spectacle (festivals for this and that, open-air concerts in central parks etc.), the exaltation of kitsch, the glorification of the superficial, the enormous investment in sports and leisure centres, the new commodification of the city's past (manufacturing a nostalgia that substitutes for continuity and tradition), the inflationary suggestions of the state-of-the-art future, its 'under-construction' technicolour present (China towns, heritage centres, gay villages, theme bars etc.) – these are the characteristics of the new city myth, the late-modern city-myth which has come to replace modernity's city-myth so powerfully evoked in Metropolis. (Ward, 2000, p. 59)

Hence, we have two intertwined processes at hand. We can recognize, first, that late-modern processes both relocate and reshape sacred spatiality (i.e., changes in location and character). Second, we can observe how religion is also located as part of the secular – for instance, the commodification of 'the postmodern city-myth'. That is, resacralization generates new semi-religious practices and symbolic spaces. Some scholars identify market religion as a core feature of contemporary Western urban space and within this perspective shopping malls are acknowledged as new sacred places because they embody the novel post-secular urban myth. In their view, shopping malls are cathedrals of commerce in a religion of the market (Pahl, 2003). This perspective needs some further clarification and discussion.

According to these scholars the shopping mall is the architectural ideal of our time; they are places where people can come together and spend their leisure time walking around, looking, feeling and dreaming and hence they form a centre. They are a place of both individuality and communality. In a more explicit manner, Jon Pahl states: 'Shopping malls, like other sacred places, use a common formula to produce enchanting effects among pilgrims' (Pahl, 2005). This is exemplified by the common design of shopping malls. The pedestrian streets with food courts, small shops, street cafes and evergreen plants are reminiscent of a genuine urban life that has disintegrated under the assault of growing mobility and urban development (Goss, 1993). This common design can be considered an imaginary construct reinforcing a sense of continuity and historicity. With the words of Hervieu-Léger (2000) we can say that the design reinforces a substitute for a chain of memory in contrast to the societal religious amnesia caused by secularization. From a more critical perspective scholars might underline that shopping malls are places where the social situation is one of disconnectedness between anonymous people constituted by an imaginary play (cf. Mäenpää, 2005).

The argument put forward by some scholars, that shopping malls represent the sacred spaces of our time, is of course also problematic. It is an interpretation that highlights a potential societal and social relevance of shopping malls, a possible relevance for identity construction, and finally how the individual and the social are located within a re-enchanted sense of imagined continuity. These kinds of interpretations are, however, dependent on a critical position that assumes a hegemonic role on behalf of the neo-liberal market economy. This perspective can be seen in line with Harvey's understanding that the neo-liberal economy produces a culture with particular values and practices and the idea of implicit religion. It is, however, important to note that the role of transcendence as a feature of the sacred is played down. This is a controversial issue and such explorations of the sacred have been questioned from a more conventional perspective (cf. Kamppinen, 2010). The perspective discussed here represents a position that does not explore religion within the market economy. It is a position that explores the market economy as a religion-like hegemonic structure in itself, i.e., a religion of the market economy.

From the perspective of our general aim to explore the assumptions that religion today is undergoing changes, we find it important to include the possibility that the market economy is a producer of new sacralized spaces, i.e., the shopping malls. At the bottom of our inquiry is therefore the tension between different possible forms of sacred places and pilgrims, the pilgrims of the shopping mall and the pilgrims of the chapel. Our interest is therefore to explore how people receive, communicate with and relate to the chapel and also the indirect negotiation within the tension of different sacred spaces. That is the core of our inquiry in this article; the concepts communication and reception are therefore important and will be covered later (see section entitled *Space as Communication – The Method of Studying Reception*).

The Big Apple and The Chapel of Silence – A Novel Public Space

The Chapel of Silence, located in the shopping mall Big Apple in Espoo, in the capital area of Finland, is a concrete result of a strategy developed by the local parish of the Evangelical Lutheran Church of Finland (i.e., Finland's majority church). The Finnish religious life of today exemplifies in an interesting manner both secularization, or at least the privatization of religion, and interest in spirituality, as well as respect for religious institutions. Finland is characterized by its relatively late, but deep and rapid, opening to the global economy, transnational cultural flows and international migration, but these influences created by the neo-liberal economic world order have been especially strong in Finland (see e.g., Heiskala and Luhtakallio, 2006; Rantala and Sulkunen, 2006). Furthermore, a large number of religious organizations operate in Finland (Ketola, 2008) and experiential dimensions of religiosity have become even more important. In addition to traditional forms of religion there are a variety of spiritually meaningful practices with more or less corresponding functions (Kääriäinen et. al., 2005).[2]

The strategy developed by the local parish expressed an effort to contest growing secularization, and accordingly the point of departure was that the Christian church 'competes with a widening range of leisure activities that is becoming more and more entertainment and consumption oriented, and segmented' (SKKIO, 2006). Based on the recognition of the changing spatial structure of late-modern urban living, the local parish decided to be a part of the people's new public place. The strategy is easy to understand taking into account that the Big Apple is estimated to attract about 100,000 visitors weekly. The priest working in the mall sheds light on this strategy:

> In my opinion the message that we have wanted to send out is that the parish is ready to meet and encounter people also in late-modern contexts. People do not necessarily need to go somewhere specific. A chapel is brought into people's everyday life, like to a mall.

A priest in the steering team of the project further noted:

> The chapel is a message of the fact that the parish is close to people, not only in celebrations, but also in everyday life. Priest is close to people when one needs a person who will walk beside you. One may meet the priest in a coffee house or while window shopping.

This particular chapel has been one of the very first shopping mall chapels in Finland – and has raised much public interest and debate. The chapel is part of a larger development project of the local parish in the Big Apple mall. This development project consists of the following elements: 1) The Chapel of Silence; 2) *Olohuone* ('Living Room', i.e., club premises); and 3) a priest working solely in the mall, both for the clients and workers/entrepreneurs (the first that was quoted above). According to the project plan, the project focuses on creating conditions and on experimenting via three elements: 1) meeting and encountering people (both the customers and the workers of the mall), 2) offering the mall a priest particularly for those working there, and 3) operation of the chapel and *Olohuone*. Out of these, it is the chapel that is our main interest in this article. The operation of the chapel is mainly administered by the mall priest and volunteer workers. The latter have duties similar to those of sextons: they open and close the chapel, prepare it for visitors and keep it in order, welcome visitors and make sure that people who visit the chapel uphold certain standards of behaviour. They are also available for people who need someone to talk to. They fulfil these duties in a small nicely decorated room with two chairs located next to the chapel.

However, in relation to the strategy of the local parish – to represent its presence in the public space – it is important to observe that the chapel is dependent on the general design of the mall. This is evident when we look at how it appears as part of the public space and design of the mall. It is common in religious architecture to emphasize the transition from the everyday order to the sacred, (see e.g., Davies, 1997; Crosbie, 2009) but the exterior walls of this particular chapel are not expressive of a distinct religious or sacred character. Rather, they repeat the general design of the shopping mall. The walls of glass reflect the surrounding commercial goods and brands, while symbols that would communicate to the visitor that he or she is entering a religious space are not very visible. Instead the chapel communicates through the media available in the mall – in the 'mall language' through a large digital commercial screen above the main crossroads in the middle of the shopping mall, as well as via the public, and continuous, voice-commercials of the mall. Here, among images and words of commodities and for sale items, visitors in the shopping mall are informed about the chapel. This exemplifies the observation made by Danièle Hervieu-Léger about the ambivalent character of the present religious landscape: '… traditional religions can hold their own by tentatively exploiting the symbolic resources at their disposal in order to reconstruct a continuing line of belief for which the common experience of individual believers provides no support' (Hervieu-Léger, 2000, p. 176).

The ambivalence addressed by Hervieu-Léger implies that the distinction between the sacred and the profane is indeed blurred. Besides the functional organization of the mall the inherent complexity of the Big Apple, as in many modern shopping malls, suggests a spiritual or existential character. The shopping mall is often referred to as a 'small city', a community of its own, in its media presentations and advertisements. On the one hand this captures the multiplicity of services and facilities provided; this also includes the particular design of the public space of the Big Apple with its large emphasis on communal space (i.e., in addition to various restaurants and coffee houses there is also a library, movie theatre and lots of open space to spend time together, or alone in the midst of all the other people). On the other hand, 'small city' as a metaphor also indicates how the shopping mall is looked upon as a miniature of urban society at large – something that may unite individuals. Such a miniature is not only of a representational nature but it resembles a city in how a city, according to Philip Sheldrake, '... represents and creates a climate of values that defines how humans understand themselves and gather together' (Sheldrake, 2001, p. 145). Further, the Big Apple follows the common forms and design of shopping malls that according to Jon Goss are an imaginary construct. The pedestrian streets with food courts, small shops, street cafes and evergreen plants are reminiscent of a genuine urban life that has disintegrated under the assault of growing mobility and urban development (Goss, 1993). The emphasis on communal space in the Big Apple is also referred to as the 'living room' of the people. This entails an understanding of the shopping mall as a social, cultural and ideological centre of our time. Finally, the name, the Big Apple, relates the place to both global heterogeneity (e.g., New York) and profound desires and temptations in a Biblical sense. Hence, all in all, what we can see here is an implicit claim in the self-presentation of the mall of being the new all-encompassing *communitas*.

Consequently, the shopping mall into which the chapel is discretely integrated is not a neutral place. Symbolic landscapes 'produce and sustain social meaning' (Cosgrove and Jackson, 1987, p. 96) and the mall can be seen as a complex spatial construct with significant social, cultural and existential trajectories. Taken together, the above-mentioned ways of depicting the shopping mall highlight Edward Soja's (Soja, 1989) critical understanding of how capitalist urban space 'reverberates complex meanings and symbols whose essence it helps construct' (Wilson, 1993, p. 75). In this sense, shopping malls can be regarded as embodiments of a new city myth. This myth involves, for instance, glorification of the superficial, emphasis on play, manufactured commodification of the past substituting continuity and tradition, and inflationary suggestions of the state-of-the-art future (Ward, 2000, p. 59). In other words, lightness, play and even superficiality are the core. Furthermore, in his article on 'market religion', David R. Loy makes the observation that it reduces our humanity, disintegrates our communities, and commodifies our world into a pool of exploitable resources for the satisfaction of our desires (Loy, 1997, p. 285). Does this leave any place for the sacred? Loy poignantly asks.

Space as Communication – The Method of Studying Reception

A central dimension of the perspectives referred to earlier is the idea that places take part in the construction of values, experiences and identities (e.g., Knott, 2009). In other words, at the core of the reflections is recognition of a communicative relationship between people and a particular context. There is a communication going on, be it intentional or unintentional. According to the Merriam-Webster dictionary, *communication* is an act or instance of transmitting, a process by which information is exchanged between individuals through a common system of symbols, signs or behaviour. According to the same source, *reception* then is the act or action or an instance of receiving – receiving, for instance, information in communication (i.e., reception as a concept is narrower than communication). Communication is a societal process working best when its targets are well-intentioned and also identified (Richardson, 1993; see also Korn et al., 2000).

As Stewart Hoover (2006) points out, the relationship between religion and communication, and the media, is timely. It is through the media that much of contemporary religion is known (see also Meyer and Moors, 2006; Hoover and Clark, 2002). Traditionally these relations have been analysed in institutional terms but today both media and the lives of individuals have changed. The power of legitimation is more and more in the hands of the seeker, and what has been missing from most discourse has been a focus on the reception and meaning making by audiences in these trends (Hoover, 2006, p. 2). This involves recognition of the role of the interpreting subject. What is communicated does not lead a life of its own, on the contrary it is reproduced in individual moments and each act of entry is thus creative and transformational (Adorno et al., 1976, p. 107; Habermas, 1996, p. 199; Bauman and May 2003, p. 178).

Our focus in this chapter is on communication, and particularly from the perspective of reception the church communicates towards individuals with its activities and the chapel at the mall. This implies a focus on what the communication evokes and how it is interpreted: what do people see, hear and experience? Reception is also always about experiencing and making value statements. The perspective of this chapter is exactly on the individual and on reception; we study reception (that is, experiences and views) of a space as communication. We pose the question about what is received by people. However, as noted earlier, *communication* is also an act or instance transmitting. Therefore, we cannot neglect the meanings embedded in signs, images and spatial constructs, and what they communicate. A discussion about this side is necessary in order to understand and shed light on the reception.

Our core aim in studying communication has thus been the reception of the mall chapel: how is the chapel appreciated and experienced by individuals? The aim has been to study how well people know the activities of the church at the mall and what kind of experiences they have of them. Furthermore, what values do these activities (in peoples' views) represent of the church? Has the presence of the church at the mall affected people's images of the church? Finally, our aim has been to investigate if and how the presence of the church at the mall transforms itself into a sacred place, particularly from the perspective of the chapel volunteers.

With the help of several empirical methods and data, both qualitative and quantitative, we will propose a more general, as well as deeper, understanding of the complex processes addressed earlier. From such mix-methods analytical perspective we will shed light on how the sacred dimension is negotiated in post-secular urban settings. In our study, the 'presumed users' of the chapel – the agents of reception (the individuals at the mall as recipients of the church mall activities) – refers to the clients of the mall, the paid workers and entrepreneurs there, the visitors to the chapel, and the visitors to the *Olohuone* club premises. Our data was collected in two waves, which were analysed both independently from each other and in relation to each other. Nynäs conducted participant observation at the mall, particularly with the mall volunteers.[3] Pessi then collected four sets of data:[4] 1) the mall customers' interviews (N = 277),[5] 2) the workers' and entrepreneurs' interviews (N = 42), 3) *Olohuone's* visitors' interviews (N = 63), and 4) interviews of the visitors to the chapel (N = 33). Our various data reveal different dimensions of the reception; from the interviews we have gained experiences, views, values and images related to the chapel as religious communication, and through participant observation profound interpretative work of the people in relation to the chapel was revealed.

Findings

In the following we will present the results from our study, both the interviews and the participant observation. We will first look at the analyses based on the interview and survey materials, then at the analyses from the participant observation.

Well Known, Well Received

As noted earlier, we analysed our data from the perspective of communication: presence and activities of the church at the mall are communication that is received, or not, by individuals. Communication is a process in which we create and maintain relations, connections via meanings (e.g., Fore 1987, p. 231) and the church exactly aimed to create relations, connections via its mall activities. Thus, Pessi analysed the interview and survey materials of individuals' views and experiences of the activities of the church at the mall as a *message* from the church to individuals (in detail, and in relation to the metatheoretical communication model by Nastasia and Rakow (2005), see Pessi (2011)). Have the activities of the church at the mall (i.e., the *message*) reached people? Have they promoted connection and relationship (i.e., the core of *communication*) between individuals and the church? That is, has communication succeeded?

The interviews revealed that a majority of the customers in the mall had heard about the activities of the church at the mall: two thirds had heard, and a third had not. Even among those younger than 25 years of age, more than half of the respondents were familiar with the activities; today, this is the group that is the hardest for the church to reach, to maintain communication with.

But what is the message received here? From those who were familiar with the church's activities at the mall, we asked what they knew about the activities. It was particularly the chapel, the sacred space, that was strongly emphasized in the replies. Interestingly, the customers of the mall were altogether even more familiar with the chapel than with the activities of the parish at the mall in general. A clear majority (76 per cent) were familiar with the chapel, and this was the case among the younger ones as well. Furthermore, the entrepreneurs and workers of the mall were even more familiar with the chapel than customers (86 per cent had heard or knew of the chapel). The clear majority (77 per cent) of the respondents who were familiar with the chapel also knew its location, and an interesting age difference appeared: the very youngest and the oldest knew the location best. Quite many indeed (40 per cent) of those customers who were familiar with the chapel had also visited it, the older ones much more often than others.

The analysis thus indicates that the basic message of the presence of the church at the mall has been well communicated, received. Many have also participated in the activities by actually visiting the mall. Still, most of these visitors (two out of three) visit the chapel only occasionally, and just a small group (one fifth) regularly (every other week or more often). Even if the chapel is not visited very often, its images are still very favourable in communication; the impressions of the chapel and the meanings ascribed to it were both deeply personal and positive, as can be seen in the following sections. The chapel makes a difference for the visitors. In this, the communication by the church has been well received.

Image via Communication? A Place for Meeting and Caring, Silence and Peace

But what really are the images of the church promoted by the mall activities? What is the message people receive here? We asked our respondents 'What comes spontaneously into your mind when you hear the expression "Parish at the shopping mall"?' No answer options were given. These spontaneous images were mostly very positive, for example 'The church comes close to people as it should'. Also ease of access was underscored; for instance, 'Easy access when taking care of other matters in the mall'. In a few spontaneous answers the chapel was even seen as an alternative to the traditional church mass and church buildings. Interestingly, to many interviewees – both to customers as well as entrepreneurs and workers – it was particularly the chapel that came into mind first in these spontaneous images of the parish. A common view, especially among younger respondents, was also: 'It is good that the chapel exists even if one does not need it for the time being'.

What concepts, from general images to more exact values, do individuals see the church communicating here? We presented the interviewees with a short list of concepts from which they should choose three concepts that in their view represent the parish working at the mall. Two concepts clearly emerged over others, as Table 9.1 indicates.

Table 9.1 A parish at the mall - customer views concerning values

	What values does a parish working at the mall represent to you?
Meeting/encountering	62%
Caring	58%
Silence	47%
Peace	45%
Communality	39%
Spirituality	24%
Tradition	15%
Commerciality	6%
Boredom	2%
Conservatism	2%
	(N = 277)

As the findings indicate, the chapel represents – in the communication from the church to individuals – a message of meeting, care and silence. This is the message received. However, there were certain relevant differences corresponding with age and gender. People under the age of 25 were over-represented in the group who chose encountering and communality; this result is indeed quite fascinating in the midst of the late-modern individualistic culture, especially in light of the difficulties the church has had in reaching the younger generation.[6] As the message in this communication is exactly from the church, it is rather striking that the value of spirituality is so low in the findings; only people over 70 years of age consider the parish activities at the mall to particularly represent traditions and spirituality. Furthermore, for women the parish at the mall tends to represent caring while men view and experience it as an example of tradition and spirituality. Additionally, for the visitors to the chapel the message seems to especially concern silence, and they also consider the activities to strongly represent caring, slowness and encountering. For the workers and entrepreneurs then, the parish at the mall represents caring – which is fascinating in the midst of the commercial values of the mall. All this together exemplifies that the chapel indeed represents a variety of messages for different people; the communication is manifold.

Those who had visited the chapel were additionally asked, with an open question, for their personal image and impression of the chapel. Surprisingly, in nearly every answer one exact word was found: peaceful.[7] For the visitors the peacefulness often represented a contrasting space in comparison with 'the rush of business' or 'the hectic, rushed place' of the mall. Peacefulness could also mean a liberating space without stressing demands and expectations, a place where 'one can just sit in peace' or 'just be quiet', to quote our data. Furthermore, the chapel also offered a connection to a parish, that is a 'home church', and hence a place of worship or 'possibilities to volunteer in a way that does not stress too much'. The meanings also involved an important dimension of comfort and consolidation; 'My sorrow, my tears unfold here'; 'One can go there if feeling down'. Finally, the chapel also represented a sense of presence, a symbol of how 'God is present in this world', even in a commercial mall.

The chapel visitors were also asked how they would develop the church's activities at the mall. The only matter they addressed concerned concrete activities: discussion groups, Bible groups, small masses and concerts. Hence, even if the visitors generally emphasized the chapel as a space of silence, the most active ones had other hopes too.

All in all, the impressions and experiences of the chapel were highly positive. By offering this space, the church has clearly established a connection with a clear need for peace and quiet.

An Important, Highly Valued Presence

But is this communication between the church and individuals at the mall needed? Our interviewees were asked: 'How necessary, in your opinion, is it that the church works and is present here at the mall?' Slightly more than half of the respondents (52 per cent) consider the activities as being at least 'somewhat necessary', and one fifth (17 per cent) very necessary or indispensible. Women and the elderly find the activities more important, and the visitors to the chapel even more so: the vast majority (70 per cent) of the interviewees consider the activities very necessary. Those who are members of the church consider the activities more important. However, as many as 39 per cent of the non-church members among our interviewees also regard the activities to be very or somewhat necessary – this is surprising. When we asked people to choose between: 'It is important that the church is present and is seen in the mall' versus 'It is wrong to use the tax money of the church for this kind of activities', an overwhelming majority (92 per cent) of all respondents chose the former.

Has the communication further power? We inquired into the personal image of the entire church from our respondents, as well as their estimates whether the church activities at the mall had affected this image. Overall, the image of the church is considered positive (this resonates with other studies, e.g., Pessi (2008)), and the majority (55 per cent) had experienced no change in the image. However, many (44 per cent) consider that the activities at the mall have indeed positively affected their image of the church. This is quite a high figure in relation to the fact that the images of the church had already been so favourable.

Furthermore, the visitors to the chapel surprised us again: a very clear majority (88 per cent) considers the activities as having altered their activities, of having altered their image of the church into a more positive perspective – and they had already had a rather positive image as they had entered the chapel.

Towards a Sacred Place?

Our findings presented so far from Pessi's empirical data (see also Pessi, 2011) are surprising in that they are overwhelmingly positive – and that the positive views of the chapel involve particular meanings, such as encountering, caring, peace, communality. This is the overall message our respondents consider the church sending, via its mall activities. The analysis from Nynäs's (Nynäs 2008; 2009) participant observation and the time spent with the church's volunteers correspond with these results. This correspondence indicates that the separate elements (such as values, meanings, impressions and opinions) in the interviews should be regarded as parts of a relevant and complex meaning-creating process.

Generally, four significant dimensions can be discerned from the volunteers' experience of the chapel. These are, of course, strongly interconnected and interdependent, but it is relevant to address them separately in order to shed light on important elements in the reception process. First, the volunteers regarded the chapel as a symbol of continuity and historicity; they thought of the chapel in terms of a link to a shared religious community, as in the interview data. The chapel was considered a sign of how the church remains present in a rapidly changing society. Second, the volunteers included in their interpretations a significant dose of emotional attitudes towards the chapel, such as respect and awe, but sometimes also darker feelings, such as melancholy and sorrow. This reinforced the personal significance and engagement, like the engagement with a home or any other part of people's individual geography.

In addition to a particular way of thinking and feeling the place, the volunteers' interpretation of the chapel involved a third dimension that could be addressed as a sense of alterity or otherness. The chapel was a place in strong contrast to the surrounding society – and this contrast further embodied a sense of presence. This is very much in line with the interview findings presented earlier where the core message from the interviewees seems to be that the church has to both be in the midst of everyday life but at the same time bring a deeper dimension of caring and peace into it. The majority of the volunteers explicitly referred to the silence or peacefulness of the chapel as a means to emphasize the strong difference between the chapel and its surrounding context. Still, such impressions did not mean only emptiness or solitude. Quite the contrary, this dimension also embodied a possibility to encounter and relate to the Other and a sense of profound meaning. Hence, we have here a significant connotation to an experience of transcendence, the wholly other. Finally, a fourth dimension shared by the volunteers was the tendency of ritualization of their engagement. They made it a special day when it was their turn to volunteer, they strived to volunteer on particular days of their own, and they had also developed individual, unique habits concerning how they spent the time and arranged the place. The volunteers indeed seemed very committed to the chapel – and for some it was their personal relation to the parish and to the wider church.

However, within this general interpretative pattern, different individuals engaged in the chapel in very different ways; the four dimensions were given an individual shape. In particular, their way of thinking about society and the chapel differed, and together with this their emotional engagement and their habits and ways of arranging the place differed as well. From listening to what they said and from observing how they arranged the room and the chapel, it was evident that they could have very different views of who the visitors are and why they visit the chapel. How did they then understand their own roles as volunteers – for whom and why were they there? The impressions and views were of course very individual and everybody had their own narrative, but some general themes or categories – patterns of interpretation – can be recognized. First, some of the volunteers had a stronger tendency to regard the chapel mainly as a *gatekeeper* of society and themselves as guards. This implied a readiness to emphasize the chapel as a vehicle of morality, order and boundaries in society. The chapel formed a link between a disoriented society and the church. This resonates to the notion above and in the interview findings: the church should bring something else, other values into the mall. Secondly, other volunteers considered the chapel rather marginalized in its present location; in their view it should be placed – both physically and mentally – more into the centre of the mall. They emphasized that the chapel should be made available to all people who needed comforting in the midst of our society of suffering. They come close to the strong message of care in the interviews. This group did view the chapel as a means of reinforcing the boundaries of society – the church should be in the middle, in the centre of society and the chapel a place of reconciliation, essentially being the heart of society. They displayed an effort to challenge and transgress societal barriers.

The final group differs from the other two in its emphasis on the withdrawnness and retreat – the chapel as a refuge from society. These volunteers did not primarily think of their duty as guards of the chapel like people in the first group, neither did they open the door and welcome everybody in need like the volunteers of the second group. They experienced their time in the chapel rather as time for personal prayer and meditation. This is also the core in what they wished the chapel to offer for other individuals. All in all, the different views seemed to correspond with their personal narratives and identities.

From both participant observation and interviews we can see that particular elements are involved in the reception of the chapel: it is a place that reinforces continuity, meaning and transcendence in society, and all this is further set apart as extraordinary through ritualizing tendencies. It represents both being at the *centre* and being something *else* in relation to the wider society. The act of interpreting the chapel in a particular direction is intertwined with the interpretation of society at large. Talking and thinking about the chapel is also talking and thinking about society. Thus, in this study, we are confronted with different but strongly interdependent views of both the chapel and the surrounding society. However, these common dimensions of interpretation gain particular patterns in the individual lives of different people.

Concluding Discussion

Our findings indicate that the church has managed to communicate with people and to get its message through with its activities at the mall. It has managed to connect. Its activities at the mall are well known and positively received, and in the case of the chapel even more so. The image and the message received seem to be one of encountering, caring and peace. From the perspective of reception, a very similar image indeed arises from both the analysis of interview and survey material and observation; three matters in particular seem to be the core of the interpreted message. The first is *presence*: it is considered very favourable that the church has chosen to search for a place in the midst of people's everyday life. Another element that people experience is an act of *caring*, in the midst of the consumerism of the mall. Finally, the chapel is particularly seen to bring elements of *peace* and (the present global trend of) slowness, that is, slow culture to the mall. These three are all elements that contrast the other mall context and its values. Furthermore, these elements are clearly linked to each other, and they are of general and existential relevance to individuals. It is noteworthy that the chapel, in particular, plays a central role in this entire threefold message. Particularly the chapel clearly functions as a 'business card' for the entire parish, and even the wider church, at the mall: it is very well known and respected, and the impressions and meanings of it are highly positive. All in all, in relation to the core aim of the parish ('to meet and encounter people'), the mall project has been successful; their message has been communicated and received.

From a critical point of view, however, one could say that these impressions may come quite easily to people when asked about church and religion. The Church of Finland is still a highly trusted and respected institution even if Finns are passive as its members. Our core findings resonate to the characteristics that we learn from our culture, and can repeat on demand. They are also common existential concerns – such as longing for care. However, two things need to be stated in contrast to this critical point of view. First, it should be acknowledged that even though the impressions may come quite easy to people and also represent basic existential values, it is noteworthy that they are directed towards the church and that the church is not excluded from this in favour of other possible alternatives. Secondly, the results surely also reflect something of the more profound inner meanings of individuals; this can be detected particularly from the participant observation of our study. The chapel, and its reception, evokes a meaning-creating process which entails complex interpretations and practices of a profound symbolic relevance in addition to values and representations. Central elements of this meaning-creating process seem to be about the making of a sacred place. All in all, the reception processes reinforce time, meaning and transcendence in society, and sets the place apart from the surrounding society through ritualizing tendencies. The chapel as such – as a conventional sacred place – seems to be a catalyst for this meaning-creating process.

The nature of the meaning-creating process involved in the reception of the chapel constitutes a relevant finding particularly in light of the surrounding context of place (mall) and time (late-modernity). The assumption that secularization and late-modernity have liberated a (possible) powerful desire for the spiritual and authentic experience of the Other, also involves an assumption that this desire for spiritual experience opens up for transformations of the socio-cultural forms of the sacred. As discussed earlier in this article, the specific condensed symbolic and the mythical character of shopping malls can be argued to form a competing semi-sacred spatiality that functions as a substitute in contrast to the assumed alienations of late-modernity and seek to restore identities and a sense of belonging in various ways. Still, this spatiality involves a disorienting character (see Pahl, 2005). This disorienting character is exemplified by how shopping malls are constituted by a symbolic order of 'authentic reproductions' or 'live recordings', which, because of the inherent contradiction and impossibility of desire, lends it increasing exigency and intensity (Goss, 2005, p. 70). 'The consumer is a person on the move and bound to remain so', writes Bauman (Bauman, 1998, p. 85). From the background of our results, however, we do not dismiss the relevance of this critical perspective and the possibility and relevance of exploring the shopping mall in terms of a sacred space, but we would like to underline that our results indicate that the chapel offers possibilities of resistance against this context. The presence of the chapel allows people to make use of it in order to make important distinctions and establish a distance to a society they, as a contrast to their expectations, perceive of in terms of disconnectedness and inauthenticity. In order to better understand this, we will address the centrality of the spatial turn in our analysis as follows.

It is obvious that the reception of the chapel is not only a matter of detecting the illustrative and representative side of the chapel. On the contrary, the chapel is a place that elicits an emotional response, and invites relationships (Seasoltz, 2005, p. 65). This means that the reception of the chapel is of an individual and personal character that connects to personal narratives and that it is highly dependent in the imaginary and interpretative work of the individual. Through the relationship meanings develop and the space gains relevance for the development of identities (Grünberg and Körs, 2009, p. 91). From our findings we can see how the engagement involved fundamentally different understandings of the role of the chapel: on the one hand to be in the middle of the society, on the other hand to bring Otherness and deeper dimensions to it. In addition, this general pattern developed in three different ways and the chapel could be experienced in different ways with different functions in relationship to the wider society; as a gatekeeper, as a hearth of society or as a place of safety. These three patterns of interpretation involve different sets of cognitions, perceptions, emotions, practices and ways of relating; that is, the making of a sacred place gains very personal forms and an individual element plays a central role in this part of the reception. This highly individual element in the interpretation process can be considered in psychological terms because it corresponds with different self–other relations and internalized attachment patterns (see Nynäs, 2008).

However, the fact that we underline an individual element of psychological nature in the reception of the chapel does not mean that we argue that the reception of the chapel and the making of a sacred place is a matter of entirely interior, nor completely individualistic, subjective mental states that are externalized or projected onto the chapel. On the contrary, in line with what is emphasized in the spatial turn we would like to underline that this individual element is not a separate process apart from social and societal – in some cases even communal – processes and practices. The emotional dimension and the subjectivities involved in forming an emotional geography should be seen as an essential part of and even form of sociospatial mediation and articulation (see Bondi et al., 2005, pp. 1–3).

The engagement that happens through the interpretations embedded in the reception involves negotiation of fundamental societal boundaries. The making of a sacred place is not only a matter of mapping reality as constituted by a distinction between the sacred and the profane. This process seems to offer the possibility for subtle but profound interpretations that strive at transforming the boundaries of society at large. This is in accordance with the idea that we live in a 'suggested society' and societies are only half-awake (Thrift, 2009, p. 91, referring to Wegner, 2002, p. 314). In our particular case we argue that the chapel plays a central role in this process of awakening. The chapel seems to function as a place through which this negotiation can take place. The personal engagement and involvement in this process is a prerequisite for this.

In conclusion, the urban religious landscape of today is of a very multifaceted character and it is relevant to examine the blurred boundaries between the sacred and the profane, and in particular the role of relocated facilities for worship and their meanings to individuals. Our research has exemplified how late-modernity has reshaped – and particularly not only marginalized but also brought more into the public life – religiosity in an urban landscape. Both the location and the design of the chapel, as well as its reception, exemplify this in several different ways. Furthermore, in this study, we have placed more emphasis on, and integrated further, a more subjective dimension of this changing religious landscape. Our main focus concerned the reception of the chapel: how is the chapel experienced by its presumed users in this particular context? From this perspective we can – again in contrast to the idea of marginalization of religion – conclude that the chapel was well known, highly appreciated and ascribed particular meanings such as presence, caring and peace. These values and meanings might be embedded in the capacity of the chapel to evoke profound processes, such as a transformative relation between place and space on the one hand, and both social and personal identities on the other. This is exemplified by how the chapel is clearly associated with a possibility or a hope of bringing something of value that is lacking in society, symbolized above by order, heart and shelter.

Further, we would like to underline that the experiences and views of individuals of the church's mall activities exemplify the current transformation of religious space towards individuality, holistic and eclectic spirituality and flexibility, but at the same time the individuals seem to receive exactly the message that the parish wants to send. For some individuals the mall chapel is even the very link to the parish community and membership (e.g., the volunteers of the chapel). According to our findings elements of individuality and of community as well as traditional and late-modern values may be more deeply intertwined than easily realized in late-modernity literature of space, communications and culture. However, despite the complexity involved in the making of a sacred place it seems to be a significant task both for individuals and societies.

Notes

[1] After this, in this chapter, referred to as 'the chapel'.
[2] Recent studies on religion in Finland indicate that the frequency of prayer has increased (43 per cent prayed at least a few times a week in 2003, 39 per cent in 1991, and 34 per cent in 1982; Kääriäinen et al., 2005, p. 122). While a third of all Finns expressed confidence in the church in 1990, no fewer than almost two thirds (57 per cent) did so in 2000 (Salonen et al., 2001), and as many as of 77 per cent of Finns view the church positively (*Gallup Ecclesiastica*, 2003). Today the overall Finnish religious environment is still intriguingly homogenous: 81.7 per cent belonged to the Lutheran church in 2008.
[3] The observation was conducted in March to April 2008, and included various elements: photographs of the mall and the chapel, observations of people coming and going in the chapel, and in particular time spent with the church's volunteers who function as wardens in the chapel. This participant observation provided us with additional observations of slightly different – and perhaps more spontaneous – responses. Thus, we are also able to focus on questions, such as how the volunteers presented the chapel and described it. How did they perceive of its use and function in the mall? How did they themselves act in and relate to the chapel? The observation data includes the volunteers' personal experiences and opinions about the chapel and the surroundings. Collection of this data involved interest in volunteers' thoughts about the chapel's use and its relevance for visi-

tors, but also observations about their way of acting in their work, their practice, and how they arranged the place. Hence, this thematic analysis of the volunteers' interpretive processes provides an in depth perspective on the reception of the chapel, even though it should be taken into account that this is a different – and more engaged – population from that of the interviews. The participant observation has been discussed in depth elsewhere (see Nynäs, 2008, 2009).

[4] All this data was collected in October to November 2008, together with student assistants (it was a part of their methodology studies). A clear majority of these interviews, those with the customers (N = 277), were conducted face-to-face, while the others were conducted on paper (including both numerical and open-ended questions, as did the face-to-face interviews too). The interview data was subjected to both descriptive quantitative analysis as well as data-determined qualitative thematic analysis.

[5] Women dominate this particular material (62 per cent versus 38 per cent), different ages are represented evenly. This domination of women actually represents the gender balance of the customers of the mall very accurately. The majority of the interviewed customers (82 per cent) belong to the Evangelical church of Finland which also represents the average of Finns well.

[6] The most common concept among people between 25–50 years of age was peace and caring, while among people 50–70 years of age it was lowness and caring, and among people over 70 years of age traditions and spirituality.

[7] It must be noted here that the name of the chapel includes the word Silence (*The Chapel of Silence*) and its visitors, particularly those who know the chapel closely, may have this in mind while pondering their impressions. However, among the wider audience, the exact name of the chapel is not necessarily known.

Bibliography

Adorno, T. W., Albert, H., Dahnerdorf, R., Habermas, J., Pilot, H. and Popper, K. R. (1976), 'On the logic of social sciences', in *The Positivist Dispute in German Sociology*. New York: Harper and Row.

Barbato, M. and Kratochwil, F. (2008), *Habermas's Notion of a Post-secular Society. A Perspective from International Relations*. EUI Working Papers, MWP 2008/25. http://hdl.handle.net/1814/9011.

Bauman, Z. (1998), *Globalization: The Human Consequences*. New York: Columbia University Press.

Bauman, Z. and May, T. (2003), *Thinking Sociologically*. Oxford: Blackwell Publishing.

Berger, P. L. (1999), 'The Desecularization of the World. A Global Overview', in Berger, P. L. (ed.), *The Desecularization of the World*. Washington: Eerdmans.

Bondi, L., Davidson, J. and Smith, M. (2005), 'Introduction: Geography's Emotional Turn', in Davidson, J., Bondi, L. and Smith, M. (eds), *Emotional Geographies*. Aldershot: Ashgate.

Casanova, J. (1994), *Public Religions in the Modern World*. Chicago: University of Chicago Press.

Cosgrove, D. and Jackson, P. (1987), 'New Directions in Cultural Geography'. *Area*, 19(2), 95–101.
Crosbie, M. J. (2009), 'Trends in Contemporary Sacred Architecture.' in Bergmann, S. (ed.), *Theology in Built Environments*. London: Transaction.
Davies, D. (1997), 'Introduction: Raising the Issues.' in Holm, J. and Bowker, J. (eds), *Sacred Place*. London: Pinter.
Dillistone, F. W. (1966), 'The Function of Symbols in Religious Experience', in Dillistone, F.W. (ed.), *Myth and Symbol*. London: S.P.C.K.
Durkheim, É. (1965/1912), *The Elementary Forms of the Religious Life*. New York: The Free Press.
Eliade, M. (1957), *The Sacred and the Profane*. San Diego, New York and London: Harcourt Brace Jovanovich, 1959 edition.
Fore, W. F. (1987), 'A Theology of Communication'. *Religious Education* 82(2), 231–46.
Frisk, L. (2009), 'Globalization: A Key Factor in Contemporary Religious Change'. *Journal of Alternative Spiritualities and New Age Studies*, 5. http://www.asanas.org.uk/journal.htm. (7 January 2011).
Gallup Ecclesiastica, data on Finns 2003. Tampere: The Research Institute of the Evangelical Lutheran Church of Finland.
Gilliat-Ray, S. (2005), ' "Sacralising" Sacred Space in Public Institutions: A Case Study of the Prayer Space in the Millennium Dome'. *Journal of Contemporary Religion*, 20(3), 357–72.
Goss, J. (1993). 'The "Magic of the Mall": An Analysis of Form, Function, and Meaning in the Contemporary Retail Built Environment'. *Annals of the Association of American Geographers*, 83(1), 18–47.
—. (2005), 'Souvenir and Sacrifice in Tourist Consumption.' in Cartier, C. and Lew, A. A. (eds), *Seductions of Place. Geographical Perspectives on Globalization and Touristed Landscapes*. New York: Routledge.
Grünberg, W. and Körs, A. (2009), ' "Symbolkirchen" as Bridges or Boundary Stones in a Merging Europe?', in Bergmann, S. (ed.), *Theology in Built Environments*. London: Transaction.
Habermas, J. (1996), *Moral Consciousness and Communicative Action*. Cambridge: The MIT Press.
Hadden, J. K. (1987), 'Towards Desacralizing Secularization Theory'. *Social Force*, 65, 587–611.
Harvey, D. (2005), *A Brief History of Neoliberalism*. New York: Oxford University Press.
Heiskala, R. and Luhtakallio, E. (2006), *Uusi jako: Miten Suomesta tuli kilpailukykyyhteiskunta?*. Helsinki: Gaudeamus.
Hervieu-Léger, D. (2000), *Religion as a Chain of Memory*. Cambridge: Polity Press.
Hoover, S. M. (2006), *Religion in the Media Age*. London: Routledge.
Hoover, S. M. and Clark Schofield, L. (2002), *Practicing Religion in the Age of the Media. Explorations in Media, Religion, and Culture*. New York: Columbia University Press.
James, W. (1902), *The Varieties of Religious Experience: A Study in Human Nature*. New York: University Books (1963 edition).
Kääriäinen, K., Niemelä, K. and Ketola, K. (2005), *Religion in Finland. Decline, Change and Transformation of Finnish Religiosity*. Tampere: The Research Institute of the Evangelical Lutheran Church of Finland.

Kamppinen, M. (2010), *Intentional Systems Theory as a Conceptual Framework for Religious Studies. A Scientific Method for Studying Beliefs*. London: The Edwin Meller Press.

Ketola, K. (2008), *Uskonnot Suomessa. Käsikirja uskontoihin ja uskonnollistaustaisiin liikkeisiin*. Tampere: Kirkon tutkimuskeskuksen julkaisuja 102.

Knott, K. (2005a), 'Space'. *Revista de Estudos da Religião*, 4, 108–14.

—. (2005b), *The Location of Religion: A Spatial Analysis*. London and Oakville, CA: Equinox.

—. (2005c), 'Spatial Theory and Method for the Study of Religion'. *Temenos*, 41(2), 153–84.

—. (2009), 'From Locality to Location and Back Again: A Spatial Journey in the Study of Religion'. *Religion*, 39, 154–60.

Kong, L. (2005), 'Religious Processions: Urban Politics and Poetics'. *Temenos*, 41(2), 225–49.

Kong, L. and Kiong, T. (2000), 'Religion and Modernity: Ritual Transformations and the Reconstruction of Space and Time'. *Social and Cultural Geography*, 1(1), 29–44.

Korn C., Morreale, S. and Boileau D. M. (2000), 'Defining the Field: Revisiting the AACA 1995 Definition of Communication Studies'. *Journal of the Association for Communication Administration*, 29(1), 40–52.

Lefebvre, H. (1991), *The Production of Space*. Cambridge, MA: Blackwell.

Loy, D. R. (1997), 'The Religion of the Market'. *Journal of the American Academy of Religion*, 65(2), 275–90.

Mäenpää, P. (2005), *Narkissos kaupungissa: tutkimus kuluttajakaupunkilaisesta ja julkisesta tilasta*. Helsinki: Tammi.

McAlister, E. (2005), 'Globalization and the Religious Production of Space'. *Journal for the Scientific Study of Religion*, 44(3), 249–55.

Meyer, B. and Moors, A. (2006), *Religion, Media, and the Public Sphere*. Bloomington: Indiana University Press.

Motak, D. (2009), 'Postmodern Spirituality and the Culture of Individualism', in Ahlbäck, T. (ed.), *Postmodern Spirituality*. Åbo: The Donner Institute for Research in Religious and Cultural History.

Nastasia, D. and Rakow, L. (2005), 'What is Communication? Unsettling A Priori and A Posteriori Approaches'. *The International Communication Association, Philosophy of Communication Division*, 1 November 2005. http://www.allacademic.com//meta/p_mla_apa_research_citation/0/9/3/2/6/pages93260/p93260-1.php. (5 August 2010).

Nynäs, P. (2008), 'Ett kapell – tre rum: ett integrerat rollteoretiskt perspektiv på tolkning och meningsskapande kring ett modernt kapell'. *Teologisk Tidskrift*, 113(4), 314–32.

—. (2009), 'Spatiality, Practice and Meaning', in Bergmann, S. (ed.), *Theology in Built Environments*. London: Transaction.

Otto, R. (1950), *The Idea of the Holy* (2nd ed.), (transl. by J.W. Harvey). London: Oxford University Press.

Pahl, J. (2003), *Shopping Malls and Other Sacred Spaces: Putting God in Place*. Grand Rapids, MI: Brazos Press.

—. (2005), 'The Desire to Acquire: Imaging the Sacred at Shopping Malls'. (Presentation at the Conference Mimetic Theory and the Imitation of the Divine, Koblenz-Schoenstatt, Germany, 6 July 2010). http://www.cla.purdue.edu/academic/engl/conferences/covar/Program/pahl.pdf. (8 May 2007).
Pessi, A. B. (2008), 'Religion and Social Problems: Individual and Institutional Responses', in Clarke, P. (ed.), *The Oxford Handbook of the Sociology of Religion*. New York; Oxford: Oxford University Press. 2008.
—. (2011), ' "The Parish must be there where people are" – A Study of Parish Mall Activities as Communication'. *Teologinen Aikakauskirja* (under review).
Rantala, K. and Sulkunen, P. (2006), *Projektiyhteiskunnan kääntöpuolia*, Helsinki: Gaudeamus.
Richardson, J. (1993), 'Communication, a Critical Pathway to Development'. *Leonardo*, 26(4), 347–51.
Salonen, K., Kääriäinen, K. and Niemelä, K. (2001), *The Church at the Turn of the Millennium*. Tampere: The Research Institute of the Evangelical Lutheran Church of Finland.
Seasoltz, K. R. (2005), *A Sense of the Sacred: Theological Foundations of Christian Architecture and Art*. London: Continuum.
Sheldrake, P. (2001), *Spaces for the Sacred*. London: SCM.
SKKIO (2006), 'Seurakuntatyön kehittämisprojekti kauppakeskus Iso Omenassa 2005–2008.' Hyväksytty Olarin seurakunnan seurakuntaneuvostossa 7.6.2005, päivitetty 6.6.2006. ['The parish development project in the shopping mall "The Big Apple" 7.6.2005/6.6.2006'].
Smith, J. Z. (1987), *To Take Place: Toward a Theory of Ritual*. Chicago: Chicago University Press.
Soja, E. (1989). *Postmodern Geographies: The Reassertation of Space in Critical Social Theory*. London: Verso Press.
Stark, R. and Bainbridge, W. S. (1985), *The Future of Religion: Secularization, Revival and Cult Formation*. Berkeley: University of California Press.
Taylor, C. (2007), *A Secular Age*. Cambridge, MA: The Belknap Press of Harvard UP.
Thrift, N. (2009), 'Understanding the Affective Spaces of Political Performance', in Smith, M., Davidson, J., Cameron, L. and Bondi, L. (eds), *Emotion, Place and Culture*. Aldershot: Ashgate.
Tillich, P. (1966), 'The Religious Symbol', in Dillistone, F. W. (eds), *Myth and Symbol*. London: S.P.C.K.
Ward, G. (2000), *Cities of God*. London: Routledge.
Wegner, W. (2002), *The Illusion of Conscious Will*. Cambridge, Mass.: MIT Press.
Wilson, D. (1993), 'Connecting Social Process and Space in the Geography of Religion.' *Area*, 25(1), 75–6.
Woodhead, L. and Heelas, P. (2000), *Religion in Modern Times. An Interpretative Anthology*. Oxford: Blackwell Publishing.
Yeung, A. B. (2006a), Beckman N. E. and Pettersson P. (co-editors) *Churches in Europe as Agents of Welfare – Sweden, Norway and Finland*. Volume 1/2. Working Paper 2:1 from the project WREP. Uppsala: DVI.
—. (2006b), *Churches in Europe as Agents of Welfare – England, Germany, France, Italy and Greece*. Volume 1/2. Working Paper 2:2 from the project WREP. Uppsala: DVI.

Part Four

Politics of the Sacred in Contemporary Urban Spaces

Chapter 10

Kinshasa and its (Un)Certainties: The Polis and the Sacred

Filip De Boeck

In Kinshasa, the capital of the Democratic Republic of Congo (D.R.C.), one of Africa's most vibrant urban environments, the two – intertwined – notions of the *polis* and of the *sacred* do not offer a lot of steady ground to sustain a straightforward understanding of what urban reality is about in this Central-African context. In the Congolese setting, it is not so clear what the notion of the polis, in its double meaning of urban community and of political community, might mean, nor is it clear to what extent Kinshasa has ever belonged to its inhabitants.

The meaning of what is sacred is no longer fixed either. Kinshasa is caught between an autochthonous, ancestral past marked by lots of (post)colonial ruptures and breaches that have often made this past inaccessible to many urban dwellers, and a model of (colonialist) modernity that for many has become as difficult to grasp, and seems to be located in a distant future that cannot easily be accessed or realized. Today, the idea of an insertion into global modernity seems to be promoted most strongly, albeit in sometimes rather peculiar ways, in the enchanting spaces of Neo-Pentecostalism. It is in these new religious movements that the terms of the polis and the sacred have become locked together today. This chapter will discuss the specific ways in which these linkages have come about, as well as the contradictions, paradoxes and uncertainties that this intertwinement has generated.

The Polis as Urban and Political Community

In terms of the polis as city, most Kinois have never had an officially recognized right to the city. During the colonial period, access to the city of Kinshasa, then still Léopoldville, was carefully controlled and regulated by the colonial authorities, and the city itself was developed along strictly defined racial as well as gender lines, which gradually turned the city into a model of urban segregation that inspired, for example, urban planning under South Africa's apartheid era. After the Second World War, Léopoldville, then a city of 40,000 inhabitants, rapidly expanded to reach 400,000 a mere ten years later, on the eve of Congo's independence from its Belgian colonial masters. In 1949, in response to growing demographic pressure, the Belgian colonial administration developed an ambitious ten year plan for Léopoldville and other major cities in the country. This plan, known as the *plan décennal*, drastically reconfigured the city by means of a vast housing scheme that also formalized the division between *La Ville*, the white European heart of Léopoldville, and *La Cité*, the term used to denote a surrounding belt of informal settlements and of regulated social housing also known as *cités indigènes*, 'indigenous neighbourhoods', constructed around and away from the downtown area. These areas still form the core of Kinshasa's current urban infrastructure. *Ville* and *Cité*, the two mirroring parts of the city, were spatially demarcated by a railroad, a market, strategically placed army barracks, as well as by belts of empty no man's land and other *zones tampons*, spaces that even today have not yet fully densified. The border between the two parts of the city, the European centre and the African periphery, were porous in the sense that Congolese were allowed into *La Ville* as 'boys', workers, watchmen, manual labourers and so on, but all of this Congolese *main d'oeuvre* needed special permits to stay in this area of the city at night, or else had to retreat into their own neighbourhoods at the end of the day. These and other measures effectively installed a tangible colour bar that ran through the city in all kinds of visible and invisible ways (De Boeck and Plissart, 2004; De Meulder, 2000).

In many ways this division retained some of its former meaning even after the sun of independence had risen over the country. Today, Kinshasa is home to an estimated 10 million inhabitants. Until very recently, however, the Belgian *plan décennal* was never followed by another formalized governmental attempt at controlling, steering and guiding Kinshasa's development. Many of the neighbourhoods of the peripheral city continued to expand at an ever increasing pace, but this expansion took place in a rather unorganized, unplanned, chaotic and often spontaneous and ad hoc manner, leaving the majority of a rapidly growing number of urban residents to fend for themselves. This greatly impacted on the quality and reliability of Kinshasa's urban infrastructure, and it also determined the access to amenities such as electricity and especially water, a precious commodity that many Kinois (inhabitants of Kinshasa) have to struggle for on a daily basis. After independence, *La Ville* remained a rather exclusive and expensive part of town, although today the divisions are no longer as clear cut as they used to be in colonial times. But even so, this still is where the country's political and economical power centres are located, and where embassies, international hotels, fancy supermarkets and residential areas for expatriates and local political and economical elites are situated. And many of Kinshasa's inhabitants still have the feeling of trespassing upon accessing this city centre. This became abundantly clear in the local interpretation of a statue of Lumumba, Congo's legendary first post-independence prime minister. The statue itself was erected a decade ago at the *échangeur de Limete*, a major roundabout on Boulevard Lumumba, the main road (Echangeur de Limete) leading into *La Ville*.

The statue portrays Lumumba with one raised hand, a greeting gesture to salute and welcome the inhabitants of the city. However, it did not take the inhabitants of Masina, Ndjili, and other parts of the peripheral city very long before they came up with their own alternative reading of what the statue conveys. For them, Lumumba was put there by the urban authorities as the gatekeeper to the city, raising his hand and telling the inhabitants of the surrounding *cités* in a loud and clear voice: 'Okokota te!' (You will not enter!). Stopping them in their tracks, the people's hero Lumumba, by an ironic twist of fate, thus prevents the slum dwellers of Kinshasa from crossing the borderline into the 'real' city, a place where they do not belong and that will never be theirs.

The exclusionist logic that informed colonial urban planning was never totally abandoned and has even made a spectacular return in recent years. For some years now, a successive series of city governors has been engaged in 'cleaning up' the city. This cleansing basically boils down to a hard-handed politics of erasure, destroying 'irregular', 'anarchic' and unruly housing constructions, bulldozing bars and terraces considered to be too close to the roadside, and banning containers, which Kinois commonly convert into little shops, from the street. The same is happening to the small street 'restaurants' known as *malewa* (which provide many women, and therefore whole families, with an income), as well as many other informal structures and infrastructures allowing urban dwellers to survive in the volatile economy of the street. The urban authorities not only started to wage a war against these 'illegal' structures and activities but also against the very bodies of those who perform or embody them. Amongst those who first fell victim to the state's effort to 'sanitize' and recolonize the city, rewrite the city's public spaces and redefine who has a right to the street and to the city, were Kinshasa's street children and youth gangs.

The same exclusionist dynamics are fuelling an even more outspoken attempt at redefining what a 'proper' city means today (De Boeck, 2011).

During the campaign leading up to the 2006 presidential elections, President Kabila launched his 'Cinq Chantiers' programme, his Five Public Works. After decades of official neglect with regard to urban planning, and fifty years after the end of the Belgian *plan décennal*, the concept presented the outline of a sort of Marshall Plan for Congo, and summarized the government's pledge to modernize education, health care, road infrastructure, access to electricity and housing accommodation in the D.R.C. In 2010, the year in which Congo celebrated the 50th anniversary of its independence from Belgian colonial rule, and a year before the next presidential elections which will supposedly take place at the end of 2011, the 'chantiers' were geared into a different speed, especially with regard to the latter three issues. Downtown Kinshasa went through a quite radical facelift, under the guidance of Chinese engineers, Indian or Pakistani architects, and real estate firms from Dubai, Zambia or the Emirates. Along the main boulevards and major traffic arteries, such as the aforementioned Boulevard Lumumba, all trees were cut down and adjacent gardens and fields were destroyed, while the roads and boulevards themselves were widened to become eight lane highways leading right into the heart of the city. Some landmark buildings were embellished or restored, while others made way for new construction sites on an unprecedented scale. Plans also exist, so the city's rumour mill has it, to build a new viaduct connecting an upgraded Ndjili International airport with *La Ville* (and more precisely with its Grand Hotel, one of the two international hotels of downtown Kinshasa). The viaduct will follow the Congo River, and run over and above the heads of the hundreds of thousands of impoverished inhabitants of the commune of Masina, commonly referred to as 'Chine Populaire', the People's Republic of China, because it is so over-populated.

Today, also, almost every main street and boulevard of Kinshasa is covered with huge billboards in a sustained politics of visibility ('*visibilité*') for the governmental 'Cinq Chantiers' policy. The boards announce the emergence of this new city and offer a spectral, and often spectacular, though highly speculative and still very volatile, vision of Congo's reinsertion into the global oecumene. The advertisements promise to bring 'modernization' and '*un nouveau niveau de vie à Kin*' (a new standard of life to Kinshasa). Apart from the classic infrastructural works (for example, bringing light to the streets, bridges and roads), the billboards also show representations of soon-to-be-constructed conference centres, five star hotels, and skyscrapers with names such as 'Modern Paradise', Crown Tower or Riverview Towers. Many advertisements sport a portrait of President Kabila alongside the statement that Congo will soon be 'the mirror of Africa'. Kinshasa, in other words, is again looking into the mirror of modernity to fashion itself, but this time the mirror not only reflects the earlier versions of Belgian colonialist modernity, but also longs to capture the aura of Dubai and other hot spots of the new urban Global South (cf. De Boeck, 2011).

But nowhere does the spectre of neoliberal global modernity conjure up the oneiric more spectacularly (and nowhere does it reveal its exclusionist logic more strongly) than in another construction project, which is currently already underway: the *Cité du Fleuve*. This is the name given to an exclusive development to be situated on two artificially created islands. These will be reclaimed from sandbanks and swamp in the Congo River. The *Cité du Fleuve* is supposed to relocate the entire Kinshasa downtown area of Gombe. According to the current plans it will span almost 400 hectares, include 200 residential houses, 10,000 apartments, 10,000 offices, 2,000 shops, 15 diplomatic missions, three hotels, two churches, three day care centres, a shopping mall and a university. The Main Island, the larger of the two, will offer mixed commercial, retail and residential properties, while North Island, the smaller of the two, will be reserved strictly for private homes and villas. The two islands will be connected to Kinshasa by means of two bridges.

According to the developers' website, *La Cité du Fleuve* will provide 'a standard of living unparalleled in Kinshasa and will be a model for the rest of Africa' and, so the website's comments continue, '*La Cité du Fleuve* will showcase the new era of African economic development'. In reality, once more, most people currently living in the city will never be able to set foot on the two islands. If all goes according to plan, the *Cité du Fleuve* will probably be accorded the administrative status of a new municipality, and will be subject to its own special by-laws. Thus, operated as a huge gated community, the *Cité du Fleuve* will inevitably redefine what is centre and what is edge in Kinshasa.

It echoes many of the ideas behind currently fashionable concepts such as the 'charter city', that is, a special urban reform zone that would allow governments of developing countries to adopt new systems of rules and establish cities that can drive economic progress in the rest of the country. But at the same time, it also replicates the segregationist model of *Ville* and *Cité* that proved so highly effective during the Belgian colonial period. It is clear that the islands will become the new *Ville* while the rest of Kinshasa, with its nine million inhabitants, will be redefined in terms of their periphery. In this way the new city map will redraw the geographies of inclusion and exclusion in radical ways, and relegate its current residents to the city's edges.

These new developments underscore the political reality of the city, namely the fact that, in political terms, the polis has always been a place of exclusion. Under Belgian colonial rule, the Congolese were defined not as citizens but as subjects (cf Mamdani, 1996), and were thereby excluded from full participation in the political life of the polis. During the Mobutu regime, a new, apparently more inclusive notion of *citoyenneté* or citizenship was generated, but at the same time Mobutu designed himself as the ultimate sovereign in a country in which the law remained in force but gradually lost all substantive meaning. Kinshasa and the country at large thereby were – and to an important extent still are – condemned to a perpetual state of exception, a zone of social abandonment with an almost camp-like urban infrastructure, in which the Congolese *citoyens* have become *homines sacri*, to adopt Agamben's notion (Agamben, 2005), people caught in a politicized form of natural or 'bare' life, subjects placed outside both the profane and the divine law, whose lives are, often quite literally, desacralized, and constantly exposed and subjugated to death (and the 2010 assassination of the leading human rights activist Floribert Chebeya in Kinshasa painfully reminded us once again of the necropolitical nature of Congo's governance).

The Sacred

This brings us to the second term, that of the sacred. The long history of contact with Christianity that Congo has maintained ever since the sixteenth century (cf MacGaffey, 1986), has turned the notion of what sacrality means today in this central African setting into an extremely complex, slippery, multi-layered and palimpsestual concept. Over the centuries, contact with Catholic and Protestant missionaries has profoundly transformed and reshaped the autochthonous ritual and cosmological horizons of Central Africa. In the Lower Congo, Christianity was translated and reinterpreted in local terms almost right from the start of its introduction. The spread and success of early Antonionist movements, such as Kimpa Vita in the seventeenth century, attests to this (cf. Thornton, 1998) as do, much later, many prophetic and messianic movements of which Kimbanguism became the best known (cf Mélice, 2011). But although much of the local cosmological structures continued to exist in spite of these historical upheavals, it is also clear that the introduction of Christianity, together with the political and economical impact of colonialism[1] (and de facto both often went hand in hand), deeply penetrated Congo's regional belief systems, occasioning far-reaching changes in local life-worlds, and causing a profound mental colonization which had a long-lasting impact that continues to have a powerful effect even today.

The breaches and ruptures thus introduced by the model of colonialist modernity that the colonial state and its religious emissaries promoted were, in a way, exacerbated even further by a second wave of religious colonization from the late 1980s onwards. During this period, in which the Mobutist regime finally started to crumble after three decades of ruinous reign, Neo-Pentecostal and other churches of Christian fundamentalist signature started to take over the local religious 'market'. One could argue that their impact has – to some extent – been even more profound than anything previously experienced – some even speak of a Pentecostal 'revolution' (cf Marshall (2009) for the Nigerian case). Preaching a radical break with the autochthonous ancestral past, which is constantly demonized in these 'churches of awakening' (*églises de réveil*) (see also Meyer (1999) for similar processes in Ghana), and promising an insertion into the 'modern' oecumene of global capitalism, this new religious wave has met with tremendous success. As such, it manages to intervene in many, often even some of the most intimate, aspects of people's daily lives. This happens, for example, by the way in which the new Christian ideologies and theologies are redefining the long-standing Central-African landscapes of lineage and kinship affiliation. They do so by propagating a move away from the extended family and its accompanying kin-based model of solidarity, by re-centring the focus towards the more 'Western' model of the nuclear family and its related forms of individual rather than collective subject-formation and singularization, and by trading the logic of the gift for a monetary and capitalist oriented logic, with all that this entails (a new work ethos, new notions of accumulation and maximization of profit, new forms of self-realization and individualism, etc.). All these changes have provoked further shifts in the city's social realm and have impacted heavily on local notions of authority and gerontocracy, on gendered labour divisions, on inter-generational dynamics as well as on multiple other domains of daily life.

Part of the success of the Neo-Pentecostal theology is certainly due to the fact that faith goes hand in hand with an emphasis on the miraculous and the promise of material success, and that salvation becomes an individual achievement, through a spirituality that is open to everyone, and potentially within the reach of all. More generally, the broader encompassing Pentecostal narrative of an Armageddon, a struggle between the forces of good and evil set within the eschatological time-frame of the Apocalypse (cf. De Boeck, 2005), is one that people easily relate to, given the harsh living conditions they endure in the city, due to the material and spiritual insecurity they encounter in their daily lives, or the more general feeling of an omnipresent nationwide multi-crisis on the political, economical and socio-cultural level.

Indeed, the Pentecostal narrative has profoundly permeated the public sphere. It has imposed new mental structures onto daily life, but it has also punctuated, marked, shaped and reconfigured the public urban space in a very physical and material way. There are church buildings emerging on every street corner of Kinshasa, and the sound of prayer accompanies one wherever one goes. It is by no means an exception for bars – these other ultimate urban spaces that are so profoundly linked to the rise of the African city, its popular culture, its notions of leisure, its time (the night), and its politics – to convert into churches, in a movement that infuses the urban public sphere with divine meaning, and visually and auditively stamps the aesthetics and moralities of a new spiritual geography onto its surface. At the same time, this spatial conversion also squarely posits the religious in the urban realm of market, capital and business. Similarly, the new religious discourse has also engulfed the city's mediascape – it is no coincidence that a majority of the radio and television channels are owned by churches (Pype, 2008).

Polis-Sacred: Beyond the Precarious Balance

It does not come as a surprise, therefore, that within this omnipresent Pentecostal whirlwind, the sacred and the polis have become intricately intertwined. The polis, the city as political community, is constantly being reshaped along spiritual lines, turning it into a City of God, a New Jerusalem.[2] Religion thus profoundly impacts upon the city's and the country's contemporary politics, in which the Pentecostal narrative of spiritual redemption is increasingly also being interpreted in terms of socio-political redemption.

However, this does by no means imply the invention or imposition of a new liberation theology. Rather, the *rapprochement* between the state and the city's main preachers and prophets has led to a further maintenance of the societal status quo. Two decades ago, political scientists tended to describe the relationship between the African state and its civil society as a 'precarious balance' (Rothchild and Chazan, 1988) between a politics from above and a politics from below (Bayart et al., 1992). Today it is clear that the relationships between the above and below are far more complex than this simple opposition allows for (cf. De Boeck, 1996). The nature of the relation between the state on the one hand, and 'civil society' on the other, is not so much, or not solely, defined by a marked opposition, or by a dialectical relationship of oppression and resistance, but it is, on the contrary, primarily marked by a lack of distance, by familiarity, complicity, connivance and 'mutual zombification', to use the famous phrase by Mbembe (1992). Like an increasing number of political parties, national NGOs and other grassroots organizations, the preachers and pastors of the new religious field have also become an integral part of this postcolonial arena, and have even started to define its terms, as is attested by the religious privatization of public functions that the state no longer seems to be able to maintain, as well as by the overall religious transfiguration of the political realm.

The existence of the state (often reduced to competing factions who follow their own pathways of accumulation) is not so much evidenced by its capacity to uphold law and order, but rather it exists by the unlawfulness and arrogant arbitrariness it constantly instigates. For decades now, the state has been forcing itself into the spaces of survival of the common citizen by means of corruption and repression. As such, the illegality initiated by the state has found its way from the centre to broader layers of society. Simultaneously, the blurred boundaries of the state apparatus provide people on the local levels of society with the opportunity to penetrate the spaces that the imploded state should but does not occupy. The blurring of the boundaries between state and civil society, the interplay between official law and unofficial practice, the interpenetration of the 'above' and the 'below', and the complex interaction between multiple, dialectically interdependent socio-political and cultural spaces and groups generates the opportunity for constant negotiation and collaboration. All this while simultaneously weakening, I would argue, the public (including the religious) realm as a whole, generating spiritual and material insecurity and other new forms of violence that, though very tangible, are often more covert.

This is not to deny that the history of the D.R.C. has obviously been marked by blatant political violence produced during a sometimes harsh colonial regime, as well as during a violent decolonization process (1960–5), which was followed by thirty years of ruinous dictatorship under Mobutu (1965–97), a long and painful political transition against the backdrop of violent warfare which involved many of the D.R.C.'s neighbours (1998–2003), and a slow and fragile process of democratization and state reform after the 2006 presidential elections. In recent years Kinshasa received its share of that violence: it lived through two massive and violent waves of looting in 1991 and 1993; it was briefly drawn into the war in Brazzaville, on the other side of the Congo River, in 1996 and 1997; it was invaded by the former Rwandan allies of Kabila Sr. in August 1998; and it saw some of its worst violence in the period immediately prior to the 2006 elections, when two presidential candidates, Jean-Pierre Bemba and current president Kabila, openly engaged in armed clashes in the streets of Kinshasa, leaving hundreds of people dead. Yet, one might argue that, in spite of this recent violent history, Kinshasa was spared the worst. Within the city, with all of its shortcomings (its unmanageable size, its poor administration, its lack of insertion into a formal economy, its insufficient policing, its failing material infrastructure and its extremely young population – a factor that greatly contributes to the growing insecurity in many parts of the city), violence is often generated on a different, much more hidden level. It is generated in the folds of the city, the shadow zones or grey areas existing in the hiatus between the practical levels of its everyday existence and the official moral discourses and practices of its administrative, judicial and religious frameworks, which are supposed to regulate, sanitize, control, discipline and uplift this unruly city life, but that often produce the exact opposite effect. While also offering opportunities and opening up possibilities, it is within this hiatus, this gap between principle and practice, that the city incessantly produces a more occult violence, a violence that destabilizes the standard meanings and terms of reference of people's daily lives, and makes (material and spiritual) 'uncertainty' the main characteristic of this postcolonial urban life.

Uncertainty

Indeed, for many in Central Africa's urbanscapes, local reality has become unfathomable, difficult to understand and interpret. More than ever before, perhaps, local reality *is* the *occultus*, in its double sense: not only the urban processes that structure local lives are often clandestine and therefore remain hidden, but local reality itself has become impossible without a 'knowledge of the hidden' and of the newly emerging spiritual realms beyond the physical reality of everyday life. Because of the recent impact of the Neo-Pentecostal wave, the meanings of these spiritual worlds have – yet again – profoundly changed and have become totally unpredictable. Ancestors no longer behave in the way people expect them to, nor do witches, who seem to become more numerous by the day. A whole library of recent anthropological work documents the continent-wide surfacing of new witchcraft beliefs in the globalizing 'modern' context of the urban arena.[3] Rather than corroborating Weber's thesis about the *Entzauberung* of the world, the rise of modernity only seems to have unleashed more powers of darkness. In former times, throughout Africa, people always used the processes of mirroring between the realities of the day and the night, or of the living and the dead, to make sense of the world. The obverse and the reverse of the world were united through links of similarity, according to a principle that Mbembe (1997) has called 'simultaneous multiplicities'. Today, however, a change seems to have appeared in the mechanisms operating this simultaneous multiplicity of the two different domains that exist in and through each other. In many urban (and rural) sites throughout the African continent, something seems to have changed in the slippage between visible and invisible, in the folds of local life, between the diurnal and the nocturnal, between reality and what we might call, for lack of a better word, its double, its shadow, reflection or image. Within the local experiential frame, the double which lurks underneath the surface of the visible world somehow seems to have taken the upper hand. The world of shadows is no longer experienced as a similar but parallel reality. On the contrary, it has come to inhabit and overgrow its opposite, thereby making the physical world more incomprehensible and even dangerous every day, as is attested, for example, by the pandemic of witchcraft accusations against children which Kinshasa has been undergoing these past twenty years (see De Boeck, 2009a). A term that is often used in Lingala (the lingua franca spoken in Kinshasa) to describe this new uncanny, elusive and confusing character of the local world that one inhabits, is *mystique*. For most in (urban) Congo it is increasingly frequent to designate people, things and situations as 'mystique', that is, as difficult to place, interpret and attribute meaning to.

Local urban experience, in summary, seems above all to be generated in the folds and shadows of the city that itself exists as a huge friction zone, marked by a generalized feeling of uncanny-ness. The spiritual insecurity in the city mirrors the material uncertainties that punctuate the urban terrain. Rather than offering a steady ground, an unchanging background or canvas against which to read the passage of time and of one's life, enabling one to generate a sense of stability and meaning and to interpret change and transformation, the urban 'local' manifests itself as a pool filled with quicksand, a topos as unstable as the sandy hills upon which Kinshasa is constructed.

This is not only true with regard to the level of an unmoored *imaginaire*, but also with regard to the very materiality that determines people's lives. Often, my interlocutors in Kinshasa tell me: 'When I leave my home in the morning I do not know if I will make it back alive in the evening. And each day, when I *do* come home in the evening, I tell myself: it is a real miracle!'

Between morning and evening, between leaving and returning, there are so many material and logistical obstacles, so many dangers lurking, so many parameters changing, that there is the constant possibility of sudden disappearance and imminent death. The local realities of one's street or one's neighbourhood never offer a steady decor for one's daily activities. The local is not necessarily the familiar. In the few hours between the time that one goes to bed and the time that one gets up again in the morning, the world as we know it might have vanished. Overnight, one's street might have turned into an unknown territory and a social minefield: prices might have changed and one's francs might have devaluated by 500 per cent; soldiers might have erected roadblocks on all the roads giving access to the neighbourhood; the power relations between local gangs might have switched; the man selling Coca Cola in the kiosk across the street might have been necklaced because he was caught stealing in an adjacent compound; sudden and inexplicable deaths might have occurred or, worse even, one's children might reveal themselves to be witches; erosion due to heavy rainfall or deficient drainage might have swept away the neighbour's house; without warning electricity might have been switched off, only to come back three weeks later, or else the main electricity cables or water pipes feeding the neighbourhood might have been stolen by the very people supposed to fix it. The material infrastructures of absence, lack and incompleteness that determine the daily rhythms of urban life, the very architectures of degradation and decay that often constitute the physicality of local living in the urban, the technologies of fixing and repairing that such an architecture generates, everything adds to the feeling that to venture into the local world of one's own street in the morning, is to venture into a vast, and increasingly exotic, unknown. '*Terrain eza miné!*' as Kinois say: 'the terrain is full of mines', and one always runs the risk of inadvertently stepping on one.

Of funeral Rites, Civic Wrongs, and a Possible Right to the Future

The city's material and spiritual crisis has clearly left its mark on the modalities of social life in the urban context, and has provoked some radical changes in it. One example amongst many others is provided by Kinois youth's dealings with death, the management of which – surprisingly – seems to escape the totalizing control of both state and church in Kinshasa.

Normally, the fathers and uncles of the deceased are the ones in charge of the funeral: they take care of all the formalities, raise the money for the coffin, address the crowd and supervise the burial. In recent years, however, the city has witnessed a powerful reversal of these norms and rules: increasingly, children and youngsters are taking over the control of the mourning and burial rituals (Fig. 10.1). This is especially true when a young person dies – and given the city's demographics (75 per cent of the city's nine million inhabitants are under the age of 25) – this has become the rule rather than the exception.

The death of a young person triggers a lot of anger and rebellious sentiments amongst age-mates (cf. De Boeck, 2009b; Vangu Ngimbi, 1997).

This anger is directed at all public figures of authority and seniority, starting with the parents and elders of the deceased. They are the first ones to be blamed for this death. In such a case, youngsters will invade the scene, single out fathers and uncles and accuse them of witchcraft. Often, such accusations lead to violent attacks. As a result, the elders are chased from the site of mourning, while the young people of the neighbourhood take over the control of the funeral and confiscate the corpse to perform the burial themselves. In the end, families totally lose the control over the burial of their young relative.

In this way, the cemetery has become the site of an intergenerational battlefield for Kinshasa's youngsters (who refer to themselves as *bana désordre*, children of 'disorder'). Their very corpses are turned into political

FIGURE 10.1   The cemetery of Kintambo, Kinshasa, 2008. (Still from the documentary film *Cemetery State* (2010), directed by Filip De Boeck.)

platforms, from which the young shout their criticisms directed at parents, elders, but also politicians, priests and other authority figures. These, the young seem to say, have not lived up to their promises, they have forsaken their responsibilities and 'sacrificed' the younger generations. Violent as their protest may seem, the political and moral criticisms voiced by this poor urban youth are not expressions of nihilism. They do not, like some exotic version of the Punks of the 1970s, shout: No More Future. Using funeral rites to address civic and moral wrongs, they actually try to convey the contrary: their right to a possible future. Unchannelled, raw, not recuperated by the official discourses of the state or the church, this urban youth's often violent and unruly singing and dancing during funerals highlight their ongoing efforts at reconceptualizing both the polis and the sacred, questioning their place in the urban space, and more broadly the meaning of the public sphere itself, or the content of a notion such as citizenship. By refusing the role of *homines sacri*, and resisting the fact that their own deaths, caused by the state of exception to which the city and the state have condemned them, remain meaningless, they reintroduce the possibility of sacrifice, in an attempt to turn their own deaths into meaningful events. In doing so, they try to renew the signification of the notion of sacrality itself. By shifting the sacred away from the official discourse of the churches, they reconnect it to much older moral matrixes and ritual vocabularies that find their origin in precolonial autochthonous pasts, a past for which this urban youth reinvents a future. The 'disorder' they thus create is the only way at the disposal of a generation that is excluded from social or political power to define a new moral ground from which to formulate alternative futures for themselves, their city and their country.

Lines of Flight and the (Im)Possibility of Futurity

In these and other, often perplexing ways, Kinshasa's inhabitants constantly generate 'moments of freedom' (Fabian, 1998), moments that represent possible lines of flight, offering the possibility for a Deleuzian move of 'decentering' (Deleuze and Guattari, 1980). They create – and this is not so much a voluntary choice but rather a bare necessity – new possibilities, through language and practice, out of the destabilized meanings with which the social and infrastructural organization of the city constantly confronts them.

If violence is generated in the cracks and folds of the city, so is opportunity. Forced by the city to step back from habitual ways of thinking and acting, an overwhelming majority of Kinshasa's residents are well trained to improvise its way through urban life and to look for feasibilities in the hiatus. Kinois know how to insert themselves in the interstices and fill in the gaps. Sometimes they do so to resist the city, but more often they seek to collude with the city in order to survive in it.

These strategies of survival come with a specific temporality, far removed from the teleological time frames of the nation state or the church. Conscious actors and participants in their own lives, people incessantly struggle to stay in control. Therefore, they are continuously busy seizing and capturing the opportunity of the moment to reinvent and re-imagine their lives in different ways. But at the same time these processes of seizure remain highly unpredictable. In these urban lives there is never a straight line between today and tomorrow, or between here and there, between possibility and the impossible, success and failure, life and death. Rather than existing through habit and routine, or rather than being formatted by the regulated temporalities of the predictable and the unchanging, postcolonial urban lives are often shaped through movements of the unexpected, which constantly seem to be steering the urbanites off course, launching them into new orbits

Such lives, therefore, are never fully autonomous projects either. Rather, they seem to consist of constant stops and starts, directed by the tricky and unforeseeable processes of seizure and capture, which in turn are structured, not only by the spatialities of various networks, of shifting contexts and haphazard connections, but also by the specific temporality of the *moment*, unpredictably wedged in-between the immobility of endless waiting, and the effervescence of sudden movement. Living in the urban local, which in itself has become an increasingly unstable and nomadic ground, constantly generates new opportunities and openings, while simultaneously also causing sudden closures, producing a lot of fall out and 'collateral damage' along the way. Urban survival, therefore, often necessitates an extreme (mental and physical) flexibility. Generated in the moment and therefore rarely knowing where they will end up, the meandering lines of local lives constantly generate conjunctures and conjectures of sudden action and passivity, power and powerlessness, expectation and disappointment, rise and fall, dream and nightmare. And because of the often instantaneous, spontaneous, improvised and random nature of individual biographies, and because of the equally unplanned ways in which these individual biographies get caught up and become entangled in other networks of physical and mental contact with other people and other discourses, practices and ideas, the line of one's life rarely is unidirectional, and one can almost never plan it ahead of time.

To deal with the city, therefore, is to deal with hazard. Prepared to open up to the unexpected, and not necessarily by choice, local lives are profoundly marked by the dynamics of the hazardous and the accidental, and that is also why their memories often remain diffuse and opaque. Therefore, perhaps, lives lived locally remain difficult to capture within the historicist approaches of modernity and its accompanying ideologies of linear development, progress and accumulation. The promise of the redemption of one's soul in a blissful afterlife often seems equally far and distant. The immediate and often dystopian quality of living and surviving in the local moment of the urban, seems to be far removed from the utopian futurities that the state and the churches have on offer. Instead, popular urban cultures, as diverse theatres of dreams and theatres of struggle, generate a world that continuously deconstructs and reconstructs itself, continuously stops and starts, and keeps history, memory and questioning in motion.

Notes

[1] For example, the Belgian colonial policy defined many urban centres throughout Congo as 'centres extra-coutumiers', that is, in opposition to the 'village', as 'modern' spaces where traditional frames of reference, ritual beliefs and customary policies could no longer be applied. The urban colonial space thus effectively represented a rupture with the rural socio-cultural context which bracketed it.

[2] The Kimbanguist church has constructed its own New Jerusalem outside of Kinshasa, at Nkamba, the movement's holy city in the Lower Congo province, erected on the spot where Simon Kimbangu was born in 1887 and started his career as prophet in 1921.

[3] See for example, Comaroff and Comaroff (1999). For a critical review of some of this recent literature on the African occult see Ranger (2007).

Bibliography

Agamben, G. (2005), *State of Exception*. Chicago: University of Chicago Press.
Bayart, J.-F., Mbembe, A. and Toulabor, C. (1992), *Le politique par le bas en Afrique noire: contributions à une problématique de la démocratie*. Paris: Karthala.
Comaroff, J. and Comaroff, J. L. (1999), 'Occult Economies and the Violence of Abstraction: Notes from the South African Postcolony'. *American Ethnologist*, 26(2): 279–303.
De Boeck, F. (1996), 'Postcolonialism, Power and Identity: Local and Global Perspectives from Zaire', in Werbner, R. and Ranger, R. (eds), *Postcolonial Identities in Africa*. London: Zed Books.
—. (2005), 'The Apocalyptic Interlude: Revealing Death in Kinshasa'. *African Studies Review*, 48(2): 11–32.

—. (2009a), 'At Risk, as Risk: Abandonment and Care in a World of Spiritual Insecurity', in La Fontaine, J. (ed.), *The Devil's Children. From Spirit Possession to Witchcraft: New Allegations that Affect Children*. Farnham, Surrey: Ashgate.
—. (2009b), 'Death Matters: Intimacy, Violence and the Production of Social Knowledge by Urban Youth in the Democratic Republic of Congo', in: Pinto Ribeiro, A. (ed.), *Can There Be Life without the Other?* Manchester: Carcanet Press.
—. (2010), *Cemetery State*. Antwerp/Amsterdam: Filmnatie/Viewpoint. (Documentary Film, 70').
—. (2011), 'Inhabiting Ocular Ground: Kinshasa's Future in the Light of Congo's Spectral Urban Politics'. *Cultural Anthropology*, 26(2): 263–86.
De Boeck, F. and Plissart, M. F. (2004), *Kinshasa: Tales of the Invisible City*. Ghent/Tervuren: Ludion/Royal Museum for Central Africa.
Deleuze, G. and Guattari, F. (1980), *Mille Plateaux*. Paris: Minuit.
De Meulder, B. (2000), *Kuvuande Mbote. Een eeuw koloniale architectuur en stedenbouw in Kongo*. Antwerp: Houtekiet.
Fabian, J. (1998), *Moments of Freedom. Anthropology and Popular Culture*. Charlottesville/London: University Press of Virginia.
MacGaffey, W. (1986), *Religion and Society in Central Africa. The Bakongo of Lower Zaire*. Chicago: University of Chicago Press.
Mamdani, M. (1996), *Citizen and Subject. Contemporary Africa and the Legacy of Late Colonialism*. Princeton, NJ: Princeton University Press.
Marshall, R. (2009), *Political Spiritualities. The Pentecostal Revolution in Nigeria*. Chicago: University of Chicago Press.
Mbembe, A. (1992), Provisional Notes on the Post Colony. *Africa – The Journal of the International Africa Institute*, 62(1): 3–37.
—. (1997), 'The 'Thing' and its Double in Cameroonian Cartoons', in K. Barber (ed.), *Readings in African Popular Culture*. Bloomington/Oxford: Indiana University Press/James Currey.
Mélice, A. (2011), 'Prophétisme, hétérodoxie et dissidence. L'imaginaire Kimbanguiste en movement'. Liège: Université de Liège. (Unpublished doctoral dissertation.)
Meyer, B. (1999), *Translating the Devil. Religion and Modernity among the Ewe in Ghana*. Edinburgh: Edinburgh University Press.
Pype, K. (2008), 'The Making of the Pentecostal Melodrama. Mimesis, Agency and Power in Kinshasa's Media World (DR Congo)'. Leuven: University of Leuven. (Unpublished doctoral dissertation.)
Ranger, T. (2007), ' "Scotland Yard in the Bush:" Medicine Murders, Child Witches and the Construction of the Occult. A Literature Review.' *Africa – The Journal of the International Africa Institute*, 77(2): 272–83.
Rothchild, D. and Chazan, N. (eds) (1988), *The Precarious Balance. State and Society in Africa*. Boulder, CO: Westview Press.
Thornton, J. K. (1998), *The Kongolese Saint Anthony. Dona Beatriz Kimpa Vita and the Antonian Movement, 1684–1706*. Cambridge: Cambridge University Press.
Vangu Ngimbi, I. (1997), *Jeunesse, funérailles et contestation socio-politique en Afrique*. Paris: L'Harmattan.

Chapter 11

The Politics of a Sacred Place: Revisiting an Israeli Development Town[1]

Haim Yacobi

Introduction

This article critically examines the Western-Modern orientation of Israeli space production vis a vis its diverse population, which in many aspects represents material culture that does not comply with the national supremacy. Specifically, this chapter will focus on the case of Netivot, a peripheral development town which offers an alternative experience of sense of place, linked to the diaspora and Mizrahi[2] identity that subverts the Israeli hegemonic production of space by creating a hybrid place.

Vast literature discusses the notion of the terms space, place and sense of place. Yet in the scope of this introduction, let me highlight only the analytical distinction between 'place' and 'space' that emerged during the 1970s, when a qualitative shift in the field of geography paved the road to the development of social and cultural geography. Tuan (Tuan, 1977), for instance, identified space as a general term in opposition to place that was defined as material. This distinction also appeared in the definition of absolute space as a container of material objects, in opposition to relational space that was defined as perceived and socially produced and emphasized the phenomenological dimension, claiming that place is not an abstract but an experienced phenomenon linked to a process which involves the perception of objects and activities that are used as sources of personal and collective identities (Madanipour, 1996).

Space and place became fundamental terms in the field of architectural theory and criticism. Christian Norberg-Schultz followed this line of argument and claimed that space is nothing but the relationship between objects. On the other hand, he argued that place is a defined built or natural space that has meaning, which stems from personal and collective memories as well as from identity (Norberg-Schultz, 1979). Indeed, space will transform into place only when we are identified with and define ourselves through it.

This work was viewed by many as a critique of the modernist movement in architecture, claiming that it had produced spaces but not places.

Simultaneous with the emergence of the phenomenological perspective, a new generation of geographers and urban sociologists pointed to the capitalist system as a social structure that may serve as a key to understanding the organization of space. For them, spatial practices such as those of planning and architecture which were seen by the phenomenologists as agents for the production of places were viewed as tools in the service of capitalism, which aim to balance private and collective capital, and thus hold potential for social oppression (Castells, 1978). Indeed, this school of thought was significant in revealing interrelations between society, space, culture and economy.

Yet, such a Marxist point of view demonstrates a lack of understanding of the everyday practices of the users and their struggle to transform space into place. Here, the work of Henri Lefèbvre who aspired to integrate theories and abstract thought with practice and the tangible daily urban experience is significant. For Lefèbvre (Lefèbvre, 1991) space is a social product and thus a 'sense of place' – though he does not explicitly use this term – cannot be seen solely as a reflection of either experience or knowledge. Rather, it is the juxtaposition of three interrelated dimensions: perceived space, conceived space and lived space. This approach enables us, analytically, to examine, on the one hand, the way in which space is appropriated by those in power who are motivated to reinforce the hegemonic narrative by using and implementing specific settlement structures or certain architectural styles. On the other hand, and most importantly, Lefèbvre also refers to the users, to their everyday life and to their ability to produce a counter-hegemonic meaning of place.

Beyond the general discussion presented earlier, the very particularity of the Israeli spatial reality calls for a localization of such theories towards the meaning of the built environment. The 'Israeli place', as I will elaborate, is the product of a contested socio-historical process, characterized by the motivation for controlling national space and framing it in a total manner. Such a decisive approach generates counter-products which are also spatially expressed. The methodological roots of my claim originate from the tendency of urban research in Israel to focus on formal processes of space production, dictated from above and burned onto the collective mind by means of plans, thus reproducing the perception of what a place is and which sites do not warrant being called places. Connected to this debate is the centrality of the argument that the production of Israeli-Zionist space can be understood along three axes: the denial of the Orient, the rejection of the bourgeois and the invalidation of the diaspora culture (Nitzan-Shiftan, 2000). However, vis a vis the short theoretical notes that open this section, let me propose that such an argument is partial since it refers to place production from above, ignoring the fact that vast parts of the built environment in Israel do not comply with standard regulations (legally as well as architecturally). Thus, they violate the spatial order created by the national culture and by so doing produce hybrid places.

It is important to clarify, already at this stage, that the notion of hybridity accordingly is not a third concept which relieves the tension between cultures, hence resulting in the recognition of the subordinate culture by the hegemonic one (Bhabha, 1994, pp. 113–14). Rather, it is formulated within a third space – a discursive junction in which the sovereign and the colonial subject are not exclusive alternatives, and the construction of their identities involves 'mutual contamination'. During this process, which involves mutual reproduction and imitation within the intervening, namely third space, the colonial power also produces its alien. Therefore, claims Homi Bhabha, the third space is potentially a site of resistance, undermining the polar perception which poses identities as opposite, authentic, ethnically and racially essentialist entities, hence it can be perceived as a site of struggle and negotiation (Bhabha, 1990, p. 211). The significance of Bhabha's argument is its recognition that power relations are the basis for the production of subaltern culture, and it proposes a wide sociological understanding of the range between the top-down power and the voice of a subaltern subject. This insight, I would suggest, is an appropriate vehicle for examining space production in social and cultural theory in general and in the Israeli case in particular.

At the core of criticism against Bhabha's third space conceptualization, highlighting the discursive aspect, lays the material question. This critical tone appears both in relation to the distinction between politics and discourse and in the call for the examination of hybrid spaces within postcolonial contexts of specific geography, history and economics. Postcolonial studies have focused on textual and literary studies, being only vaguely concerned with what happened. In the context of these criticisms, there is a necessity to engage in material practices, actual spaces and real politics that have increasingly, if belatedly, brought into the debate recent as well as earlier studies of colonial urbanism and architecture, largely ignored by the literary discourses on the postcolonial context (King 2003, pp. 167–83). Indeed, it is important to ground the formulation of the third space in meaningful practices; hybrid places are the result of interactions that are located in concrete differing positions of power, which must nevertheless cohabit (AlSayyad, 2001).

This chapter joins that call; it aims to acknowledge the centrality of practices that are being conducted in the third space as a tangible site where the diaspora place is produced within a national-sovereign space. To put it differently, the discussion concerning the Israeli place, on which I will focus, allows for recognizing the significance of practices occurring within the third place, not merely as a metaphor, but also as a concrete site in which material practices, producing the physical space, are activated. My argument follows Raz-Karkotzkin's suggestion that disavowing the diaspora past in the Israeli context is part of the implementation of the regime of modernity. It should be recognized that a strict denial of the diaspora exists owing to the formulation of cultural identity in terms of disavowal, and more importantly, the fact that repudiating the diaspora means repudiating the Jewish memory (Raz-Karkotzkin, 1993, p. 113).

Jewish Place and Sovereignty

The general debate concerning the Israeli production of space-place focuses on the 'local' versus the 'other', ignoring the dynamic nature of identities. The same applies to the examination of the role of architecture and planning within the Zionist enterprise, which has so far been focused on the Jewish–Arab or Israeli–Palestinian issue. This is connected to a very common point of departure – 1948 – and to the discussion of the appropriate spatial form of habitat for the Jewish people in their motherland. Yet, it is important to follow this debate from an earlier period – the pre-state period – as I will discuss in the following section by means of an analysis of the architectural discourse of the 1930s as presented in the first issues of a journal named *Habinyan*.[3]

The journal exposes a serious discussion concerning the commitment of architects and planners to defining the appropriate form of Jewish habitat and its relevance to the construction of identity and the attempt to prove territorialization. In the first issue of *Habinyan* there is a clear expression of the tension between the Western approach to planning and the local geographical and economic conditions in Eretz Israel:

> In the course of our adaptation to the conditions of the Land we learned . . . that neither American or European models of development, even the most progressive of them, are not appropriate to our capability . . . since in the future they will cause the growth of public expenditure. (Schiler, 1937, pp. 28–9)

In the above, Schiler recalls then existing development options (American and European), which were not relevant to the Israeli economic reality at the time. Yet, the important issue is the possible option, i.e., that 'the level of ancient habitat of our land can teach us a lot', but Schiler restricts this statement by adding, 'without being dependent on the sentimental memories attached to it' (ibid.). In the next issue of *Habinyan*, a clear modernist statement is presented by Posner (1938, p. 2) who elaborates on the correlation between national identity and the architecture of the housing unit. According to him, 'the people can be recognized by the form of its habitat. A good example is the German settler in Sarona who replicates his father's estate from his native homeland to a foreign land'. In reference to the Jewish people, he notes that 'while a Jew returns [to his land] he does not bring from his previous country the specific form of habitat suited to his characteristics. As he did not appreciate other forms of material life, so he did not appreciate the form of his [previous] house'. Posner further explains that 'in central Europe, a place where attention was given to the form of habitat, the Jews appreciatively accepted the customs of the German and the English'.

For Posner, it is significant to adopt a neutral modernist attitude. Thus he argues that 'lately Jews have taken part in the development of European taste'. This is expressed by the fact that the Jewish people 'are distancing themselves from traditional forms, they are learning to appreciate cleanliness and simplicity, and are thus liberating their homes from the memories of the past'. This liberation from the past has a considerable impact upon the presence of Jews in the Land of Israel – not just as a denial of the diaspora, but also, as a denial of the Orient that is presented by means of Oriental morphology:

> First of all, people are no longer captivated by the Oriental appearance. Anyway, we have relinquished the Oriental character created from constructing domes and arcades. This reaction is necessary as well as suitable to the real demands of Jewish taste. (Posner, 1938)

The third issue of the journal that deals with villages in the Land of Israel draws attention to the dichotomous attitude towards the Oriental-Arab landscape. In the opening essay, Posner categorizes settlements and cites their disadvantages and merits. He suggests that the village in the Land of Israel 'is ancient and has hardly changed'. Thus, he asks:

> what we can learn from such ancient experiences? Probably we can learn from their economy, their social relations, their collective agricultural

manners... Some people claim that the home in the Arab village protects one from the climate better than our homes in the moshavot. (Posner, 1938, p. 1)

Beyond such an Orientalist approach, Posner continues to argue that the journal equally avoids romantic superlatives concerning the wholeness of the Arab agricultural villages, stating that 'we would not say that we must build so traditionally and we would also say it is prohibited to build so badly and oddly. The Arab village is not a model for replication by us . . .'. (ibid.). This approach indicates the centrality of architectural discourse and space production to identity. More specifically, it reveals the duality in relation to the Oriental landscape – it is on the one hand an authentic object of desire that might inspire the shape of the habitat of the Jewish people, and on the other hand it is the signifier of the underdeveloped Oriental-Arab society. Yet the spatial implementation of such an approach was limited. As I will discuss in the following section, it was only when the geopolitical conditions had changed and the Israeli state was established that a modernist paradigm in planning and architecture became central to the production of the new Jewish place.

But which landscape was supposed to replace the built environment that was marked as Oriental? The answer to this question was obvious at the time and can be related to the modernization project that provided justification for the rejection of an Oriental past and present as I have discussed earlier. In addition, it should be related to the manner in which power relations enable the implementation of a plan aimed at providing the means to create social transformation. Realizing this plan requires the extensive involvement of the state and a centralistic planning approach to enable the fulfillment of a vision that provides 'an opportunity to rewrite the national history' (Holston, 1989, p. 5).

Modernity and urbanism in this sense are not part of an uncontrolled evolutionary process. Rather, as sociological and political processes, they crawl along and in most cases erupt via their various agents – settlement, nationalism, immigration, professional experts and capital – guaranteeing a change in society and consciousness that will eventually lead to an inevitably better future (Taylor, 1999). Indeed, modernity as a social project includes a doctrine of progress accompanied by the creation of a new subject, the agent of modernity, which is freed from the bonds of tradition in order to fulfil himself as an individual. Seeing modernity as a neutral process strengthens the dominance of Western culture and transforms it into the sole default option to which to aspire in order to justify being termed 'modern', and this is a condition for benefiting from the distribution of rights and goods.

Let me illustrate the above argument while using one of Israel's iconic architectural objects – the *shikun* (the Hebrew word for a tenement housing block), whose political and architectural meaning has been the subject of many papers[4] indicative of its dominance in the Israeli landscape of development. Apart from being a manifestation of a certain school of planning, it is also linked to an ideology that perceived the formation of modern space as a means of constructing a sense of collective belonging. The shikun in its modernistic form assumed a double function in the Israeli context: it reflected sovereignty over national territory, and at the same time served as an incentive to economical, social and identity production and reproduction (Kallus and Law-Yone, 2002).

Indeed, the construction of the shikunim during the 1950s was considered revolutionary. The project, which was part of a comprehensive national plan for spatial development in Israel conducted by Arieh Sharon, head of the Planning Division of the Prime Minister's Office, presumed to provide housing for a population that doubled in size during the first decade of the state. The plan, entitled 'Physical Planning in Israel', reflected the centralistic statehood that characterized the Israeli regime in the 1950s. The Sharon Plan defined three dimensions of spatial design (and in my opinion, a pedagogic objective as well) – land, people and time – as a basis for a professional physical construction plan. These imaginary concepts facilitated the formation of the new national space:

> This assorted immigrants' ingathering will become uniformly consolidated only if supported by comfortable physical, social and economical conditions . . . A social composition and a planning framework should be provided in order to facilitate assimilation and stimulate the process of integrating different types of settlers . . . into one unified creative whole. (Sharon, 1951)

This approach enhanced the importance of the home as a vehicle for the creation of a collective sense of identity and belonging, as a means of transforming immigrants into locals; or in spatial terms, to produce place in the new territory. Golda Meir confirms this claim by stating that:

> . . .inadequate accommodations are evident everywhere around the globe. In Sweden, no Swedish born individual whose ancestors resided there will cease to be Swedish just because he has no home. Here, how-

ever, this is severely problematic. The housing problem is highly significant, and it will determine whether that same family that emigrated with its children, foreign and unacquainted with the language, the conditions and often also the goals – it will determine whether these family members will become Israeli or remain foreign, albeit holding Israeli citizenship. (Meir in Zaslevsky, 1954)

The necessity for domesticating the immigrants' culture coincided with the modernist approach of planning that took it upon itself to design the housing unit. This fact had social implications that came to bear over the everyday use of private space, since it aimed at liberating the family from its traditional domestic perceptions. This planning and architectural paradigm dovetailed with the objectives of the Israeli regime in the 1950s that aimed to transform the immigrants through a process of de-Arabization (Shenhav, 2006). Architectural modernism can therefore be contained within the parcel of national belonging under the guise of civil and secular culture – terms that according to Bhabha were exploited to draw people into the human community, but at the same time were used to exclude them from it as 'others'. These clearly reflect the double mechanism that produced the new habitat in Israel – a modernistic approach of efficiency, order and planning, and the application of ethno-national logic which replaces what has been considered as underdeveloped.

It seems that Amos Oz's description encapsulates the transformation of the *shikun* – from a pedagogical architectural object:

The large distance between the buildings, planned by the architect, make the shabbiness more marked than it would be if the buildings were close together – a Mediterranean town, house touching house, spaces of more human proportions. Were these neglected lots intentional, in the planners imagination perhaps, meant to be vegetable gardens, small orchards, sheep pens, and chicken coops: a North African Nahalal on the rocky slopes of Judea? What did the town planner know or want to know about the lives, the customs, the hearts' desires of the immigrants who were settled here? Was he aware of, or partner to, the philosophy prevailing in the fifties that we must change these people immediately – remake them completely – at all cost? (Oz, 1983, pp. 28–9)

As noted by Oz, North Africa has been one of the main origins of immigration to Israel since the establishment of the state. The new national project referred to the Oriental immigrant culture as an object that demands special treatment by pedagogic Westernization and modernization aimed at reshaping the immigrant's everyday life. This was the contribution of the architectural practice and discourse to affixing antinomies such as east/west, third world/first world, modernity/backwardness and sovereignty/diaspora.

Definitely, images of the tenement housing block, as a signifier of the Mizrahim, appear in several representations that deal with the Mizrahi culture, political activism and protest (Yacobi, 2008). Over the years, the users have transformed their housing environment. These additional constructions, which are not the product of professional logic and aesthetics, undermine the power of national logic, supported by professional knowledge. In other words, the modification of the housing environment is a counter act of place determination that goes beyond the inhabitants' motivation to improve their physical quality of life, but rather as a manifestation of their past cultural affiliations – a debate to be discussed in the following section.

Towards a Diaspora Place?

In the year 1956 the first settlers arrived at Netivot from the Maghreb countries. The Olim [new immigrants] were loaded on trucks and taken in the middle of the night to the place, the object of their yearning. Many of them believed that they were taken to Jerusalem, but under cover of darkness they were transported to the town of Netivot. (Netivot Municipality website)

The above quotation narrates in a nutshell the reterritorialization of Israel and the attempts to stabilize its sovereignty by the establishment of new development towns (Tzfadia and Yiftachel, 2004). As part of the physical plan for Israel discussed in the previous section, the town of Netivot was established in 1956, as a regional centre for the northwestern Negev agricultural settlements and the first wave of Netivot's inhabitants was primarily characterized by Jewish emigrants from North Africa. Several reports since the establishment of the city point to its economic underdevelopment, attributing this to its ethno-demographic composition (Zaslevsky, 1969). Even more recent data from the Central Bureau of Statistics indicates that the city is ranked at socio-economic level 3 (out of 10). In the year 2000, Netivot was officially declared a city by the Ministry of Interior and its population, as of 2004, stands at 26,000 inhabitants (Central Bureau of Statistics, 2005).

To a visitor arriving in Netivot, the city looks like many other development towns in Israel that conform with the modernist form of space. The housing blocks and the semi-detached houses are in accord with the road system that marks the planned neighbourhood units. This urban scheme, designed by Tzion HaShimshoni, is based on modernistic planning principles such as zoning; green open, public spaces linked to pedestrian paths; and efficient road systems that link between the different zones.[5] Nevertheless, this schematic urban morphology is visually and spatially disrupted by indications of a different layer of urban life and experience that reflect diverse perceptions of what constitutes a city – an approach that highlights the way in which 'people are never passive recipients of external initiatives, but rather always struggle within their own immediate contexts of constraints and opportunities to produce meaningful life with their own particular values and goals' (Beng-Lan, 2002, p. 202).

Jerusalem Street is the main entrance to Netivot – other streets branch out from it, bearing names of Jewish Moroccan saints and rabbis. At the main streets' corners, on top of the official street signs, an additional placard is placed with an image of Rabbi Yisrael Abuhatzeira known as the Baba Sali (Praying Father in Moroccan Arabic) who was born in Morocco, immigrated to Israel in the 1950s and several years later settled in Netivot. Following his religious, spiritual and political influence, with the subsequent construction of such sites, they have also gained political importance at the municipal as well as the national level (Ben Ari and Bilu, 1997, p. 246). Netivot has also begun to attract Jews who have returned to their religious roots.

The Baba Sali died in 1984. His funeral in Netivot's cemetery drew an estimated 100,000 people. The influence of the Baba Sali has grown and the city has become a renowned focus of pilgrimage for the Moroccan Jewish community in Israel as well as from abroad, i.e., for Moroccan Jews residing in France and Canada. His gravesite in Netivot has become a popular pilgrimage site in Israel, especially on the date commemorating his death.

It is important to mention Kosansky's remark that the Jewish pilgrimage shares similarities with saint veneration as practised by both Muslims and Jews in Morocco (Kosansky, 2003, p. 553). Though several anthropologists have extensively written about this phenomenon, exploring the cultural, social and political dimension of it (Bilu and Ben Ari, 1992), no special attention has been given to the spatial influence of it, or to its contribution to creating Netivot as a place – a void that the following section aims to fill.

If the visitor to the city were to follow the signs along Abuhatzeira Street, s/he would begin to recognize a different architectural expression of the buildings – contradicting the modernist space and commemorating the past of the Jewish community in the diaspora. This issue was raised in an interview with the representative of the Baba Sali Institutions[6] who claimed that the use of such architectural style that 'purposely does not fit the Netivot cityscape... is the appropriate way to commemorate the Tzadik[7] ... The buildings in Morocco in the Tafilalt region (an oasis in the Moroccan Sahara) are similar. We replicated them here in Netivot, in order to symbolize the past'.

Down the road, Abuhatzeira Street leads to the edge of the city, where the modernist housing blocks mark the end of the urban constructed area. The back of these buildings faces a neglected open space, which according to the planning regulations detaches the city from its cemetery. Nonetheless, Netivot's cemetery is not a dead place – the Baba Sali burial site has become a focal point of religious, spiritual and social encounters, especially at the time of the Hillulah, or celebration day. From the architectural point of view, the place constitutes an attempt to establish an icon that commemorates not only the Baba Sali legend but the memory of the Jewish community in Morocco as well. This notion was raised by several people during the last Hillulah when I asked them what the significance of Netivot is for them. A man in his fifties told me that he was a child when his family immigrated to Israel from Morocco: 'I do not remember myself what it was like there, but we come here every year with my mother... She has told us that it is exactly the same. I feel as though I were there' (Interview, January 23, 2007). Let me suggest that here lays the notion of the diaspora experience for those who are here but still attached to there.

Interestingly enough, the modification of the cemetery into a pilgrimage site has been done by official planning procedures. The new urban scheme that has been authorized enables the modification of land use from a cemetery into a pilgrimage site: 'the objective of [the] plan is ... c) Altering the existing land use from public, open space into a burial plot of 4,339 square meters ...' (Urban scheme No. 103\03\22). Moreover, the modified urban scheme of the cemetery acknowledges the pilgrims' needs according to their tradition and allocates space for the construction of a 'feast shelter' for use by the pilgrims, the establishment of a structure for commercial activity and the construction of three rest units:

There is a custom among some ethnic groups that the terminally ill seek healing at saints' graves by praying and seclusion, as well as by adjacent sleeping accommodations. The purpose of the rest units is to enable these people to realize their wishes under the same roof [as the other activities]. (Urban scheme No. 103\03\22)

Spatially speaking, on the day of the Hillulah, the neglected space between the edge of the city and the cemetery is transformed into a meeting place of the pilgrims. Thousands of people visit the Baba Sali burial site and a lively market of religious goods, food and clothing serves the crowds.

The extensive city life takes place in a public space, which is actually a parking lot, while the modernist shikunim that house many of the Baba Sali's community members serves as the backdrop. The modernist urban order is further transformed by means of the cemetery. The new religious and educational institutions that have been established by the Baba Sali Foundation are designed with reference to the 'old-new' architecture and are used as landmarks on the urban scale (Fig. 11.1).

The effect of the diaspora–Mizrahi religious notion of the city is acknowledged by the municipality that participates (in terms of budget) in the Hillulah events and acknowledges the contribution of the institutions to the city, stating that 'On its 50th anniversary, all Netivot's inhabitants

FIGURE 11.1   A new building in Netivot. Photo by Michael Jacobson.

appreciate the contribution of the Baba Sali to the development and progress of the city. The municipality is committed to act, by all means, in order to commemorate the Baba Sali legend and to support its institutions' (Yehiel Zohar, Mayor of Netivot in the Baba Sali Foundation brochure, 2006). The reconstruction of Netivot's Tefilalt-like sense of place coincides with Oren Kosansky's observation of the considerable Jewish element of the city in Morocco in the mellah (the segregated Jewish quarter in Morocco) and its Jewish cemetery. Architecturally speaking, he suggests that there is a specific Jewish architecture expressed in the mellah. The main road is lined with exceptionally elevated buildings with distinct decor marking their elevation in the front. Also, he observed that the balconies extend beyond the lanes below – an element not to be found elsewhere in the old city (Kosansky, 2001). Moreover, the interim space created in Netivot has also constructed a virtual network of places. Praying and imploring of the Baba Sali is possible via several Internet sites which also broadcast the burial site and prayers twenty-four hours a day.[8] I would suggest that Netivot appears to offer some insight into the potential of diaspora communities within a forceful national context to express, and often glorify, their ties to their homeland.

Let me elaborate on the relevance of the notion of the diaspora to our case. The concept of the diaspora has traditionally referred to cases of communities living outside of their homeland. The term is used extensively while referring to emigrants, expellees, alien residents and ethnic minorities. Beyond the different definitions, there are shared characteristics of the notion of the diaspora as referring to a given social group that has dispersed from its territory to a different, foreign region. In this process, the specific group constructs its collective memory concerning its origin, location, history and culture. More importantly, Safran argues, the diaspora group perceives itself as an excluded social entity which can not be fully integrated into the host society (Safran, 2005).

The definition above stems from the very specific case of the exile of the Jews from the Holy Land and their dispersion throughout several areas of the world. Such an approach must be seen as an ideal type since a comparison to other cases demonstrates that most diasporas do not match this definition. In contemporary postcolonial literature, there is a wider understanding of the term that broadly refers to it in relation to displacement, dislocation and reformation of the 'double consciousness' of being 'inside and outside' (Levy, 2001). Indeed, the diaspora discourse 'is loose in the world, for reasons having to do with decolonization, increased immigration, global communications, and transport – a whole range of phenomena that encourage multi-locale attachments, dwelling, and traveling within and across nations' (Clifford, 1997, p. 249).

The notion of homeland is an inherent component and is used as a raison d'être for the production of space (as presented in the previous sections) which is related to the ideological and political circumstances that caused these people to immigrate to Israel, while at the same time, Israeli-Zionist ideology denies the notion of the diaspora past, the geography and culture of these immigrants. More specifically, as already suggested by Levy, though Jews perceive the Land of Israel as the core of their collective history, they furthermore 'conceive of Morocco as a symbolic center; a homeland for those who remained behind as well as for those who migrated' (Levy, 2001, p. 245). Likewise, as in other cases, the role of religion in the diaspora experience and place making is central; places accumulate meaning beyond their function for religious practices and thus gain value and become social, cultural and political signifiers of diaspora identity (Fenton, 1988).

Discussion

This chapter examined the transformations in the discussion of the Oriental nature of the Israeli built environment, supporting the claim that identity – as a political and cultural construct – is related to the formulation of new time and space created by communal imagination processes that intertwine past, present and future. This process is a manifestation of hegemonic culture, which frames the place while intervening and generating spatial transformation, using space production as an instrument for their realization. Thus is formed the pedagogic landscape, the spatial fabric which teaches us about our past and our identity, and within which the built environment assumes its structured symbolic significance, being justified as a representative of the collective desire and thought.

The discussion points out the role of the built environment in the production of Jewish place in the old-new space, and, as indicated, this is the site of ongoing struggles, in which top-down power creates counter-reactions that do not adhere to the desire to modernize/westernize space. Indeed, within the Israeli space, as a product of counter-acts, the modernist housing machine became a hybrid twice. First, it became transformed from a site that expressed a unified modernist national identity into a site that symbolized the excluded *Mizrahi* population. Second, it became transformed from a site based on the notion of progressive modernity into a site of alternative modernity, where individual place production violates the top-down initiatives.

Indeed, space is not a static container of social relations; people create alternative local narratives that do not necessarily reflect the rationale of the nation or of capital, nor the social hierarchy or the power relations that create them. In relation to this article, the counter-production of urban order, I would propose, is a direct result of the Zionist ideology based on the denial of a diaspora past. However, this conclusion does not aim to idealize or essentialize the Arab character of Jews in the diaspora. Following Raz-Karkotzkin, historically there had been tension among the Jews as a minority in their Arab countries of origin. However, this tension was not defined as a cultural gap to be overcome. It is the Eurocentric model of the Israeli national project that contains the East-West dichotomy as an objective category of modernity and space ordering that leads to the conclusion that being included in the Israeli collective is both the tangible and symbolic act of Jews foregoing Arab culture and place construction (Raz-Karkotzkin, 1993, p. 126).

Theoretically, I have indicated the relevance of postcolonial theory to the understanding of the Israeli space/place production.[9] First, the postcolonial body of knowledge critically examines the social structures that result from ideologies of domination stemming from colonial histories. Secondly, postcolonial criticism has enabled an analysis of the ways in which subaltern cultures are shaped while internalizing hegemonic culture. Thirdly, a significant issue in the postcolonial theory is hybridism which is linked to the notion of the diaspora. Here, allow me to rephrase the notion of the diaspora as it is exposed by the case study. The concept of the diaspora indeed incorporates the transnational experience of those who returned home according to Zionist ideology, a situation producing negotiable multidirectional ideas and spatio-cultural urban topographies.

Through these lenses, this chapter rethinks the traditional view of architecture that assumes the national category as the natural realm for space production – a perspective that lends high priority to official planning and architecture practice as an apparatus for the production of national sovereignty, an issue discussed in the first section. Yet, it also suggests that the multiple loyalties of people is simultaneously moulded in different spaces/places, locating themselves between here and there, within sovereign, state boundaries, and at the same time in their diaspora experience that produces a hybrid place. This term is not a fixed topographical site of negotiation between different locales (i.e., societies, cultures), but rather a zone of deterritorialization which in turn produces identity.

Hybridity as a site of negotiation was not confined merely to the tenement housing blocks environment. The new social, economic and political structure as indicated in Netivot enabled the shifting of the excluded imagined place and desires to be included in the official mapping of the city, and the extensive infiltration of this architecture into other spheres became visible. In fact, the modernist model that seeks to level the range of identities has become an indication of a multicultural option that grows from the bottom up and enables a discussion of Netivot as a project of alternative modernity – a concept focusing on the significance of modernity in daily life among societies and spaces that are not part of the 'first world'. This type of modernity rejects the bourgeois ethos of modernity, and, instead, seeks recognition of the fact that different modernization projects have not produced uniform results (Appadurai, 1996). At the basis of this cultural theory lies recognition of the many expressions of modernity. The capitalist economy, technology and bureaucratic organization of the state are inherent elements of modernity, but they lead to different types of modernity that diverge from the binary view of modernity versus traditionalism.

In this context, the peripheral city of Netivot can be seen as a third space, where the recognition of planning authorities enabled the expression of communal architecture that is not subjected to the hegemonic narrative. A similar argument is presented by Ben Ari and Bilu who suggest that the emergence of sacred sites of Jewish saints in Israeli development towns is not just rooted among the North African diaspora, but rather it strengthens people's sense of belonging to their places:

> By constructing these sites people in development towns come to terms with their peripheral status in Israel. This phenomenon is related to what maybe termed an internal Israeli cultural debate centering on its identity as a "Middle Eastern" society; to the extent which Israel shares with its Arab neighbors a set of cultural concepts and guidelines by which public life is carried out. (Ben Ari and Bilu, 1997, p. 61)

The question that remains is to what extent it is possible to view the third space as an arena of subversive struggle and negotiation, as suggested by Bhabha. Let me suggest that though the third space can be seen as an element that challenges the hegemonic perception of space, it does not transform it strategically. If we would return to the peripheral characteristics of Netivot (in terms of socio-economic, class and ethnic stratification that

I have cited earlier),[10] this recognition cannot come in place of or be separated from distributive questions. Rather, it should not draw attention away from distributive issues, as then the city would fall into the trap of perpetuating the hierarchy as dictated by the state's spatial ordering.

Notes

[1] A version of this article was originally published in: Yacobi, H. (2008), 'From State-Imposed Urban Planning to Israeli Diasporic Place: The Case of Netivot and the Grave of Baba Sali', in J. Brauch, A. Lipphardt, A. Nocke (eds), *Jewish Topographies: Visions of Space, Tradition and Place*. Ashgate: London, pp. 63–82

[2] Mizrahi Jews, Mizrahim in plural, are those who come from Arab and Muslim countries.

[3] 'The Building' in Hebrew.

[4] See, for example, Shadar (2004), Kallus and Law-Yone (2002).

[5] For a detailed discussion see Efrat (2004).

[6] Interview with the representative of the Baba Sali Institutions in Netivot, September 25, 2006; translated by the author.

[7] Tzadik is a righteous person.

[8] See, for example, www.po-ip.co.il

[9] In the scope of this chapter, I did not address the relevance of postcolonial discussion to the understanding of social and political structures in Israel (e.g., in *Theory and Criticism*, 20 and 26). However, one topic that postcolonial discussion has not included is the position of space designing practices, such as urban planning and architecture, which challenges this chapter.

[10] New research findings point to the way in which Netivot's image among the Israeli public has been improved. One explanation for this is the transformation of the city into a spiritual node that exposes it to the public. Furthermore, in comparison to other development towns, Netivot's economy is improving, independent of state subsidies or intiatives (*Ha'aretz* Newspaper, January 26, 2007).

Bibliography

AlSayyad, N. (2001), 'Hybrid Culture/Hybrid Urbanism: Pandora's Box of the "Third Place" ', in AlSayyad, N. (ed.), *Hybrid Urbanism: On the Identity Discourse and the Built Environment*. New York: Praeger Publishers, pp. 1–20.

Appadurai, A. (1996), *Modernity at Large: Cultural Dimensions of Globalizations*. Minneapolis: University of Minnesota Press.

Ben-Ari, E. and Bilu, Y. (1997), 'Saint's Sanctuaries in Israeli Development Towns', in Ben Ari, E. and Bilu, Y. (eds), *Grasping Land Space and Place in Contemporary Israeli Discourse and Experience*. Albany: State University of New York Press.

Beng-Lan, G. (2002), *Modern Dreams: An Inquiry into Power, Cultural Production and the Cityscape in Contemporary Urban Penang, Malaysia*. Ithaca, NY: Cornell Southeast Asia Program.

Bhabha, H. (1994), *The Location of Culture*. London & New York: Routledge.
Bilu, Y. and Ben-Ari, E. (1992), 'The Making of Modern Saints: Manufactured Charisma and the Abu-Hatseiras of Israel'. *American Ethnologist*, 19(4), 29–44.
Castells, M. (1978), *City, Class and Power*. London: Macmillan.
Central Bureau of Statistics (2004), *Characterization and Ranking of Local Authorities According to the Population's Socio-Economic Level in 2001*. Jerusalem: Central Bureau of Statistics.
Clifford, J. (1997), *Routes: Travel & Translation in the Late Twentieth Century*. Cambridge MA: Harvard University Press.
Efrat, Z. (2004), *The Israeli Project: Building and Architecture 1948–1973*. Tel Aviv: Museum of Art [Hebrew].
Fenton, J. (1988), *Transplanting Religious Traditions – Asian Indians in America*. New York: Praeger Publishers.
Holston, J. (1989), *The Modernist City – An Anthropological Critique of Brasilia*. Chicago & London: University of Chicago Press.
Kallus, R. and Law-Yone H. (2002), 'National Home/Personal Home: Public Housing and the Shaping of National Space in Israel'. *European Planning Studies*, 10(6), 765–79.
King, D. A. (2003), 'Actually Existing Postcolonialism: Colonial Urbanism and Architecture after the Postcolonial Turn,' in *Postcolonial Urbanism*, Ryan Bishop and John Phillips (eds). London and New York: Routledge, pp. 167–83.
Kosansky, O. (2001), 'Reading Jewish Fez: On the Cultural Identity of a Moroccan City'. *The Journal of the International Institute, University of Michigan*, 8(3), 8–9.
—. (2003), 'All Dear Unto God: Saints, Pilgrimage, and Textual Practice in Jewish Morocco'. Unpublished dissertation, University of Michigan.
Lefèbvre, H. (1991), *The Production of Space*. Oxford, UK & Cambridge, USA: Blackwell.
Levy, A. (2001), 'Center and Diaspora: Jews in late-twentieth-century Morocco'. *City & Society*, 13(2), 245–70.
Madanipour, A. (1996), *Design of Urban Space – An Inquiry into a Socio-spatial Process*. Chichester: John Wiley and Sons.
Netivot Municipality website: netivot.muni.il
Nitzan-Shiftan, A. (2000), 'Whitened Houses'. *Theory and Criticism*, 16, 227–32 [Hebrew].
Norberg-Schultz, C. (1979), *Genius Loci – Towards a Phenomenology of Architecture*. New York: Rizzoli.
Oz, A. (1983), *In the Land of Israel*. Tel Aviv: Am Oved.
Posner, Y. (1938), 'The Village in Eretz Israel'. *Habinyan*, 1–2 [Hebrew].
Raz-Karkotzkin, A. (1993), 'Exile within Sovereignty: Towards a Critic of the 'Negation of Exile' in Israel Culture'. *Theory and Criticism*, 4, 23–56 [Hebrew].
Safran, W. (2005), 'The Jewish Diaspora in a Comparative and Theoretical Perspective'. *Israel Studies*, 10(1), 36–60.
Schiler, A. (1937), 'Land Development Problems for Housing', *Habinyan*, 28–33 [Hebrew].
Shadar, H. (2004), 'Between East and West: Immigrants, Critical Regionalism and Public Housing'. *The Journal of Architecture*, 9, 23–48.

Sharon, A. (1951), *Physical Planning in Israel*. Jerusalem: Israel Government Press [Hebrew].

Shenhav, Y. (2006), *The Arab Jews: A Postcolonial Reading of Nationalism, Religion, And Ethnicity*. Stanford: Stanford University Press.

Taylor, C. (1999), 'Two Theories of Modernity'. *Public Culture*, 11(1), 153–74.

Tuan, Y. (1977), *Space and Place: The Perspective of Existence*. Minneapolis: Minneapolis University Press.

Tzfadia, E. and Yiftachel, O. (2004), 'Between Urban and National: Political Mobilization among Mizrahim in Israel's "Development Towns" '. *Cities*, 21(1), 41–55.

Urban Scheme no. 103\03\22: Netivot Municipality Archive.

Yacobi, H. (2008) 'Architecture, Orientalism and Identity: A Critical Analysis of the Israeli Built Environment'. *Israel Studies*, 13(1), 94–118.

Zaslevsky, D. (1954), *Housing for Immigrants – Construction, Planning and Development*. Tel Aviv: Am Oved [Hebrew].

—. (1969), *A Survey of Netivot's Development*. Jerusalem: Ministry of Housing [Hebrew].

Chapter 12

The Sacred in the City: Havana. Alejo Carpentier or 'Fieldwork' in the Urban

Liliana Gómez

The Search for the Sacred in Havana's Urban Spaces

Rare is the popular window in Havana that does not have a mould of the Virgin of Charity, or any other merciful divinity. In some, the votive images constitute real museums . . . Museums whose cathedral is at the old Plaza de Vapor where a window is placed under the patronage of big porcelain and ceramic figures that are worthy of being placed – because of their authentic value – in a gallery of popular arts . . . A figure of an enormous rooster that seems to announce in victory the golden dawn of a major prize; figures of a very fine Virgin, of a San Lazaro on an Italian altar, and of a delicious Chinese dog on a grey horse – ceramics that would inspire an intelligent antiquary. The frame is completed with four vases full of artificial roses, a Chinese painting accomplished in silk, and a lithography that comes from the area of Zanja and that shows us the mayor court of Chiang Kaishek meeting with the counsellor. (Carpentier, 1996a, pp. 46–7)[1]

It is with the insights from everyday life, viewed in terms of aesthetics and popular cultural dynamics that the Cuban writer, Alejo Carpentier, observes his native city of Havana, Cuba. By the time of his return to Havana in 1939, he tried to decipher the constitutive elements of Havana's modern spaces: he captured the sacred as the experience of the heterogeneous, the incongruent and the hybrid. His observation is supported by a series of both theoretical and methodological questions he attempted to answer through (new) ethnographical lenses: by decentring himself as an 'observer who observes himself observing', the city is narrated in a different way, from the margins of what is constituted as the sacred. What are Havana's modern urban spaces? Which urban popular culture does Carpentier describe in his writings? What was going to be the socialist project's legacy after the Cuban

Revolution of 1959? And what is the cultural and social cohesion of the urban society that is experienced in these modern urban spaces? To follow these questions I will look in particular at the urban chronicle 'La Habana vista por un turista cubano', which is a key – point of entry into Carpentier's urban writings and experience of the city, and hence also his ethnographic observations, all of which reflect his encounters with the surrealist movement in Paris in the years before returning to Havana. This chronicle in particular helps us to decipher the sacred as a notion and experience which Carpentier described by looking at Havana's modern urban spaces and urban popular culture. There are two main paths I try to follow. First, I will look at Carpentier's urban (ethnographical) writing and his concept of everyday life that describes the modern and urban cultural transformations in Cuba. Secondly, I will try to decipher the sacred in Havana's modern spaces that, according to Carpentier's search, was to become a key concept in understanding these processes of transformation. Both paths will show how Carpentier's work oscillates between an ethnographical and hence epistemological positioning, that of a new kind of observation, and a political project of society proposed by a novel narrative strategy. Both paths follow the different influences and transatlantic encounters present in Carpentier's work. Both paths point to the (actual) state of modern Cuban society, its incorporation of Afro-Cuban mythology, and the importance of the city of Havana with respect to the Cuban socialist project that followed.

'La Habana vista por un turista cubano' (1939)

I understand Carpentier's chronicle 'La Habana vista por un turista cubano' as a precursor of his later major literary work: it is part of a novel ethnographic observation, present in his later narratives and writing. The chronicle shows in particular the writer's interest in deciphering the 'modern' in Havana's urban spaces as well as new forms of everyday culture, which reflect the (his) experience of the sacred. Published as a series in the Cuban weekly journal *Carteles* in 1939, the chronicle proposes some unknown methods of (ethnographic) observation and decipherment of the emergence of the modern in the city of Havana. It makes 'visible' some of the constitutive elements that I understand as relevant for a kind of archaeology of approaches to the urban medium and to the conceptualization of the urban cultural transformation processes that make us perceive the modern as 'modern'. These elements, or newly invented methods, belong to two (aesthetic) strategies that characterize the chronicle. The first concerns the question of the constitution of the cultural, while the second points to the writer's decentred perspective that I will look at in a moment. From within this decentring perspective of observation Carpentier approaches cultural phenomena that are characteristic of the urban transformations of the 1920s and 1930s experienced in Havana. However there are also two other aspects present here: the chronicle performs a practice of theory which Carpentier translates from his own experience of everyday life in Havana, that is 'lo popular' – the popular. This experience is shaped by his intimate, 'new' contact with Havana, when he returned to Cuba in 1939 after eleven years of exile in Paris. The other conceptual and historical moment has to do with the crisis of modernity that Carpentier experiences through the modern city against the background of the crisis, equally present, of the Second World War, which started in September 1939, the same year as the chronicle's publication. This moment certainly defines his restless search for rethinking the history as an alternative one, as well as the cultural appropriations between the metropolis, Paris and the Caribbean. Not only does this chronicle record the conceptual re-emergence of the Caribbean, by projecting an alternative and therefore hybrid modernity, but it also assembles multiple, polyphonic transatlantic voices that were part of the intellectual group called the 'surrealist dissidents', such as Robert Desnos, Ribemont Dessaignes, Georges Bataille, Michel Leiris, Walter Mehring, Roger Vitrac and others, in Paris at that time. Not only does this chronicle give form to and sketch out Carpentier's later and most important cultural concept, 'lo real maravilloso' – the real marvellous, that characterized the new programme of Latin American literature projected by him, and which much later emerged as the so-called 'boom literature' – but it also searches for the deepest recesses of an alternative and hybrid modernity whose possibility he identified in everyday life, that is 'lo popular'.

I would like to briefly recall the context of Carpentier's chronicle 'La Habana vista por un turista cubano'. It seems that the chronicle is an answer to, and a conceptual questioning of, the European cultural crisis of 1939. How could we read Europe's cultural crisis, manifested in the violent eruption of the Second World War in September 1939? In 1931, the German writer Walter Mehring, who was invited by Carpentier to write a short article for the journal *Imán* – place of a constellation of so-called 'surrealist dissidents', reminded us of the necessity to understand the European catastrophe of the period in-between the wars years against the background of Europe's colonial project and its transatlantic limits:

> Before the war they showed us, in a Berlin exhibition, two strange beings with noses in the form of a pecker and maxillaries in the form of a proboscis that were meant to represent – they assured us – the last remaining Aztecs. The schoolboys were brought there en masse to contemplate these figures because it was a scientific curiosity – that is a charlatanry . . . How would it be with the last Europeans? Wouldn't they be exhibited some day in a similar manner in a museum in Montevideo? . . . And if the culture of the United States lived as long as the Incan civilization, would it leave us comparable ruins? (Mehring, 1931, p. 211)[2]

Carpentier certainly responded with this chronicle to the crisis as a disaster of progress that also announced the defeat of the city's modernization project. He and the 'surrealist dissidents' conceptualized Europe's cultural crisis from within that transatlantic perspective and it was at that same moment that he left Paris for Havana after his long years of exile and his French experience. This complex moment is present in the chronicle. Carpentier tried to decipher it through the emergence of modern urban spaces and the new metropolitan reality of Havana when he returned to his homeland, Cuba. Nevertheless, the real marvellous is *experience* of those urban spaces from which the sacred, the magic and everyday life – 'lo popular' – gain new meanings and become a constituting force.

Ethnographical Imagination: The Chronicle

Without doubt the chronicle elaborates an ethnographical and sociological imagination which describes the city and its urban spaces as a laboratory where it is possible to observe processes of social constitution whose heterogeneous elements produce a new social configuration that we identify as 'modern' (Rincón, 1998, p. 335). The experience of the sacred in these modern spaces, and in particular its heterogeneous elements, are part of that ethnographical imagination – or ethnography of the (modern) self – manifested in the chronicle. Carpentier introduces a new modern figure, that of the tourist sui generis – in its double Gestalt as 'modern tourist' and 'tourist in his own country' (Rincón, 1998, p. 337) – who is configured by the author's own displacement of cultural identity. The modern tourist incarnates the modern gaze fixed on the Caribbean metropolis. This gaze, similar to what Mehring detected in the Berlin exhibition at the end of 'colonial' times, seems to reorder Havana's urban spaces. In the chronicle, the 'tourist in his own country' is in that particular and unique position of an 'observer who observes himself observing' and of an 'observer who observes himself while observing' (ibid.). Carpentier invented novel tools of observation that oscillate between the methods of modern ethnography and the new approach performed by his surrealist friends and orchestrated in the modern metropolis, Paris. The modern urban development of Havana, the so-called 'Paris of the Caribbean', in the 1920s and 1930s under the influence of the United States, following the short US-occupation of the island from the Spanish–Cuban–American War in 1898 until 1902, can be characterized by a new distribution of the city spaces, orchestrated for leisure activities and pre-occupied with the modern commercial tourism then emerging. Carpentier critically took these circumstances into account with the figure of the modern tourist. He wrote:

> The entrance to the port [of Havana] seems a work by a most skilful stage manager ... where an architect had the ingenious idea to install the central station in a gothic cathedral, the tourist finds himself with a vision that does not rob him of his romantic illusions; those of the colonial castles, with moats and look-outs, that are a tangible materialization of images imposed on his mind by the reading of novels and historic tales. ... A young American tourist who stood next to me made this adorable question, pointing with the index finger towards the Morro and Cabaña: But ... these are real castles? (Carpentier, 1996a, p. 29)[3]

It has been observed by sociologists that the sociological view is confirmed through the perception of the modern metropolis. The questions that the theoreticians and researchers, among them Émile Durkheim and Max Weber, tried to answer when examining phenomena of societies that were considered less complex, the so-called 'primitive' societies, became relevant for the perception of the modern city. The modern city was the laboratory where they could observe that the perception or the experience of living there not only exercises its effects at the level of the characteristics of a sociological view, but also that the construction of sociological concepts refer themselves in relation to the perception of the modern city (Rincón, 1998, p. 335). When Carpentier returned from his exile in Paris endowed with (these) novel tools of observation, which made the chronicle 'La Habana vista por un turista cubano' in particular a decipherment of Havana's urban modernity, he also witnessed a 'second view' dispensed by a modern ethnology and surrealism (ibid., p. 337).

We can thus observe in the chronicle that the crisis is conceptualized and narrated through novel images that open up new cultural perspectives of an alternative (Latin American) history. These novel images narrate the changes in the modern city of Havana, the spaces of everyday life that intersect with those of the experience of the sacred, or the heterogeneous elements of a modernity-*other* that define Havana's urban spaces. The author's wonderment when walking Havana's streets decipher the constitutive elements of the Afro-Cuban culture which intermingle with the Spanish Catholic ordering grid of the historic town, the cathedral, the places, the Spanish sacred relics of Saints, the sculptures. He finds the juxtaposition of everyday things from urban and rural culture in the city's modern spaces: the driving forces of a heterogeneous modern society, the Cuban society that includes the Spanish cultural heritage and the Afro-Cuban appropriation of Christian divinities, all constitutive elements of a marvellous new syncretistic reality.

The chronicle exposes at least two different operations of cultural critique with which to confront the crisis of the twentieth century: first, Carpentier operates with an exteriorized perspective – that of the 'tourist in his own country' – which allows him to displace the once familiar by seeing the non-familiar. Second, the chronicle is the favourite narrative space for experimenting with novel tools to observe and experience the rapidly transforming city. Due to this epistemological decentring, that of positioning oneself as observer of everyday life and thinking with (and from within) the perspective of 'lo popular', practised by walking the city of Havana, the 'tourist in his own country' now registers and perceives other details that he 'no había sabido ver' – that he could not see before – that of the modernization of the 'vida habanera', of life in Havana (Carpentier, 1939, p. 37). The familiar is related to a basic determination of the tourist's world, and, according to Roland Barthes, it is part of the domestication of the foreign in the form of exoticism. In that sense, Carpentier observes:

> Today it is indisputable that the concept of the suprarealist poets [. . .] is part of the intellectual baggage of every informed traveller. This traveller does not ignore that one of the first things which have to be visited in a city is the market place – the place where humble manifestations of popular art always flourish. Also, the market place is the place of contrast, and the contrast is the maximum generator of poetic images. For many years European and American travellers have learned to feel lo popular. (Carpentier, 1996a, p. 39)[4]

The chronicle demonstrates a powerful poetic-utopian potential, nourished by experienced images of everyday life, and is a projection of an alternative modernity that includes rather than excludes heterogeneous elements, such as the different experiences of the transformed forms of the sacred and its manifestation in urban culture and urban spaces. Heterotopic spaces emerge out of 'lo popular', out of the vibrant streets of Havana, out of the cultural hybrid. Carpentier conceives of everyday life – 'lo popular' – in its limits between social rationality and the aesthetical potential of opposition, as a sort of resistance or subversion of the modern world's crisis and rationality. We can certainly decipher this form of writing as a cultural critique of the homogeneous modernity that characterized Europe's cultural crisis: its totalitarian regimes. Carpentier searches for other spaces, other than those of totalitarian logic. He searches for the utopian that is no longer subjected to the logic of war. Indeed, the chronicle lives with and from within the 'peripheral' urban spaces of everyday life, 'lo popular', which has decentred the city centre itself. The sacred in the city can only be comprehended from within these popular dynamics, which form modern Cuban urban culture, and which would later be incorporated, in 1959, by the project of the Cuban Revolution.

Magical Formulas between Paris and Havana

Carpentier's chronicle 'La Habana vista por un turista cubano' is indebted to another project that illuminates his search for novel tools to observe the transformations of the modern city of Havana. His search makes clear that the sacred in its social function participates in what I recognize as the realm of magic and in particular the magic in modern urban spaces. I would like to recall in this context the radio programme, which was elaborated and invented by Desnos and Carpentier himself, between 1931 and 1939 during his stay in Paris, as a response to his encounters with the surrealist movement. The radio art that Desnos practised and for which Carpentier organized the music opened up a space for collective imagination that allowed the radio listeners to participate and intervene with their own images and imaginaries. Here everyday experience is the capacity for social cohesion that I try to decipher as the sacred. There were two radio programmes that made particularly clear how the city was conceived and deciphered as an imaginary order or imaginary principle that was collectively shared: one is 'Fantômas' and the other 'La clef des songes'. The radio formats developed by Desnos make especially clear the social role of the (surrealist) imagination, which reflected both the imagined and the collective projections. Not only can we recognize here the interweaving of a certain 'collective conscience' – following Émile Durkheim – with different visual modern urban superficies, but we can also identify the practice of novel methods of decipherment of the constitution of culture and of urban society's transformations. Within these transformations new forms of the sacred meet with what I like to call here the magic. Let me explore this a little bit more.

The programme 'La clef des songes' was a radio-montage realized between 1938 and 1939 and was shaped by, and based on, the different stories of the dreams sent in by the radio listeners every week. Desnos aimed to crystallize a sort of collective image or collective imagination that would represent the listeners' unconscious or collective unconscious. He wanted to discover a shared fear, a collective dream, or the desire for a possible common space that is the magic sphere of modern social cohesion. The programme played with a novel representation of the modern city. It approached the projective energy of the image: an image depicted by the dreams and urban imaginaries of the audience. This particular relation between image and collective imagination, between perception and observation of the city, also captured the subversive forces of everyday life, 'lo popular'. If there is a convergence between everyday life and the sacred then, without doubt, the programme 'La clef des songes' played with it. The sacred and its subversive forces, following Carpentier and the dissident surrealists, was looked at from the elements that were less visible, the elements that capture the driving forces of modern urban society. As the radio programme unfolded it became clear that the key to the sacred in the city lays in the deciphering of the experience of everyday life in modern urban culture. The sacred adopts here the cultural forms of magic which help us in identifying the 'collective unconscious' as social cohesion. Desnos wrote about these aspects in the article 'L'Imagerie moderne', which was published years earlier in 1929 in the journal *Documents*. There he pointed out the magic energy of the popular figure Fantômas that eventually became the title for one of the radio programmes. Desnos identified in it the superimposition of the modern city and its urban imaginaries and representations, which are the modern city's magical forms. He noted:

> ... because it is these popular manifestations which are affected the most by sudden fashions. Disdained today, we will explore tomorrow the extraordinary covers of the illustrated supplements of the *Petit Journal* and *Petit Parisien*, which give a perfectly expressive snapshot of actuality and history. . . . aspects of capital cities and in particular of Paris, worldy manners . . .how the people imagine them, bourgeois manners, police manners, and for the first time the presence of the marvellous proper to the 20th century, natural utilization of machines and recent inventions, mystery of things, of people and of destiny. (Desnos, 1929, p. 377)[5]

Desnos captured the actuality of history: the coloured covers of the popular series 'Fantômas' certainly represented how the city and its uses were imagined reflecting a wide spectrum, and opposing itself to the all too rationalistic discourse of modern city planning. The everyday rescued the collective and therefore heterogeneous (urban) spaces. The covers of the 'suppléments illustrés', which were almost magic representations and collective imaginaries, were also documents and visualizations of the modern city as experienced and perceived. They formed, nevertheless, an archive of the cultural constitution of urban society. Presented as archaeology of the urban medium that excavated past and actual life forms, the popular manifestations of everyday life made visible the transforming power of modernity:

> ... the nightmares of which a poster of the epoch gives a very precise idea. . . . If Fantômas was the agent of all these revolutions, he would have been powerfully supported in his psychic action by the posters which . . . were pasted on the walls. . . . It was in this way an entire series of magical formulas which were disseminated in the world. . . . (Desnos, 1929, pp. 377–8)[6]

How does the sacred manifest itself in its new cultural forms in the city? Although utopian energy is part of the posters of Fantômas's diffusion in the city, the series of magic formulas is embodied in the urban fabric. Is this series of magic formulas part of the sacred realm of the city? Without doubt, Desnos and Carpentier were looking with the radio programmes for heterogeneous spaces and an alternative modernity that could include the magical as well as the heterogeneous experience of the sacred in its modern cultural forms.

Back in Havana, Carpentier observed the heterogeneous spaces where urban popular culture was present in different objects related to Spanish Christian belief, superimposed with and incorporated in Afro-Cuban mythology, which had shaped the city spaces in their own way. Carpentier was always interested in the city's architecture and urban spaces – in his youth he wanted to become an architect – as well as in the Afro-Cuban elements of the hybrid Cuban culture, both present in his writings and ethnographical observations. In the short chronicle 'Regla, la ciudad mágica', written in 1941, he observed the manifestation of popular urban syncretism in the modern city of Havana as follows:

> A bit further, beyond the park, there is another heterodox altar, which is one of the most beautiful that I ever have seen in my life . . . Also, I could

almost affirm that it is unique in its category, because it is an 'aquatic altar'. Imagine a fountain full of vital water that serves as a harbour for a marine fauna of fishes, snails, and sponges. There are sea anemones, sea horses, and stars. In this swimming pool, floating eternally, there are a sailing boat whittled in timber by a devoted sailor and a British lead grey armoured cruiser named Southampton. There are also some vessels of lesser importance . . . But this entire convoy serves as an escort for the main piece in this miniature ocean: a timber boat in which the three Juanes of the most popular of the Creole prayers, Juan Indio, Juan Odio, and Juan Esclavo are rowing, hands together. And over this aquatic landscape, enclosed in a room, a double altar floats, carried by Solomonic columns and embellished with baroque angels with hands full of garlands of flowers. On the lower level, there is a big Virgin of Charity, with a rich headdress. On the upper level, a Virgin of Regla, of the same size as the previous, who with her authority dominates the whole of this maritime world, which encloses in itself, like a little universe, all the elements of modern poetry. At the foot of this extraordinary altar, that is more than three meters high, I could hear . . . the admirable beats of the drums batá that I have known during the long years of travel for the Afro-Cuban folklore . . . Only a few meters away there is another altar, dedicated to Saint Barbara, goddess of war, which loyal believers have adorned with lead soldiers, tank toys, planes, artillery, and many other bellicose attributes or red motifs – ritual colour of Changó . . . (Carpentier, 1996b, pp. 78–9)[7]

Syncretism and Urban Cultural Practices

Oscillating between architecture and ethnography, Carpentier's interest in popular urban syncretism and its different forms manifested in the city's spaces, would form the framework for most of his later literary works. In a very early but significant attempt, in 1933, Carpentier published an article that tells us about his interest in the sacred in Havana's modern spaces. He published an extraordinary series of photographs in the journal *Le phare de Neuilly* that makes this interest in Afro-Cuban mythology particularly clear. Indeed, these very elements of Afro-Cuban mythology inform the emerging modern urban spaces in Cuba. This life-long interest also defined his later well-known novels and determined aspects of the movement of Latin American literature of 'lo real maravilloso'. The series of photographs published for the first time were accompanied by the following short text 'Images et Prières nègres':

> The photographs which accompany these lines were taken by me – autumn 1927 – in the small room, "*famba*" or forbidden small room, of a black sorcerer, Taita José, whose cabin, surmounted by the horn of a billy goat, loomed in the heart of one of the most isolated regions in the province of Santiago in Cuba. The negatives of these photographs, of which only one copy exists, have been destroyed in the presence of the sorcerer. I hasten, however, to add that it is not necessary to go thus far, in Cuba, to find black sorcerers. There are even some at the gates of Havana. But those turn out to be so suspicious of the white man that it would have been impossible to take pictures of their altars. These images represent predominantly Christian divinities, interpreted or clothed according to the worshippers' predilection. But it is the rites of witchcraft that give them a secret life, a role, and a totally different identity. Saint Lazarus, which a grotesque statuette shows us leaning on his crutches covered in wounds symbolizes the power of Babayou-Ayé, medical divinity of the blacks. The Spanish virgins, which are in the centre of the altar, figure Yemayá, goddess of waters, and Ochúm, one of the women of Saint Barbara. The latter, changing sex, has become Shangó, god of thunder and tempests. As for the crucifix, it is named Obatalá, king of the creative forces of nature. Near by these images, the statuette of an adolescent (Eshu), brandishing a small axe, protects the labourers. The *diablito*, – little devil – masked with a black hood surmounted by a panache of raffia, personifies the sorcerer himself, transformed into a minor divinity. And the horns, the coral, the necklaces, the stones, the wooden pearls are adored for the materiality itself which constitutes them as elements of the universe and ritual attributes of the *orishas* – or powers – to which they are tied. These *orishas* have well-determined functions. Shango-Saint-Barbara, Eshu-the tiller, Elegbá-the-solitary-soul are invoked for their enchantment. Others are destined to watch over pregnant women or the sick. . . . Every image, every symbol, every object possesses its anthems and prayers. (Carpentier, 1933, pp. 44–5)[8]

Because Carpentier visited the sacred spaces of Afro-Cuban rituals and transcultural practices in Cuba, he became a witness to the vivid religious practices of resistance to modernization and, therefore, also to the suppression of Afro-Cuban culture during the preceding centuries and its peripheral, hidden, heterodox spaces. As a result, he could decipher the modern urban processes of transformation from a perspective of 'observer who observes himself observing' and of an 'observer who observes himself while observing' that would change any city narrative, once centred on the city centre. Within this decentring perspective of observing the city and of participating in popular urban culture and everyday life, Carpentier reverted to the urban myth and tale of the centre itself so that the city's symbolic, attractive forces and its urban topography received a different coloration. The city's narrative, from then on, would certainly be that of the peripheral but constitutive elements of its urban spaces. It could no longer be the narrative of the urban myth of the classic, symbolic centralization that is the cathedral of Notre-Dame of Paris (Rincón, 1998, p. 345), from within which cities' topologies had been narrated and perceived, defining, following Carpentier, the urban appropriation of the modern tourist. The topography of the Caribbean metropolis, the locus that is the cathedral, where all imaginations meet, would include – through Carpentier's writings – other heterogeneous spaces and syncretistic spaces. The window of the Plaza de Vapor, in this sense, is an allegory: 'the personifications are there as archetypical images. The idea of *métissage*, of heterogeneity, the poetics of the heteroclite and the marvellous are there. And there is something else too, the essence of these personifications: the utopias that have . . . incarnated them' (Rincón, 1998, p. 345, my transl.). This decentring perspective restores the sacred as heterogeneous experience in the city. Here a cultural and social cohesion can be lived and dreamt of and opposes an all too homogeneous modernity, a too rationalistic modern city planning.

Havana's Legacy of a Socialist City

In 1959, the Cuban Revolution had started to transform the city. With it emerged a new, modern project of nationhood, or 'cubanía'. At the centre of this project was the modern city of Havana facing the questions: 'How to deal with the Spanish colonial urban heritage?' and 'How to re-order the Republican city of Havana which should represent the ideal of a socialist city?'. It was clear that the birth of the 'new man' should go together with the re-semantization of the city of Havana. But how were the heterogeneous, syncretistic and hybrid spaces to be incorporated into the new project? What happened with those spaces of urban popular culture that Carpentier had observed and written about in the preceding decades?

When I travelled to Havana in 2002 for fieldwork I visited the housing project and city projection of Habana del Este located just at the opposite side of the entrance to the Bahía where the historic city centre begins. This socialist urban project of the 1960s was meant to initiate a new Cuban urban era by providing high quality housing for everyone. I arranged a meeting with the person responsible for the administration of Habana del Este. I took the *guagua*, the bus, or let us be more precise the *camello* as the Habaneros used to say, which is the rusty old bus in the shape of a camel which mainly serves the East. Departing from the historic city centre, 'la ciudad colonial', just across the Capitolio from the Republican era, it was quite a long drive outside the city, crossing the Bahía entrance through a tunnel built in the 1960s to connect and extend Havana to its East. But Havana didn't become an extended or amplified city. It seemed to me to leave the city and to leave behind all the heavy and overwhelming legacy of Cuban (Spanish) urban history, which the socialist project didn't really know how to face. The *camello* left the ruins of Havana to approach the promise of a new project. I arrived. I was sure that a narrative of the city of Havana nowadays is only possible from that angle, from within the point of view of the peripheries of Havana, from the new Havana.

I followed my guide with whom I had arranged that meeting and I was wandering through the big green open spaces between the modern building blocks. Housing, the promise of new housing in a variety of architectural forms and colours. Of course, these spaces were the same kind of spaces you find in other 'socialist cities' too: a monotonous, homogeneous but a generous open space. Here in Havana, here at the Caribbean Sea, the housing blocks had lost their colours already. The moisture had taken over; it dominated the facades without pity. Indeed, it seemed as if the Cuban environment might even resist this kind of modern urbanization. 'Would it be possible to enter the apartments?' I wanted to know. Suddenly he received me warmly with a smile: '¿Estás interesada en la vida habanera y no sólo en el urbanismo, verdad?' he asked me. Yes, I was rather interested in knowing about urban life and urban popular culture there. Determined, he brought me to a block set a little apart form the big housing units, just in front of the Sea. 'Conozco a la gente que vive aquí', he added. He explained that he wanted to make sure that they were not in any ceremony when entering the apartment in Block D, first floor. The door opened and a tall white woman appeared all dressed up in white clothes. She kindly let us in and showed us the rather small and dark apartment that was packed with too much furniture, mostly old pieces, possibly a kind of family heritage, some historic paintings, and black and white pictures hanging on the wall. I was a little bit disappointed about the highly lauded housing interior design. After all, the housing of Habana del Este gained many important international design awards. She apologized for the disorder in the apartment and offered a black and very sweet coffee. I accepted. As I got more comfortable in her space, she asked me to follow her into another room. 'No uses la cámara', she said. Proudly she opened the door and I couldn't believe my eyes: In this little inconspicuous apartment was hidden a beautiful marvellous altar. Brightly coloured Saints embellished it, and food and drinks were placed in front of it to calm the Orishas. In her old apartment in Centro Habana, she told me, she had not much space for this altar. But here in Habana del Este she was so happy to have an extra room for her rituals.

I remembered the imaginary of the unorthodox altars that Carpentier had described when returning to Havana in 1939. It is well known that Santería practices, religious practices from the Yoruba religion that the slaves brought once from Africa to the island, are common among the Cubans in Havana. And it is not as if these religious practices were only shared among the Afro-Cubans in Havana. I was reassured that everyone, or at least many, secretly practise this religion. The socialist (urban) project with its desire to homogenize was unable to include these religious practices. It had feared the constitutive heterogeneous elements, which could threaten the Revolution instead of serving it as a binding social force. Maybe this was one component of the popularity of Santería practices and beliefs among urban Habaneros. Maybe it was this kind of sacred space that opened up as a critical discourse opposing the socialist project. For me it became clear that to understand the modernization of Havana in the twentieth century, before and after the Revolution, it was important to understand that these heterogeneous spaces are part of the sacred which plays a crucial role in the configuration of the (modern) city. Indeed, the superimposition of the sacred and everyday life is the key to Havana's urban spaces: the practices of Santería in its various guises, the different sacred objects incorporated into the city space, the different holy gods, the Orishas, the colour of the sacred, the banished spaces in which the sacred cohabitates, the people's driving force to resist the everyday struggle of scarcity and control, the spaces for escape, the dynamics of the social and the cultural that bind the Habaneros together. A long time ago, in 1939, this similar idea of an alternative modernity, the poetics of the heteroclite and the marvellous, were projected by Carpentier as well as by the other 'surrealist dissidents' who looked for other spaces, for the sacred in the city, one that would resist totalitarian logic.

Notes

[1] 'Rara es la vidriera popular habanera que no tenga por alguna parte una estampa de la virgen de la Caridad, u otra divinidad propicia. En algunas, las imágenes votivas constituyen verdaderos museos... Museos cuya catedral se encuentra en la vieja Plaza de Vapor, donde una vidriera aparece colocada bajo el patronato de grandes figuras de porcelana y cerámica, dignas de situarse, por su auténtico valor, en una galería de arte popular... Figura de un enorme gallo en actitud de anunciar victoriosamente el alba dorada de un premio mayor; figuras de una virgen finísima, de un San Lázaro de altar italiano, y de un delicioso guerrero chino, montado en caballo gris – cerámica que sabría entusiasmar a un anticuario inteligente. El cuadro es completado por cuatro jarrones llenos de rosas artificiales, una pintura china ejecutada en seda, y una litografía procedente del barrio de Zanja, que nos muestra el estado mayor de Chiang Kaishek reunido en consejo' (Carpentier, 1996a, pp. 46–7). (English translation by the author.)

[2] 'Antes de la guerra nos mostraban, en una exhibición berlinesa, dos extraños seres, con narices en forma de pico y mandíbulas en hocico, que debían representar – según nos aseguraban – los últimos aztecas. Los chicos de las escuelas fueron llevados en masa para contemplar estas figuras, porque se trataba de una curiosidad científica – es decir, de una charlatanería... ¿Cómo serán los últimos europeos? ¿No los exhibirán de la misma manera, algún día, en un museo de Montevideo? . . . ¿Y si la cultura de los Estados Unidos llega a vivir el tiempo que vivió la civilización incaica, nos dejará ruinas comparables?' (Mehring, 1931, p. 211). (English translation by the author.)

[3] 'La entrada de su puerto parece obra de un habilísimo escenógrafo. [...] donde un arquitecto ha tenido la idea genial de instalar la estación de ferrocarril en una catedral gótica, el turista se encuentra con una visión que no defrauda sus ilusiones románticas; la de castillos coloniales, con fosos y atalayas, que son una materialización tangible de imágenes impuestas a su espíritu por la lectura de novelas o relatos históricos. [...] Una joven turista americana que se encuentra a mi lado me hace esta pregunta adorable, alargando el índice hacia el Morro y la Cabaña: Pero [...] "son castillos de verdad" ' (Carpentier, 1996a, p. 29). (English translation by the author.)

[4] 'Hoy es indiscutible que el concepto de los poetas suprarealistas [...] forma parte del bagaje intelectual de todo viajero enterado. Ese viajero no ignora que una de las primeras cosas que deben visitarse en una ciudad es el mercado – lugar en que florecen siempre manifestaciones humildes de arte popular. Además, el mercado es el lugar de contraste, y el contraste es el máximo generador de imágenes poéticas. Desde hace muchos años, los viajeros europeos y americanos han aprendido a sentir lo popular' (Carpentier, 1996a, p. 39). (English translation by the author.)

[5] '... car ce sont les manifestations populaires que pâtissent le plus souvent de ces vogues soudaines. Méprisées aujourd'hui on recherchera demain les extraordinaires couvertures des suppléments illustrés du *Petit Journal* et du *Petit Parisien* qui donnent à l'actualité et à l'histoire un commentaire si parfaitement expressif. ... aspects des capitales et particulièrement de Paris, mœurs mondaines... telles

que les imagine le peuple, mœurs bourgeoises, mœurs policières et présence pour la première fois du merveilleux propre au XXe siècle, utilisation naturelle des machines et des récentes inventions, mystère des choses, des hommes et du destin' (Desnos, 1929, p. 377). (English translation by the author.)

6 '... les cauchemars dont une affiche de l'époque donne une idée très exacte ... . Si Fantômas était l'animateur de toutes ces révolutions, il était puissament secondé dans son action psychique par les affiches qui ... étaient collées sur les murs ... . C'était ainsi toute une série de formules magiques qui étaient répandues dans le monde ...' (Desnos, 1929, pp. 377–8). (English translation by the author.)

7 'Un poco más lejano, más allá del parque, se encuentra otro altar heterodoxo, que se encuentre entre los más hermosos que he visto en mi vida ... Además, casi puedo afirma que es único en su género, ya que se trata de un "altar acuático". Imaginad una fuente llena de agua viva, que sirve de albergue a una fauna marina de peces, caracoles y esponjas. Hay abanicos de mar, hipocampos y estrellas. En esa piscina, flotando eternamente se encuentra un velero, tallado en madera por un devoto marino, y un acorazado británico, color gris ploma, que lleva el nombre de Southampton. Hay también algunas embarcaciones de menor cuantía ... Pero todo este convoy sólo sirve de escolta a la pieza capital del océano en miniatura; una barca de carpintería, en que bogan, con las manos juntas, los tres Juanes de la más popular de las oraciones criollas, Juan Indio, Juan Odio y Juan Esclavo. Y sobre este paisaje acuático encerrado en una habitación, se cierne un doble altar sostenido por columnas salomónicas y adornado por dos ángeles barrocos, con las manos llenas de guirnaldas de flores. En el piso inferior, hay una gran virgen de la Caridad, con riquísimo tocado. En el piso superior una virgen de Regla, del mismo tamaño que la anterior, que domina con su autoridad todo un mundo prodigiosamente marítimo, que encierra, en sí mismo, como un pequeño universo, todos los elementos de la poesía moderna. Al pie de ese extraordinario altar, que mide más de tres metros de alto, he podido escuchar, hace un año, los más admirables toques de tambores batá que yo haya tendido el privilegio de conocer en largos años de andanzas por el folklore afrocubano ... A pocos metros de éste, se halla otro altar, dedicado a Santa Bárbara, diosa de la guerra, que los fieles adornaron con soldados de plomo, tanques de juguetería, aviones, baterías antiaéreas, y cuantos atributos bélicos o motivos rojos –color ritual de Changó- fuese posible hallar ...' (Carpentier, 1996b, pp;. 78–9). (English translation by the author.)

8 'Les photos qui accompagnent ces lignes ont été prises par moi – automne 1927 – dans la chambre "*famba*", ou chambre interdite, d'un sorcier noir, Taita José, dont la cabane, surmontée d'une corne de bouc, s'élevait au cœur d'une des régions les plus isolées de la province de Santiago, à Cuba. Les négatifs de ces photos, dont il n'existe qu'une seule copie, ont été détruits en présence du sorcier. Je m'empresse toutefois de dire qu'il n'est pas nécessaire d'aller si loin, à Cuba, pour trouver des sorciers noirs. Il y en a même aux portes de la Havane. Mais ceux-ci se montrent si méfiants envers les blancs, qu'il aurait été impossible de photographier les images de leurs autels. Ces images représentent surtout des divinités chrétiennes, interprétées ou habillées selon le goût des fidèles. Mais les rites de la sorcellerie leur confèrent une vie secrète, un rôle et une identité toute différente.

Saint-Lazare, qu'une statuette hideuse nous montre appuyé sur ses béquilles, couverts de plaies, symbolise la puissance de Babayou-Ayé, divinité médicale des noirs. Les vierges espagnoles qui se dressent au centre de l'autel, figurent Yemayâ, déesse des eaux, et Ochúm, une des femmes de Sainte-Barbe. Cette dernière, changeant de sexe, est devenue Shangó, dieu du tonnerre et des tempêtes. Quant au crucifix, on le désigne sous le nom d'Obatalá, roi des forces créatrices de la nature. Auprès de ces images, la statuette d'un adolescent (Eshu), brandissant une hachette de fer, protège les laboureurs. Le *diablito* – petit diable – masqué d'une cagoule noire surmontée d'un panache en rafia, personnifie le sorcier lui-même, transformé en divinité mineure. Et les cornes, le corail, les chaînes, les cailloux, les perles de bois, sont adorés pour la matière même qui les constituent, comme éléments de l'univers et attributs rituels des *orishas* – ou puissances – auxquels ils se rattachent. Ces *orishas* ont des fonctions bien déterminées. Shango-Sainte-Barbe, Eshu-l'agriculteur, ou l'Elegbá-l'âme-solitaire, sont invoqués pour les envoûtements. D'autres sont destinés à veiller sur les femmes enceintes ou les malades. ... Chaque image, chaque symbole, chaque objet possède ses hymnes et ses oraisons' (Carpentier, 1933, pp. 44–5). (English translation by the author.)

Bibliography

Carpentier, A. et al. (1931), 'Conocimiento de América'. *Imán*, 1, 189–211.
—. (1933), 'Images et Prières nègres'. *Le phare de Neuilly*, 1, 44–8.
—. (1939), 'La Habana vista por un turista cubano'. *Carteles*, 8 October–17 December.
—. (1987a), 'Robert Desnos et ses trois maisons magiques', in Dumas, M. (ed.), *Robert Desnos*. Paris: L'Herne, pp. 329–34.
—. (1987b), 'Un homme de contraste', in Dumas, M. (ed.), *Robert Desnos*. Paris: L'Herne, pp. 363–6.
—. (1996a), 'La Habana vista por un turista cubano', in Carpentier, A. (ed.), *El Amor a la ciudad*. Madrid: Alfaguara, pp. 17–57.
—. (1996b), 'Regla, la ciudad mágica', in Carpentier, A. (ed.), *El Amor a la ciudad*. Madrid: Alfaguara, pp. 75–80.
Desnos, R. (1929), 'Imagerie moderne'. *Documents*, 7, 377–80.
Dumas, M. (1980), *Robert Desnos ou l'exploration des limites*. Paris: Klincksieck.
Durkheim, E. (1912), *Les formes élémentaires de la vie religieuse*. Paris: Alcan.
Hollier, D. (ed.) (1995), *Le Collège de Sociologie 1937–1939*. Paris: Gallimard.
Leiris, M. (1995), 'Le sacré dans la vie quotidienne', in Hollier, D. (ed.), *Le Collège de Sociologie 1937–1939*. Paris: Gallimard: pp. 94–119.
Mehring, W. (1931), 'Conocimiento de América'. *Imán*, 1, 209–11.
Nelle, F. (1996), *Atlantische Passagen. Paris am Schnittpunkt südamerikanischer Lebensläufe zwischen Unabhängigkeit und kubanischer Revolution*. Berlin: Tranvía.
Rincón, C. (1980), 'Antes de lo real-maravilloso americano, Le Merveilleux'. *Eco*, 220, 417–41.
—. (1998), 'Simulacro e imagen: Huitzilopochtliburg hoy, La Habana ayer', in Armbruster, C. and Hopfe, K. (eds), *Horizont-Verschiebungen: interkulturelles Verstehen und Heterogenität in der Romania*. Tübingen: Narr, pp. 331–46.

Chapter 13

Remaking Sacred Spaces after Socialism in Ukraine

Catherine Wanner

The earliest art works were created in service of ritual, first magical rituals and later religiously oriented ones. The aura of a work of art can never be separated from its ritual function, although that function is endlessly malleable. In cities and towns throughout the Soviet Union monumental art was central to political and popular rituals, at times venerated and later held in contempt as ominous idols. Monuments provided the sites for rituals and anchored those rituals in space, forging close associations in people's memories among practice, place and meaning. Yet, over time the primary function of monumental art, and art more generally, along with the rituals associated with them, shifted under the weight of Soviet ideology. The doctrine of 'l'art pour l'art', which Walter Benjamin referred to as a 'theology of art', was suppressed in favor of placing art in service, not to ritual, but to politics (Benjamin, 1968, p. 224). In the Soviet Union, artists became agitators for a particular ideological worldview and art became an instrument to transmit socialist ideals.

Monumental art in socialist societies played a key role in the statecraft of remaking citizens in a particular image to reinforce an ideological redesign of society that promised to lead to a 'bright future'. A repertoire of symbols, images and themes were cast in predictable forms as part of an effort to forge a 'socialist realist' style of art which would dominate the urban landscape in Eurasia during the 74 years of Soviet rule. These monuments were designed to illustrate supernatural (state) power, ideal type empowered citizens and the glories of socialism. Paul Connerton has argued that general abstract linguistic oppositions, such as imperial/Soviet, private/public, and importantly for our purposes, sacred/secular, are often effectively articulated in material spaces. He writes, 'Topography is a rhetoric, a set of well-tried discursive formulae' (Connerton, 2009, p. 32).

Given the recent outpouring of interest in memory, a number of scholars have turned their attention to analyses of monuments in formerly socialist countries as cultural artifacts and analyzed how they have influenced historical understanding, political mobilization and identity construction (Forest and Johnson, 2002; Fowkes, 2002; Ladd, 2002). They have considered the role of architectural artifacts in socialist societies in terms of how they shape memories, and by extension identities. The use of monuments for such purposes among Soviet officials was so deliberate and so pervasive that this legacy has imposed itself on post-Soviet leaders. Current political leaders have to contend with an urban landscape dotted with monuments that hark back to a fallen past that the monuments materialize. These monuments have become important *lieux de mémoire* (sites of memory), which Pierre Nora defines as places, practices or objects in which 'memory crystallizes and secretes itself' (Nora, 1989, p. 7). Furthermore, monuments – as the sites of rituals where habitual actions and mores associated with these rituals are embodied – allow memories of a certain past to graft onto current habits and remain visible and potentially meaningful today. In this way, they also serve as *milieux de mémoire*, or realms of memory, where mentalités are articulated and maintained.

After the collapse of socialist regimes, these dynamics became quite problematic. For example, the Mausoleum of Georgi Dimitrov, the first prime minister of Communist Bulgaria who died in 1949, is illustrative of the potential political benefits during one period and the perils during another that monuments can offer. Following Dimitrov's death and the establishment of communism in Bulgaria, his body was interned, preserved and put on public display in a special mausoleum, modeled on the Lenin Mausoleum on Red Square, which was specially constructed for this purpose in the center of historic Sofia. As Maria Todorova describes, without much fanfare and even less protest, in 1999 the mausoleum was blown up, erased from the urban landscape, and Dimitrov's body was cremated (Todorova, 2006). In no time at all, an old new vista of the monarch's palace was restored, resurrecting the importance of a more desirable history by destroying the painful lieu de mémoire of a more troubling one.

Elsewhere in the region, some monuments to a similar period remain unaltered, such as the memorial complex in Volgograd, Russia to the 'heroes of the Battle of Stalingrad', analyzed by Scott Palmer (Palmer, 2009). World War II monuments played a pivotal role in promoting a commemorative cult of the war, which included Soviet solidarity and sacrifice in the face of extreme adversity, and of mythic military prowess capable of repelling fascism and delivering superpower status to the Soviet Union. This commemorative cult of the war served to redeem and to legitimate the Soviet state and state socialism after the tumultuous 1930s which were laced with convulsive change and repression (Weiner, 2000). Because the suffering during the war was indeed real and is recalled by so many, this monument, and many others like it, retain much of the original meaning and ritual function in society and remain in place. While Scott Palmer examines the process by which this war monument was built in Volgograd and what the implications are for memory, Maria Todorova explores what it means for the memories and everyday lives of Sofia urbanites when monuments are removed. In both instances there are powerful implications for historical understanding and for politics.

In this chapter, I take a somewhat different perspective. I consider not just the fate of Soviet era monuments in post-Soviet society, but depart from the assertion that Soviet monuments constituted sacred spaces that shaped everyday cultural practices and political rituals in socialist cities. Given such inherited cultural practices, political habits and developed patterns of urban planning, all of which position monumental art as both a *lieu de mémoire* and a *milieu de mémoire*, I consider some new ways in which the sacred is deployed in monumental art in Kyiv, the capital of Ukraine. Whereas most studies of sacred spaces in urban landscapes have focused on buildings used for religious worship (Miller, 2001), I explore how the sacred permeated lived urban space. I consider the distinctively sacred qualities that were inputted to monuments previously and what the relevance of that sacredness has been for new uses of monuments and urban public space after the fall of socialism in Kyiv, the capital of Ukraine.

Conflated as Soviet ideology was with a sacred vision of worldly salvation, and as reflective of that ideology as monuments were, the urban landscape then – and continuing on today – reveals an ongoing presence of the sacred, not only in political ritual, but in the lived urban spaces of everyday social and cultural practices as well. Along with secularized uses of the sacred, this was part of a broader vision of socialist modernity. By contrasting the shifts in the sites and meanings of representations of history and of the national self in monumental art from the Soviet to the post-Soviet periods, we see the way understandings of what constitutes 'the sacred' have been articulated and imparted in the urban landscape.

Centrally located and designed to inspire worship and awe, monuments became theologized forms of art that characterized the urban landscape in socialist societies. The meanings of the sacred and the profane were transformed more than once over the course of the twentieth century in Ukraine. Initially, they were a key component of a greater project to create the 'new Soviet man', and since 1991 and the collapse of the Soviet Union, they have been used to help forge nationalized, ethical citizens of independent Ukraine.

Monuments as cultural artifacts have a historical genesis whose meanings also change over time in tandem with the normative and political functions they perform. Using a few of the most poignant examples, I will consider how the current remake of monuments in the urban landscape of Ukraine is using concepts of the sacred in novel ways to re-enchant public space on the ruins of socialism in an effort to purge the urban landscape of fallen idols and misguided convictions. Such changes are part of an effort to recreate meaningful sacred spaces in the urban landscape.

Monuments as Sacred Spaces in the USSR

I consider Soviet state monuments as iconic representations of Soviet power, as objects infused with a mystical aura of omnipotence, and designed to prompt feelings of worship and awe. The effectiveness of monuments as tools of statecraft, as tools of ideological instruction and indoctrination, lies in the fact that they can be constituted as sacred and sublime spaces. The process of viewing is often accompanied by bodily, sensory forms of experience which pass as knowledge of something 'true'. Moreover, the iconic, visual forms of monuments communicate a message accessible to all regardless of educational achievement or linguistic abilities.

Lenin envisioned Soviet cities adorned with monumental propaganda that would directly deliver 'the artifacts of a museum, the teachings of a school, and the reverent milieu of a church' (Stites, 1989, p. 90). Monuments evoked – and by extension helped to maintain – religious sensibilities by trading on associations of the sacred melded to the state to secure political legitimacy for its mission. Ironically, this political practice worked at cross-purposes with other state policies that were intended to foster a secular worldview that would rely on a cognitive, science-based understanding of knowledge and authority to determine if something were 'true'. The aesthetic value of a monument was a distant secondary concern after its ideological and political effectiveness. This was particularly true given the confines of the socialist realist style, which was characterized by a state approved thematic uniformity and highly censored aesthetic range in which to depict the permissible subjects. By obliging monuments to conform to a narrow selection of thematic and aesthetic elements, they also served to homogenize public space across this enormous country, much like 'big-box' chain stores and strip malls do in the US today.

The project to create uniform urban space contributed to the highly ambitious ideological project of Sovietizing and secularizing a sprawling, eleven time-zone multinational empire into the first socialist state. The uniformity of monumental representation created a sense of familiarity and unity across an otherwise geographically, culturally, linguistically and religiously diverse terrain. It was at once a means of muting difference and forging commonality and familiarity. The creation of a 'new Soviet man' vitally depended on undermining the salience of alternative sources of identity, such as religion and ethnicity, and animating and making magnetic newly invented and highly ideologized ones. Spatial expressions of ethnic and historical particularities that were manifest in the organic growth of city centers and their narrow winding streets were often erased and replaced with Soviet-style urban planning that advanced 'modern' models of urban design featuring large open squares, grand boulevards and industrial clusters that fused production with living space. These ideas, which stemmed from the particularities of socialist modernity, were designed to spatially reinforce the perceptions of the Soviet people as a reality.

The Soviet project to realize a 'bright future' characterized by a 'withering of the state' and the social equality and the new understandings citizenship communism was believed to yield, would have to be achieved by first destroying old bourgeois allegiances to reactionary forces, such as religious institutions. These initiatives to secularize the citizens of the USSR by liberating them from their religious superstitions were also manifest in the urban landscape. Anti-religious campaigns and atheist ideology mandated the destruction of numerous churches, synagogues, mosques and other institutionally-related sacred places. Those that were not destroyed were converted to mundane, profane uses, such as swimming pools, dancing clubs or warehouses, in an effort to destroy their aura of otherworldly, transcendent, sacred space. These attempts to transform sites of religious worship into something unrecognizable were part of a two-pronged broader effort to purge Soviet society of the influence, power and authority of religion and the institutions that supported a transcendent worldview.

Secularizing Public Space in the USSR

The motivation for anti-religious policies was twofold. Initially, the Bolsheviks had to contend with the Russian Orthodox Church as a competing institution that commanded the allegiance of the Empire's populace and, even more significantly, was an institution that was closely allied with the absolute tsarist monarchy. For the Bolsheviks to secure political power, they had to compound the internal difficulties the Russian Orthodox Church was already experiencing to weaken its standing during this tumultuous period. Secondly, following the dictates of Marxist ideology, the Bolsheviks believed religious superstitions and practices to be an impediment to progress. Religious beliefs fostered false consciousness and impeded the masses' ability to address social problems and the sources of poverty-related suffering in the here and now.

A series of anti-religious campaigns throughout the Soviet period, combined with the at times coercive and vigorous promotion of atheist ideology, was the means used to deliver a secularized society. In many respects, the efforts of Soviet officials to divest religious institutions of political power and to eliminate their role in key spheres of public life, such as education and social service provision, did yield their intended results. Over time, Soviet society radically differentiated the spheres and functions of the church and state. The society did indeed secularize as the authority and power of organized religion in the lives of individuals and in various spheres of social and political life plummeted.[1] Perhaps most significantly, the highly critical stance towards organized religious activities that the Soviet government promoted led to not only diminishing religious convictions but also to a legitimation of unbelief. Ultimately, Soviet-style modernization, much as Max Weber had predicted, led to disenchantment, secularization and a complete crisis of meaning, finally climaxing in the dramatic and rapid collapse of communism in the former Soviet Union in 1991.

If the fall of the Soviet Union took scholars by surprise, they were shocked by the religious revival that quickly took root in the fifteen independent successor states to the USSR. How can these seemingly contradictory trends of steady unidirectional secularization followed by a quick religious revival be explained? I will argue that Soviet policies of secularization, which have been well researched, were also accompanied by a prominent dynamic that has been overlooked, namely, processes of sacralization.

In writing about the particularities of socialist space and how these practices impinged on everyday life, David Crowley and Susan Reid urge scholars to go beyond simply charting a spatial ideological cartography of the urban landscape and ask a provocative question: 'Marxist-Leninist ideals of progress and principles of social justice, based on an equitable redistribution of all resources through the agency of the State, were claimed to be the basis of a new spatial economy. Measured against these ideals, such "socialist spaces" will no doubt be found wanting... Should we not, rather, consider a wider field of spatial relations, uses and discourses that goes beyond rhetoric?' (Crowley and Reid, 2002, p. 4). I think they have a point and this is the challenge I intend to take up. By focusing on something as ever present, visible and as key to the formation of memories and identities as monuments in the urban landscape, I aim to explore how spatial relations in lived everyday urban life connect individuals to the supernatural and thereby contribute to the process of sacralization in a society that professed to be secular.

Soviet efforts to secularize the social and political order by purging it of religious elements under the banner of squelching superstitions were predicated on evoking transcendence, triumphalism and the magical might it would take to realize a Soviet social order devoid of conflict and want.[2] I will argue that by pursuing both goals simultaneously, Soviet policies served to displace the sacred out of traditional sites, such as churches, and into everyday urban spaces and integrate them with mnemonic practices where the sacred permeated spatial relations of urban life in unintended ways. Monuments are perhaps the most vivid example of this phenomenon of evoking the sacred to create a secular political order.

Not all would agree that the sacred can permeate everyday life. Rita Felski, for example, considers everyday life to be a fundamentally secular concept. In tracing the historiography of the term 'everyday life', Felski claims that it 'conveys the sense of a world leached of transcendence: the everyday is everyday because it is no longer connected to the miraculous, the magical or the sacred' (Felski, 1999–2000, p. 16). I will argue that an analysis of Soviet monuments suggests precisely the reverse. The power and usefulness of monuments to the regime hinged on the fact that they were sites of commemorative ritual as well as the ritualized behavior of everyday life. They at once created sensibilities, imparted values, and defined identities through the ritual inscription of memories in commemorative ceremonies and individual rites de passage in sacred spaces, all of which crafted shared meanings.

Sacred-Secular Continuum

I make this argument predicated on two others. I propose to consider the secular in tandem with the sacred, which might seem unusual at first, but I will argue that the processes of realizing both are interconnected. I concur with Nicholas Demerath who defines secularization as 'the process by which the sacred gives way to the secular, whether in matters of personal faith, institutional practice, or political power. It involves a transition in which things once revered become ordinary, the sanctified becomes mundane, and things other-worldly lose their prefix' (Demerath, 2003, p. 213).

I believe he is right to suggest that secularization is not simply a matter of subtraction, of eliminating religion in part or totally from certain spheres of political and social life, and of diminishing belief. Rather secularization should best be conceived of as a recasting of the sacred, which in the case of the Soviet Union resulted in a displacement of the sacred into profane domains, which then became infused with sacred attributes through ritual. When I evoke the sacred, I am referring to things, issues, practices, beliefs and the like that are sanctified and held to be otherworldly. This kind of an amorphous, experiential view of secularization that is not tied directly to religion is radically different from the conceptions that have dominated the literature on secularization for decades now (Martin, 1978; Casanova, 1994; Bruce, 2002). Secularization has primarily been framed and 'measured' by considering such factors as church attendance, professed belief, membership rosters and the like. These are all relevant indicators of secularizing trends, but we should not let them limit our analysis.

Many years ago, Eliade argued that religion by no means exhausts the possibilities for the sacred (Eliade, 1959). He proposed the term 'hierophanies' to connote vehicles to the sacred, rather than religion itself. Certain sites and practices, often embodied in myths, according to Eliade, afforded a breakthrough to the sacred, which he called hierophanies, and provided 'ideal models' of value and orientation for the social order. I am arguing that monuments, rituals and the national myths associated with them offered such hierophanies even though sacred monumental artifacts existed in a largely secularized public sphere in Soviet society.

A displacement of the sacred – as the essence of processes of Soviet secularization and distinct from those that evolved in Europe – occurred variably in terms of degree, velocity and location. On the relationship between the two processes, secularization and sacralization, Demerath writes, 'sacralization is the process by which the *secular becomes sacred or other new forms of the sacred emerge*, whether in matters of personal faith, institutional practice or political power' (Demerath, 2003, p. 214, emphasis in the original). And I would add in terms of spatial relations as well. Most notably, Demerath contends that these processes flow in a tug-of-war, back and forth motion, full of tension and oscillation. He writes, 'every episode of sacralization generally follows a preceding period of secularization . . . the two tendencies often oscillate and even play off one another' (Demerath, 2003, p. 215).

The key point I am arguing is that one should embrace an interconnected view of the sacred and the secular that includes an expansion of the scope of secularization that is not limited to religion. Conceptualizations of secularization should be expansive enough to include cultural domains where various hierophanies, or manifestations of the sacred, occur. The shift away from formal religion when considering secularization allows us to consider how aspects of everyday life and lived spaces were rendered either 'sacred' or 'secular'.

Especially in a Eurasian context, these finer shades of the secular and the sacred are more useful. In terms of public displays of religion and overt religious participation, incontrovertibly, the USSR secularized rapidly and profoundly. Church attendance, allegiance to religious organizations and observance of religious rituals and traditions all drastically decreased within a generation. Yet, I have argued elsewhere that it would be a mistake to assume that the society was secularized and Soviet citizens were converted to atheism (Wanner, 2007). Rather, the religious sensibilities of Soviet citizens were not destroyed, nor were levels of belief significantly reduced, although non-belief was indeed legitimized. Soviet policies of secularization, above all, displaced religious practice out of the public sphere and atomized it in private or 'invisible' domains. Over time, this produced ignorance of religious doctrine and practice. It did not, however, diminish reverence for the transcendent and a respect for things, people and places deemed sacred. Ignorance of doctrine and unbelief are two very different outcomes. The latter was intended but the former was produced.

In the Soviet Union, we have a paradoxical example. We have an instance of a state willfully instigating a process of public sacralization of monuments along with its other policies of secularizing the public sphere and public life. Formal religious institutions that aspired to hold some power over believers became the target of the Soviet state's repressive policies. The sharp reining in of the number and visibility of religious buildings as well as the activities of clergy and believers were the primary targets of repression. In response, personal piety, professed belief and manifest religious practices became oriented towards non-religious spheres of social life.

As Demerath reminds us, 'The quality of sacredness is not inherent in a thing or idea: rather, sacredness is imputed from within a social context' (Demerath, 2003, p 217). Therefore, monuments and the images, myths and concepts they represent, among other markers in the urban landscape, can take on sacred overtones as easily as more traditionally religious images and concepts can. The sacredness simply has to be imputed. Monuments became intentionally bathed in a transcendent aura and always had the potential to create the Geertzian 'long-lasting moods and motivations' that religion can command. From the beginning, the goal was to make monuments sanctuaries of contemplation, to integrate them into the urban landscape as spaces that would generate awe and deep respect and thereby create a sacrosanct silence before a sacred shrine. Like museums, which served the same purpose, these urban spaces had a didactic function. They were designed to impart a message predicated on communicating the meaning of one's identity and the meaning of one's membership in a group. When considering how Soviet monuments were infused with sacred qualities, I do not think in terms of a 'religion' or even a 'civil religion'. Rather, in keeping with my conceptualization of secularization, my focus is on sacralization and evocation of the sacred in an effort to generate meaning and allegiance. Monuments were positioned as sacred and revered objects, the site of specific ritualized practices, designed to trigger certain experiences of metaphysical authority and meaning.[3] As such, the bodily sensations that Soviet monuments generated authenticated religious experience and religious sensibilities even as the state tried to stifle them through the promotion of atheism and waves of anti-religious campaigns.

Secularizing and Sacralizing Public Space

Maria Todorova has written, 'The symbolic language of monuments and how it is mobilized in bringing about or sanctioning social change has become a favorite topic of research, especially with the rich variety of examples that have accompanied the nervous transformation of the cultural landscape in the post-Communist world' (Todorova, 2006, p. 394). Monuments can be effectively mobilized because they can be used to authenticate and validate certain historical interpretations and myths laden with political implications to help secure the legitimacy of particular ideologies, initially communism and now capitalism. Monuments have the power to transcend time, to remove events and personalities from a forgotten and forlorn past and reinsert them in the present in a vibrant and animated way by evoking empathy towards 'victims' of unjust suffering. This is why they can take on such symbolic value for social movements, especially national movements of consolidation that identify with them.

Two examples illustrate how sacred space surrounding monuments created a certain habitus that permeated everyday life in Soviet Ukraine and shaped the memories and knowledge of history.[4] The most visible landmark of the Kyivan skyline is the 'Motherland' statue, or *Mat' Rodina*, the mother of the motherland, although it is popularly referred to as the '*baba*', a derogatory term for a peasant woman. It was completed in 1981 and erected to commemorate the Soviet victory over fascism. The Soviet victory in World War II came on the heels of a decade of Stalinist rule notable for its terror and ruthless use of violence to stifle dissent. Because the superpower status Soviet victory bequeathed to the USSR renewed allegiance to the state and became a source of national pride, it was widely and often garishly monumentalized. To commemorate this achievement in the Ukrainian capital, a woman warrior, weighing 450 tons, made of stainless steel, clad in Roman-like robes and wielding a shield and brandishing a sword was erected on a hilltop on the banks of the Dnipro River alongside the glistening gold domes of the coupolas of the Kievo-Percherska Monastery, which dates back to the eleventh century. With churches by her side, her sword, proudly reaches towards the heavens and extends upwards of 102 meters, making the Motherland statue the third highest in the world. The woman warrior is the centerpiece of a sprawling monumental complex. The base of the enormous statue houses a museum to the Great Patriotic War and is surrounded by a park that features a display of World War II-era military hardware, including tanks and helicopters, which children climb on as if it were playground equipment. Having integrated iconic images of power in the monument, museum facilities to instruct and a park area to generate contemplation and leisure activities, – all in a highly visible manner – the Motherland statue has become the single best known marker of the Kyivan landscape.

To date, individuals commemorate Victory Day and the suffering the members of the 'imagined community' of the nation endured during World War II on May 9 by placing flowers at the base of this and other monuments to the war. The warrior woman, as the symbol of the nation in maternal form, evokes an image of the protector of the dead and the yet to be born. In viewing the monument, individuals are linked in this way to a larger collective and a common history of suffering and sacrifice. This monument – much like the monumental complex in Volgograd to World War II – remains in place, unaltered precisely because the suffering of the war is still remembered and commemorated as a common tragedy. As a traumatic event, the commemoration of the war in monument and ritual remains meaningful. Many Soviet holidays have been eliminated from the official calendar, such as Great October Revolution Day on 7 November, and have been replaced by new national holidays, such as Independence Day and Constitution Day. Even the popular celebrations of International Women's Day on 8 March are being gradually supplanted by the more commercial Valentine's Day and Mother's Day. However, commemorations of Victory Day on 9 May, much like this monument, remain in place.

A second monumental complex in Kyiv is the Arch of Peoples Friendship, also located in a very visible site, at the base of the city's main boulevard, Khreshchatyk, just behind the Philharmonic Concert Hall.

'Peoples Friendship' was a core ideological principle integrated into the governance of Soviet society to obfuscate the imperial, center-periphery workings of the Soviet state as well as to mask ongoing efforts to Sovietize the population into an assimilated, new civic-based understanding of a multi-national federation. This monument features a 50 meter rainbow linking two groups of sculpted individuals, with two young men proudly standing beneath. These men, much like the Mother of the Motherland, also have their arms extended to the heavens and are holding a banner with the symbol of the USSR, a hammer and sickle, in the center. The rainbow-linkage is meant to symbolize the unity of the Russian and Ukrainian peoples, and the two men underneath, the enthusiastic endorsement of this concept.

Precisely because the imperial legacy of the Russian state was so difficult to overcome, the Soviet state erected numerous such monuments all over the federation to illustrate the creation of a Soviet people. Having issued a resounding condemnation of this project with independence, Ukrainians refer to the rainbow as 'the yoke'. The monument has lost its intended meaning and has become a secularized space, unlike the Motherland monument which retains its reverence and sacred attributes. As a secularized space, fully integrated into worldly, mundane concerns, does this monument still function as a lieu de mémoire shaping sensibilities and identities? Paul Connerton would say no. He writes, 'The relationship between memorials and forgetting is reciprocal: the threat of forgetting begets memorials and the construction of memorials begets forgetting. If giving monumental shape to what we remember is to discard the obligation to remember, that is because memorials permit only some things to be remembered and, by exclusion, cause others to be forgotten. Memorials conceal the past as much as they cause us to remember it' (Connerton, 2009, p. 29). Devoid of any ritual or routine practices, this monument permits very little to be remembered and therefore its intended meaning and current relevance fades into the landscape. Like bleak ever-present advertisements, it is simply seen and ignored.

Imparting Sacred Elements to New Monuments

With independence in 1991, it became incumbent on the new Ukrainian state to articulate a sense of individual and collective self that carries qualitatively new attributes than those bequeathed by Soviet ideology. The new collective self would have to be purged of the transgressions Soviet power is thought to have foisted on its subjects. The multitude of new monuments that now dot the urban landscape in Ukraine serve as important indicators of new orientations, some of which are accepted and others challenged. Nonetheless, they all are designed to generate a sublime experience that trades on a highly selective remembrance of the Soviet period in order to forge another kind of collective memory, or a particular version of history. The vision of a 'bright nationalized future'[5] that can serve as the springboard from which to launch an alternative means to navigate this second social experiment as the country transitions into something approximating a nation-state with democratic forms of government and a capitalist market economy. Such religiously-infused concepts as evil, goodness, repentance, forgiveness and rebirth are cultivated in the aesthetics of the sites of these new monuments and are designed to prompt an experience of the transcendent. They communicate a moral message, thereby bequeathing sacred qualities to the monument. The bodily sensations produced by viewing inscribe knowledge on the body and can potentially validate the new cultural history and the moral premise a monument proposes.

Efforts to remake urban space have to reckon with the material manifestations of the communist period. This is a dilemma faced throughout the former Soviet Bloc in Eastern Europe and Eurasia, and perhaps will soon also be a significant issue in places like China, Vietnam and Cuba. There are several shared trends that can already be observed regardless of the specifics of location. For example, the closer to power, the more drastic the remake of the urban landscape has been. Taking Russia as an example, Bruce Grant has argued that a series of monuments designed by Zurab Tsereteli and erected in Moscow that depict characters and animals from Russian children's fairy tales amounts to an infantilization of public space (Grant, 2001). Grant argues that this infusion of fairy tale characters in urban space, which is quite controversial among Muscovites, projects a 'state of innocence', or timeless youth, that harks back to a simpler, earlier time and evokes precisely the realm of order that remains elusive in post-Soviet society. Ultimately, these monuments, like all others, have the potential to serve a political project of creating new subjects with new cognitions, thanks to the presentation of new perspectives on one's own personal history and on the nation's collective historical experience. The political leaders that authorize the financing of such monuments amidst economic difficulties bank on the fact that the monuments will help deliver new forms of political legitimacy amid widespread public dissatisfaction with the pace of positive change in Russia. These fairy tale monuments, as Grant suggests, serve as both a '*detour* around questions of Soviet accountability after the fall of the USSR, as well as a *deferral* of expectations for a rise in standards of governance and standards of living among many Russian citizens who long saw themselves as excluded from the dividends of the 20th-century economic growth' (Grant, 2001, p. 351).

In other words, by representing the national self in fantastic, fairy tale-like terms, the Russian government, artists, and by extension the Russian people are spared the process of introspection and the harsh reality of coming to terms with the failed socialist experiment and the excruciating high cost in terms of lives lost, suffering inflicted and humiliation endured. The realm of the make believe becomes a buffer, or a detour to use Grant's phrase, around the need to discuss the truth and reckon with issues of culpability for the horrors of the past. To date, in neither Russia nor Ukraine has there been anything like a Truth and Reconciliation Commission, as there was in South Africa, nor the likes of the Nuremburg Trials, as there was in Germany after World War II, or even a policy of lustration as there was in the Czech Republic to review individuals' secret police files to determine degrees of culpability, albeit unaccompanied by the standard forms of punishment, such as fines or imprisonment. Here, in contrast, a harsh gaze towards 'the dust heap of history' is averted by the playful, fantasy figures that adorn Moscow's streets as of late.

A different type of political project is underway in Ukraine and, as a result, a different aesthetic is emerging in monumental art. The center-periphery structure of rule in the USSR makes it is easier for many Ukrainians to see themselves as 'victimized' rather than as 'victimers' simply because they did not constitute the privileged, majority nationality in the USSR. The willingness to recast the collective self and recast the historic relationship with Russia is predicated on the distance from guilt that not being the home of the 'center' of the Soviet Empire affords. As a result, new monumental art in Ukrainian urban spaces does not make use of fairy tale, surreal, non-human figures, as has been the case in Moscow. Different political challenges have mandated different aesthetic styles while maintaining the Soviet-era traditions of using monumental art as indications, as points of orientation, for the *narod* [people] amidst massive social and political change. Ironically, this new aesthetic reintroduces differences in the urban landscape that Soviet leaders worked so hard to standardize.

Many of the new monuments that are being erected in Ukraine project an atmosphere of tranquility and calm. This is created first and foremost by the setting. The new monuments in Ukraine are often referred to as 'garden sculptures' to affirm that human figures have shed the massive, Herculean proportions that characterized Soviet idols, like the young men symbolizing People's Friendship, and they are no longer adorned with weapons, no longer locked in struggle. The new sculptures are not made to be the focal point of a busy intersection or designed to intrude on a wide vista. Rather, they are often integrated into smaller thoroughfares, in parks, or in some other setting that lends itself to greenery, contemplation, a slower pace, and above all, human over mythic proportions.

The essence of many of the new monuments is an articulation of a new relationship between Ukrainians and Russians and a recasting of relationships among those who live in Ukraine. Underlying this presentation of a revised sense of relatedness is a new mode of ethical living. Engagement in lived urban space with images of reinvigorated ethical living and frequenting of this public space, which is set aside as sacred space within the city, generates possibilities for moral action. Much like earlier Soviet uses of religious frameworks and sensibilities to present secular ideology, here we see again a purposefully blurred distinction between the origins of ethics and morality in religiously-based faith and in secular reasoning and presented in a sacralized setting surrounded by secularized public space. In essence, the new monuments and their sacred-secular continuum constitute new aesthetics, a domain of everyday life where images of morally and ethically-informed interaction are articulated.

For example, new monuments to the *Holodomor*, or man-made Famine of 1932–3 in which approximately 7 million Ukrainians died, are perhaps the best illustration of a morally-informed aesthetics that recasts the relationship of Ukraine to the Soviet Union and by extension of Ukrainians to Russians. The Famine is represented in monuments that carry connotations positioning it as an extraordinary act of evil. Monumental commemorative representations of the Famine use religious imagery designed to merge the sacred qualities of an eternal, transcendent nation with remade urban space in an effort to generate a 'born again' experience for viewers. Sacred connotations of purity, triumph and rebirth are rendered thanks to evocations of religious symbolism, motherhood and gendered images of the nation that play off a contrasting subtext of evil. The immensity of the suffering inflicted on Ukrainians during this period of Soviet rule, many Ukrainian scholars now argue, is such that it constitutes genocide against the Ukrainian people. Although the Famine occurred in rural eastern areas of the country, it is monumentally commemorated in cities in central and western Ukraine, where such evocations of 'them' inflicting evil on 'us', the innocent victims, finds a much more receptive audience. Such depictions, however, serve a political agenda that aims to reinforce the need for independence from Russia, in spite of a shared 350-year long historical

FIGURE 13.1 Monument to the Ukrainian Famine of 1932–3 (photo by the author).

tradition and the cultural commonalities such a long historical experience has bequeathed in the form of religion and language. Most notably, the main Holodomor monument not only renders the nation as a woman once again, but she is now with child and the impending birth, or rebirth, suggests hope (Fig. 13.1). Mother and child are encompassed by a cross, symbolizing protection and an organic restoration of nation and religion, individual and faith, death and life. The monument was erected to commemorate the sixtieth anniversary of the Famine and placed outside the newly reconstructed Mikhailivsky Cathedral, which was destroyed in the 1930s by Stalin.

As modest as the size of the monument is, the power of its symbolism evokes a Christ-like triumph over death and over evil rulers. In addition to annual commemorative ceremonies on the fourth Saturday in November, the monument is also the site of numerous ritualized behaviors on commemorative occasions: couples are photographed before the monument on their wedding day; graduating classes of schoolchildren are photographed there on the last day of school; and it is a popular tourist destination. The integration of this monument into national ceremonies as well as individual rites de passage and ritualized everyday acts ensures that these practices will inscribe an ongoing relevance of the Famine as a national and individually meaningful event and suggests that this new post-Soviet monument will retain the sacred qualities that the Bolsheviks once imparted to some of their monuments across the land.

Conclusion

Since the collapse of the Soviet Union and the discrediting of socialism, there has not been a complete break with Soviet monumental traditions, practices of political indoctrination and patterns of urban design. There rarely is. New monuments representing the nation and reflecting national experience continue to function as mechanisms of power, serving the needs of governance and trading on sacred imagery to advance a particular ideology. New national monuments carry the burden of articulating images of the nation and the core values of a particular national identity. This process is predicated on recasting the relationship of Ukrainians to Russians by challenging the relationship as a fraternal and eternal one embodied in the concept of 'Peoples' Friendship', and replacing it with another biography that includes conflict, oppression, and exploitation, leading to eventual separation. In post-Soviet monuments the nation is still rendered in a non-sexualized, maternal feminine form. However, she is no longer depicted as mighty and triumphant, but rather is now more modest, pure and fertile. Most importantly, representations of the nation are now shrouded in religious symbolism, constituting new public displays of sacredness and suggesting a return to the historic pattern in Orthodox countries where an organic relationship is posited as linking nationality to Orthodoxy.

To take on a national identity is now to take on a religious one as well, even if it is understood in a more cultural sense that evokes the sacred in broad, visceral terms, rather than in direct appeals to doctrinal belief and institutionally sanctioned forms of religious practice. This new mode of relatedness, which is being cultivated in national monuments placed throughout urban centers in Ukraine, constitutes an attempt to re-enchant urban space based on a revised sense of nationhood. In this way, the Soviet tradition of creating sacred spaces around monumental art has been reinvented and perpetuated. Monuments are once again used in Ukraine as sites to re-enchant public space by rendering the collective national self sacred for all to see.

Notes

[1] Mark Chaves (1994) makes the case that the essence of secularization is the loss of authority that religious belief and religiously-affiliated organizations formerly claimed. Indeed, it was the authority, even the moral authority, of the Russian Orthodox Church as an institution that was compromised during the Soviet period.

[2] The same could be said of monuments more generally. The Soviet case simply provides a more extreme example because the politicization and manipulation of urban space was so extensive.

[3] When considering how Soviet monuments were infused with sacred qualities, I do not think in terms of a 'religion' or even a 'civil religion'. Rather, in keeping with my conceptualization of secularization, my focus is on sacralization and evocation of the sacred in an effort to generate meaning and allegiance.

[4] For more on Soviet monuments in Ukraine see Wanner (1998, especially Chapter 6).

[5] It is important to note that none of the monuments built to adorn private graves have been altered. Monuments erected in public space for the living have been remade but those acknowledging the dead have not.

Bibliography

Benjamin, W. (1968), 'The Work of Art in the Age of Mechanical Reproduction', in Arendt, H. (ed.), *Illuminations*. New York: Schocken Books.

Bruce, S. (2002), *God is Dead: Secularization in the West*. Malden, MA: Blackwell.

Casanova, J. (1994), *Public Religions in the Modern World*. Chicago: University of Chicago Press.

Chaves, M. (1994), 'Secularization as Declining Religious Authority'. *Social Forces*, 72(3), 749–74.

Connerton, P. (2009), *How Modernity Forgets*. Cambridge: Cambridge University Press.

Crowley, D. and Reid, S.E. (eds) (2002), *Socialist Spaces: Sites of Everyday Life in the Eastern Bloc*. New York: Berg.

Demerath, N. (2003), 'Secularization Extended' in Fenn, R. K. (ed.), *The Sociology of Religion*. Malden, MA: Blackwell, pp. 211–28.

Elide, M. (1959), *The Sacred and the Profane: The Nature of Religion*. New York: Harper & Row.

Felski, R. (1999–2000), 'The Invention of Everyday Life'. *New Formations*, 39, 15–31.

Forest, B. and Johnson, J. (2002), 'Unraveling the Threads of History: Soviet-Era Monuments and Post-Soviet National Identity in Moscow'. *Annals of the Association of American Geographers*, 92(3), 524–47.

Fowkes, R. (2002), 'The Role of Monumental Sculptures in the Construction of Socialist Space in Soviet Hungary' in Crowley, D. and Reid, S. (eds), *Socialist Spaces: Sites of Everyday Life in the Eastern Bloc*. Oxford and New York: Berg, pp. 65–84.

Grant, B. (2001), 'New Moscow Monuments, or, States of Innocence'. *American Ethnologist*, 28(2), 332–62.
Ladd, B. (2002), 'East Berlin Political Monuments in the Late German Democratic Republic: Making a Place for Marx and Engels. *Journal of Contemporary History*, 37(1), 91–104.
Martin, D. (1978), A General Theory of Secularization. New York: Harper & Row.
Miller, S.G. (2001), 'Apportioning Sacred Space in a Moroccan City: The Case of Tangier, 1860–1912'. *City & Society*, 13(1), 57–83.
Nora, P. (1989), 'Between Memory and History: Les Lieux de Mémoire'. *Representations*, 26, 7–24.
Palmer, S. W. (2009), 'How Memory was Made: The Construction of the Memorial to the Heroes of the Battle of Stalingrad'. *Russian Review*, 68(3), 373–407.
Paperny, V. (2002), *Architecture in the Age of Stalin*, (trans. John Hill and Roann Barris). Cambridge: Cambridge University Press.
Stites, R. (1989), *Revolutionary Dreams: Utopian Vision and Experimental Life in the Russian Revolution*. Oxford: Oxford University Press.
Todorova, M. (2006), 'The Mausoleum of Georgi Dimitrov as lieu de mémoire'. *Journal of Modern History*, 78, 377–411.
Wanner, C. (1998), *Burden of Dreams: History and Identity in Post-Soviet Ukraine*. University Park, PA: Penn State Press.
—. (2007), *Communities of the Converted: Ukrainians and Global Evangelism*. Ithaca: Cornell University Press.
Weiner, A. (2000), *Making Sense of War: The Second World War and the Fate of the Bolshevik Revolution*. Princeton: Princeton University Press.

Index

abstract space 9, 143, 145, 147, 157
accursed share 40
aesth/ethics 7–8, 73, 75, 78–9, 88, 90
Agamben, Giorgio 10, 196
agonistic 55, 65
amnesia 85, 87, 91, 167
apocalypse 197
atheist bus 57, 63, 66–7
atmosphere 79–82, 85–6, 89–91, 257
Augustine 112–15, 142–3, 148, 150–1, 154–5, 158

Bachelard, Gaston 142–3, 148, 150–4, 157, 160
Bataille, Georges 35, 37–43, 46–7, 49, 229
Brazil 1, 8, 96–7, 101, 104
Busshinji-Temple 101–3, 105

Carpentier, Alejo 11, 227–38, 240–3
Casey, Edward 147–8, 157
cemetery 89, 203, 217–20
chapel 9, 20, 161–2, 164, 167–70, 172–84
Cité du Fleuve 195
College of Sociology 7, 34–9, 44
commemoration 254
communitarian 59, 61–2, 65
community 4, 7, 10–11, 17, 19, 21, 23–8, 42, 54–5, 58–9, 83–4, 90, 101, 108, 111–12, 121, 135, 141, 143, 146–8, 153–5, 164, 170, 177, 183, 191, 195, 198, 215, 217–19, 254
cosmos 9, 19, 73, 99–100, 103, 141–3, 145, 147–56
Cuba 6, 10–11, 227–30, 236–7, 242, 256

Derrida, Jacques 130, 137
Desmond, William 142–3, 156–7
development town 10, 208, 216–17, 223–4

diaspora (diasporic) 208, 210–12, 216, 218–23
Dubai 194–5

elemental 9, 141–3, 145–57
ethnic 9, 101, 127, 130–1, 134, 136, 210, 218, 220, 223, 248
everyday life 7, 11, 37–8, 41, 44–8, 54–5, 62, 148, 153, 168, 178–9, 200, 209, 216, 227–30, 232–5, 238, 240, 249–50, 252–3, 258
exchange 26, 32, 34–41, 46, 78, 90, 171
expansion/expansionism (colonial) 51–3, 109, 115, 192, 251

fieldwork (ethnographic) 227

globalization 56–7, 108–9, 112, 116–18, 120–1, 128

Havana 10–11, 92, 227–33, 235–40
headscarf 53, 66
Hereford map 141–2, 149, 155–6, 158
Holy Blood 6, 20, 27
humanist 58, 119
hubris 128, 136
hybrid 11, 208, 210, 221–3, 227, 229, 233, 235, 238

identity 7–8, 11, 17–19, 21–2, 27, 31, 35, 40, 53, 55, 60–1, 74, 80, 82, 108, 110–11, 117–18, 121, 134–6, 162, 167, 208, 211–14, 221, 223, 230, 237, 245, 248, 253, 260
interview 103, 106, 172–4, 176–9, 184, 218, 224
Israel 6, 10–11, 208–18, 221–4

Kabila, Joseph   194, 200
Kimbanguism   196
kinhin   8, 96, 99–101, 103, 105
Kinshasa   10–11, 191–6, 198–200, 202–6

late-modernity   161–2, 165, 180–3
Lefèbvre, Henri   66, 165
Leiris, Michel   35, 37, 44–5, 47, 229
liberal (liberalism, liberal theory, neo-liberal)   4, 19, 53–5, 62–4, 104, 165, 167–8, 195
life stance   8, 108–9, 111, 113, 115, 117, 119–21, 123
lifestyle   4, 25, 56–7, 63–5, 98, 100, 109
lived religion   7, 75, 77–9, 91
lived space   45, 75–9, 81–3, 85–6, 90–1, 144, 149, 209, 252
Lumumba, Patrice   193–4

magic (magical)   5–6, 23, 31–5, 47–9, 230, 233–5, 244, 250
mana   31, 34, 48
mappa mundi   141–2, 158
Mbembe, Achille   199, 201
memory   7, 10–11, 18, 73, 75, 78, 85–8, 90–2, 102, 167, 206, 211, 218, 220, 244–6, 256
Mizrahi Jews   224
Mobutu   196, 199
modernity (modernization)   2, 4–7, 18, 33–40, 45–6, 57, 90, 112, 149, 153, 161–6, 180–3, 191, 195, 197, 201, 206, 211, 213, 216, 222–3, 229, 231–3, 235, 238, 240, 246, 248
monumental art   244, 246, 251, 257, 260
morality   178, 258
multicultural (multiculturalism)   7, 27, 54, 62–3, 65–6, 136, 223
museum   6–7, 22–4, 29, 78, 84, 86–8, 132, 137, 227, 230, 247, 253–4

national (nationalist)   11, 24, 53–4, 58, 63, 87, 104–6, 108, 118, 135, 199, 208–17, 220–2, 246, 251, 253–4, 256–7, 259–60
nation-state   54, 60, 256
non-place   17–19, 24–5, 27, 29

occidentalization   99
oriental (orientalism)   121, 212–15, 221

Pentecostal (Pentecostalism, Neo-Pentecostalism)   6, 10, 191, 197–8, 200
plan décennal   192, 194
pluralism   6, 24, 26, 55, 64–5
postcolonial (postcolonialism)   6, 35, 129–30, 199–200, 205, 210, 220, 222, 224
post-secularity   53–5, 60, 64, 66
procession   6, 15, 19–20, 27, 52, 61, 82
public/private distinction   53

real marvellous   229–30
recognition   6–7, 15, 25–7, 55–6, 60, 66, 129, 132, 136, 168, 171, 210, 223–4
religious diversity   54, 56
remembrance   8, 47, 82, 85–8, 90–1, 256
republican (republicanism, republican theory)   7, 55, 59–62, 64, 238–9
ritual (ritualized, ritualization)   7–9, 15, 20–5, 43, 53–4, 56–7, 61–2, 75, 78, 81–5, 90–1, 110, 114–15, 156, 161, 165, 178–80, 196, 203–4, 206, 236–7, 242, 244–6, 250–5, 259–60
Russia   245, 255–8, 260–1
Russian Orthodox Church   248, 261

Saint Barbara   9, 127, 132–4, 137, 236–7
Sao Paulo   8, 96–7, 101–3, 105–6
secular (secularity, secularized)   4, 6, 15, 43, 47, 54, 56, 64, 66, 78, 141,166, 215, 244, 246–52, 255, 258
secularism   115
secularization   2, 4–5, 9, 39, 43, 53, 56, 60, 74, 161–3, 167–8, 180, 249–53, 261
sense making   111–16, 119, 121
shopping mall   9–10, 18, 161–2, 164–70, 174, 181, 195
socialism   11, 244–7, 260
Soto school   99
Souza de Murayama, Claudia   8, 97, 99–101, 105
spirit   34–5, 76, 80, 82, 87–8, 91, 97, 100, 105, 155

Straus, Erwin 149, 157
syncretism 11, 235–6

Thich Nhat Hanh 100, 102
thirdspace 75–6, 78, 88, 90
Tower of Babel 8–9, 127–37
transcendence 81, 141–3, 146–51, 153–6, 167, 178–80, 250

Ukrainian famine of 1932–3 258–9
unity 4, 17, 20–1, 24, 33, 38, 65, 74, 130, 136, 248, 255
urbanity 24
urbanization 1–5, 8, 31–2, 34–9, 44–8, 75–6, 98, 108, 115–18, 120–1, 123, 239

urban jungle 24–5
urban space 2, 4–7, 10–11, 24, 36–8, 41, 43–4, 48, 73–4, 78, 81–8, 90, 166, 170, 189, 198, 204, 227–8, 230, 232–3, 235–6, 238, 240, 246–7, 250, 253, 256–8, 260–1

van Eyck, Jan 127, 132–7

walking meditation 8, 96–9, 103, 105
World War II 52, 192, 229, 245, 253–4, 257

Zen 8, 96–7, 99–102, 104–6
Zionist 209, 211, 221–2